Ethereum for Web Developers

Learn to Build Web Applications on top of the Ethereum Blockchain

Santiago Palladino

Apress®

Ethereum for Web Developers

Santiago Palladino
Ciudad Autónoma de Buenos Aires, Argentina

ISBN-13 (pbk): 978-1-4842-5277-2   ISBN-13 (electronic): 978-1-4842-5278-9
https://doi.org/10.1007/978-1-4842-5278-9

Managing Director, Apress Media LLC: Welmoed Spahr
Acquisitions Editor: Louise Corrigan
Development Editor: James Markham
Coordinating Editor: Nancy Chen

Cover designed by eStudioCalamar

Cover image designed by Freepik (www.freepik.com)

Distributed to the book trade worldwide by Springer Science+Business Media New York, 233 Spring Street, 6th Floor, New York, NY 10013. Phone 1-800-SPRINGER, fax (201) 348-4505, e-mail orders-ny@springer-sbm.com, or visit www.springeronline.com. Apress Media, LLC is a California LLC and the sole member (owner) is Springer Science + Business Media Finance Inc (SSBM Finance Inc). SSBM Finance Inc is a **Delaware** corporation.

For information on translations, please e-mail rights@apress.com, or visit http://www.apress.com/rights-permissions.

Apress titles may be purchased in bulk for academic, corporate, or promotional use. eBook versions and licenses are also available for most titles. For more information, reference our Print and eBook Bulk Sales web page at http://www.apress.com/bulk-sales.

Any source code or other supplementary material referenced by the author in this book is available to readers on GitHub via the book's product page, located at www.apress.com/9781484252772. For more detailed information, please visit http://www.apress.com/source-code.

Printed on acid-free paper

To Ale, my soon-to-be-wife, who supported me through the many days that went on while writing this book.
To my parents, both computer scientists, who passed down their passion on to me.

Table of Contents

About the Author

 **Santiago Palladino** has been working as a professional software developer since 2005, working extensively in web applications for over 10 years. He entered the Ethereum space in 2017, when he joined the OpenZeppelin team as one of the first employees. There he worked as security researcher in several audits, and led the development of open source tools and services for building Ethereum applications. He has an MSc in Computer Science from University of Buenos Aires, where he was a TA in Algorithms and Numerical Methods for a total of 7 years. He has written several online articles on Ethereum development and Blockchain in general. You can find him on Twitter @smpalladino, or Github @spalladino.

About the Technical Reviewer

**Alexander Chinedu Nnakwue** has a background in Mechanical Engineering from the University of Ibadan, Nigeria and has been a front-end developer for over 3 years working on both web and mobile technologies. He also has experience as a technical author, writer, and reviewer. He enjoys programming for the web, and occasionally, you can also find him playing soccer. He was born in Benin City and is currently based in Lagos, Nigeria.

Acknowledgments

I want to thank, first and foremost, the awesome team at OpenZeppelin. OpenZeppelin was my first contact with the mind-blowing world of Ethereum, and where I learned everything that you will read throughout this book.

I also want to thank all the colleagues with whom I shared my professional life as a developer, in particular those at manas.tech, where I worked and learned for almost a decade. Those years got me to be the developer I am today.

A big thank you also goes to the entire Ethereum community. Many of the buidlers[1] and maintainers of the infrastructure that keeps everything running often go unnoticed or unappreciated. It is through their great efforts that this ecosystem thrives and grows.

I also have eternal gratitude to the teachers of the public and free University of Buenos Aires, where I got an invaluable education in computer science. Even if blockchain did not even exist during my time as a student, the foundations I learned there still help me today when approaching any topic.

Last but not least, a special thanks to the team at Apress who helped me in putting this book together, and in getting it to your hands.

And of course, to my cat, who unrelentingly slept by my side every single hour I spent writing this book.

---

[1]Typo intended: "buidl" is a meme in the Ethereum community, in response to the "hodl" cryptocurrency meme.

Introduction

It was not easy to write a book on Ethereum. Ethereum is one of the fastest evolving technologies I have ever seen. It builds on an entirely new computing model that did not even exist five years ago, and has undergone countless transformations since its conception. Writing something as static as a book feels an almost futile attempt to try to capture it. Combining this with web development, another area known for its rapid-changing environment, seemed like a daunting task.

Nevertheless, there are concepts that have become fundamental to developing blockchain-based applications. Even if the space is new, we are seeing many new chains being launched[1] after Bitcoin and Ethereum, and all share many of its basic building blocks. Those are the concepts that this book attempts to capture, seen from the perspective of a web developer. I believe they will be as helpful in several years' time as they are today, even if the tools and practices we rely on change completely.

Throughout the book, you may read many disclaimers in the form of *at the time of this writing*, to emphasize things that are bound to change in the near future – some of them even did in the time it took me to write and review each chapter. However, it is important for you to keep in mind that the disclaimer applies to the entire book, as the Ethereum ecosystem is in constant evolution.

Who this book is for

This book is for me a few years ago, before entering the blockchain space. I had worked as a full stack developer for several years, and moving into Ethereum rocked the foundations of how I had been building and thinking applications.

At that moment, it was surprisingly difficult to find comprehensive material to understand all the aspects of Ethereum needed to build a decentralized application. And it still is today, for information is mostly fragmented, and often tailored for a specific toolset.

So, this book is for developers experienced in web applications, who want to apply their skillset to this new decentralized platform that is Ethereum. What we are seeing is

---

[1]Facebook's new Libra coin is being announced as I am writing these words.

much like the mobile revolution, which completely changed how we interacted with the web over a decade ago. It required developers to relearn and adjust to a new paradigm. The same is happening now.

With that in mind, this book presents, on top of traditional web development, the new concepts that come from having an Ethereum network at your disposal.

What you should know

Being written for web developers, this book assumes that you already know and master what a web application is, are comfortable with javascript as a development language, and understand concepts such as client-server architecture, relational databases, the HTTP request/response cycle, and DNS.

In particular, we will make use of React as a front-end library to simplify the development of many examples throughout the book. Considering that React has existed for longer than Ethereum itself, and given its popularity today, it seems like an adequate choice. We will not rely on any framework or state-management solution, as we will keep our examples simple and focused on the Ethereum side of the picture.

Even though we will be working with a cryptocurrency, it is not necessary to have prior knowledge of cryptography or currencies to approach this book. We will be covering the basics of hashing and public key cryptography in the first chapter, and briefly go through financial incentives in the last ones. Of course, if either of those areas are of interest to you, blockchain is a fantastic place to exercise them.

The working environment

Much of this book is composed of code samples. Even if the value of this book relies on the concepts it attempts to pass on to you, each chapter includes several code snippets or full applications to help illustrate them. With that in mind, you may want to have an environment ready to reproduce the experiments listed.

All code samples are written in Javascript ES6, were developed and tested on an Ubuntu Linux system, and run on nodejs[2] 10.16 from a bash shell. With Javascript being multiplatform, the samples should seamlessly run on OSX or Windows environments,

---

[2]`https://nodejs.org/en/`

though your mileage may vary. That said, having npm[3] working and being able to run a create-react-app[4] locally should be enough for most code samples. Certain chapters may also require you to install and run an Ethereum node, such as Geth[5] or Parity Ethereum.[6] Refer to their websites for platform-specific instructions for installing them.

We will make very limited usage of Ethereum-specific tools and libraries throughout the book. We will limit ourselves to a single Javascript library for interacting with the Ethereum network,[7] plus a tool for simplifying the compilation of smart contracts,[8] and a library of standard contracts to avoid reimplementing them from scratch.[9] The tooling and framework space in Ethereum changes fast, and I wanted to avoid tying the book to one of them. Nevertheless, when you start your new Ethereum application, relying on an existing framework such as OpenZeppelin, Buidler, Truffle, Embark, or Etherlime may help you speed things up.

A walkthrough of the chapters

The first chapter will be the only one free of code. It will introduce what a blockchain is, with a bit on history going from Bitcoin to Ethereum, plus the fundamental concepts of accounts, transactions, and blocks, along with the basic bits of cryptography that will be needed throughout the book. It will also briefly cover blockchain use cases, and introduce the concept of decentralized applications.

Chapter two is fully hands-on. It compensates for the lack of code on the previous one by going heads-on to develop a complete decentralized application from scratch. Many concepts will be quickly glossed over, but this chapter should help you understand in a practical way how all the components fit together, so you have a clear idea of their role when they are explored in depth later.

Chapter three is the only one unrelated to web development. It provides a crash-course on smart contracts, a key construct in Ethereum. Having a good understanding of smart contracts and knowing what they can and cannot do will help

---

[3]https://www.npmjs.com/
[4]https://facebook.github.io/create-react-app/
[5]https://geth.ethereum.org/
[6]https://www.parity.io/ethereum/
[7]https://github.com/ethereum/web3.js/
[8]https://sol-compiler.com/
[9]https://github.com/OpenZeppelin/openzeppelin-solidity

you design the architecture of your applications. Most of the chapter builds on Solidity, the most popular high-level language for writing contracts.

Chapters four and five go back to web development, going in-depth with very basic tasks: reading and writing data from the blockchain. Gathering blockchain data is not like sending a SQL query to your average relational database, and sending a transaction requires managing concepts like gas and signatures. In blockchain development, long confirmation times and reorganizations may dwarf the challenges you know from NoSQL databases' eventual consistency. These two chapters will present those issues, and several techniques for dealing with them.

Chapter six will challenge decentralization itself. Up to this point, all samples were built as a static single-page application using the blockchain as its only back end. This chapter will introduce centralized components to the architecture of a decentralized application, such as indexing and storage solutions.

Finally, chapters seven and eight deal with two of the most pressing challenges in Ethereum development as of today: user onboarding and scalability. Getting started in the Ethereum space for a non-technical user can be challenging, as they get bombarded with concepts like private keys or mnemonics, in an unforgiving space where they could lose all their funds if they make a mistake. Furthermore, having a platform with a global throughput of a dozen transactions per second severely limits the applications it can run – think of a cloud provider that offers no more than twelve database writes per second shared across all its clients. These two chapters explore these problems in depth, and include a survey of the current solutions available. These are also the two scenarios most rapidly changing, but the chapters will give you the basics to help you navigate this space, so you can then build an outstanding Ethereum application.

The mandatory disclaimer

Security in software development is hard. Security in blockchain development is even harder. Smart contract applications potentially manage large amounts of funds, and are like sitting ducks to attackers in a public executable environment.

I want you to write a program that has to run in a concurrent environment under Byzantine circumstances where any adversary can invoke your program with any arguments of their choosing. The environment in which your program executes (and hence any direct or indirect environmental dependencies) is also under adversary control. If you make a single exploitable mistake or oversight in the implementation, or even in the logical design of the program, then either you personally or perhaps the users of your program could lose a substantial amount of money. Where your program will run, there is no legal recourse if things go wrong. Oh, and once you release the first version of your program, you can never change it. It has be right first time.

—Adrian Colyer, "Zeus: Analyzing safety of smart contracts"[10]

Even though all code samples in this book have been reviewed, they have not been formally audited. And even if they were, there could still be an overseen security bug. The goal of the code in this book is to teach you, not to be copy-pasted into your application – we already have StackOverflow for that. Neither the author nor the publisher of this book can offer any warranties on the security of the code you will find here.

Bottom line is that you should not blindly trust any code snippet from this book – or from any other source, for that matter. Always make sure you have a good understanding of what you are doing, and have your code reviewed and audited by third parties before going to production in the Ethereum network.

THE SOFTWARE IS PROVIDED "AS IS", WITHOUT WARRANTY OF ANY KIND, EXPRESS OR IMPLIED, INCLUDING BUT NOT LIMITED TO THE WARRANTIES OF MERCHANTABILITY, FITNESS FOR A PARTICULAR PURPOSE AND NONINFRINGEMENT. IN NO EVENT SHALL THE AUTHORS OR COPYRIGHT HOLDERS BE LIABLE FOR ANY CLAIM, DAMAGES OR OTHER LIABILITY, WHETHER IN AN ACTION OF CONTRACT, TORT OR OTHERWISE, ARISING FROM, OUT OF OR IN CONNECTION WITH THE SOFTWARE OR THE USE OR OTHER DEALINGS IN THE SOFTWARE.

Without further ado, let's get started.

---

[10]https://blog.acolyer.org/2018/03/08/zeus-analyzing-safety-of-smart-contracts/

CHAPTER 1

Blockchains

We will begin our journey with a brief introduction to Ethereum and blockchain technology in general, starting with Bitcoin. We will explain what makes a blockchain and when it makes sense to use one. We will also cover some cryptography basics before we start and later provide an overview of decentralized application development before we implement our first one in Chapter 2.

A Refresher on Cryptography

Before we go into blockchains, we will go over two cryptography concepts that are key building blocks in most blockchains: hashes and public key cryptography. Feel free to skip this section if you are already familiar with them.

Hash Functions

A *cryptographic hash function* is a pure deterministic function that maps inputs from a large space to outputs in a fixed set. These outputs are usually called the *digest* of the input. For instance, the input could be the entire text of the prologue of this book, and its digest could be the hexadecimal `01cc88cda97d50346743ae58bb3ebe75` from the space of 128-bit values.

Without going into formalisms, a secure hash function should be *collision resistant*. This means that it should be practically impossible to find out two different inputs that yield the same digest. Hash functions should also be *non-invertible*: given only the digest, it should be practically impossible to find out an input that yields that digest. Also, a small change to the input should yield a large change to the output digest – two similar inputs should have very different digests. Hash functions should also be relatively fast to calculate from their input, so verifying that an input matches with its digest is an easy task.

1

© Santiago Palladino 2019
S. Palladino, *Ethereum for Web Developers*, https://doi.org/10.1007/978-1-4842-5278-9_1

Hash functions are at the core of maintaining a blockchain's integrity and also form the basis for the proof-of-work consensus mechanism. We will see both uses in a few pages.

Public Key Cryptography

Public key or *asymmetric cryptography* is an encryption system that relies on pairs of keys: a private key, known only to its owner, and a corresponding public key, shared with the world. A string encrypted with the public key can only be decrypted with the private key. Anyone who wants to send a secret message to a user can use the recipient's public key to encrypt it, knowing that only the holder of the private key can decrypt it.

Key pairs can also be used inversely as *digital signatures*. A user can send a message, along with its digest encrypted with his private key. Any recipient can then use the public key to verify that the digest was signed by the owner of the private key.

These signatures are the authentication mechanism in public blockchains. Every public key has an associated private key that should be kept secure by its owner and grants access to the owned assets in the blockchain.

Public key cryptography can be implemented via many different algorithms, one of the most popular ones being Rivest–Shamir–Adleman (better known as RSA). Ethereum, however, relies on an Elliptic Curve Digital Signature Algorithm, or ECDSA. This algorithm also allows to *recover* the public key, given a message and its signature.

Armed with these two cryptography concepts, we can now finally get started and take on how a blockchain is built.

Blockchain 101

A blockchain is a decentralized indelible public digital ledger. We can think of a blockchain as a distributed database, where, once a record has been confirmed, it can never be removed or altered and where no single authority has control over this database, which is replicated across all nodes in a peer-to-peer network. What is actually stored in this database may vary: it could be a currency, a registry of assets, or even executable code.

Transactions and Blocks

In a blockchain, every state change is part of a *transaction*. Think of a transaction as an atomic write operation from a user in the global database that may alter one or more records. Any user in the network can submit a transaction to be executed.

How transactions are processed is part of the blockchain *state transition rules*. The blockchain transitions from one state to another by processing each transaction it receives. For instance, a blockchain that manages a currency may process transactions as transfers of its currency between two accounts: it reduces the sender's balance and increases the recipient's by the same amount. Other blockchains even allow transactions to create and execute full programs on the chain.

When a user sends a transaction, they must cryptographically *sign* it with their private key. This way, the blockchain can enforce that only a specific user can move a certain asset or alter a certain record. This introduces a notion of *ownership* by the holder of a key.

Note   Public blockchains do not require their users to sign up. They can just create a new key pair to start signing transactions to participate in the network. However, they may require their users to have a currency associated to the blockchain for their transactions to be processed.

Transactions are batched together in *blocks*, which are then chained together to form the actual blockchain. The blocks constitute the history of the blockchain, each of them packing a set of transactions that change its state. How transactions are chosen and ordered in each block depends on the blockchain *consensus rules*, which we will see in a few pages.

When a block is added to the blockchain, it is propagated through the peer-to-peer network to all nodes. Each node will re-execute all transactions in the block locally in order to check if they are indeed valid, rejecting the block if they notice any illegal change. This means that each transaction is actually executed once per every single node in the entire network. This allows the blockchain to be completely decentralized, since each node checks all transactions that are run. However, it comes at a cost: the computational overhead imposes a cap on the number of transactions that can be processed per second by the network. In other words, performance is traded in exchange for decentralization.

Given this high cost of processing a change in a blockchain, all transactions require a *fee* to be paid. This fee is usually paid in a currency native to the blockchain (such as bitcoin in the Bitcoin network[1] or ether in Ethereum). Regardless of who is the beneficiary of this fee, which we will see in a few pages, the goal of the fee is to prevent attackers from flooding the network with transactions that need to be processed by every single node, and to provide an incentive to the nodes that add new blocks to the chain.

Chain of Hashes

Blockchains are resistant to changes by keeping a *digest* of their entire history on every block. Each block in the chain is identified by a hash computed over its own transactions, as well as over the hash of the previous block (Figure 1-1).

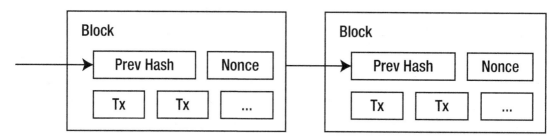

Figure 1-1. *How a blockchain is constructed. Each block is identified by a hash of the previous block, plus all its own transactions. We will see the role of the nonce in the next section. Image from the Bitcoin paper[2]*

With this scheme, any change on any transaction on any block in the chain will cause all subsequent hashes to change, making any modification trivial to detect. For instance, if an attacker tried to alter a transaction that happened ten blocks ago, not only the digest of that block would change but also that of the next block (since it is calculated based on the previous block hash) and so forth until the head of the chain.

However, for this mechanism to be useful to prevent an attacker from modifying the blockchain and distributing a spurious copy in the network, it must be *difficult* for the attacker to regenerate all blocks. That's where the proof-of-work comes in.

---

[1]Bitcoin (with uppercase B) is used to name the blockchain network that controls the bitcoin (with lowercase b) cryptocurrency.

[2]https://bitcoin.org/bitcoin.pdf

Reaching Consensus

How the transactions are ordered and included in the blockchain's blocks will depend on the *consensus algorithm* of the network. Since we are dealing with a decentralized database, we need a way for all actors to agree on how changes are added to the chain. For instance, if a seller is offering an asset on the blockchain and two buyers rush to purchase it, how can a decentralized network decide who got first? Even worse, how do we prevent the seller from telling both buyers that they made the purchase and cash in twice?[3] We need a way to determine how transactions are chosen and ordered in order to have a single state of the blockchain. In other words, we need a way to establish a *consensus* on which blocks are added to the chain.

Many public blockchains like Bitcoin or Ethereum rely on a consensus algorithm known as *proof-of-work*. A proof-of-work is a cryptographic proof that a significant amount of CPU cycles were spent performing a computation; in this case, computing a difficult number based on a block. In order for a block to be added to the blockchain, it must be accompanied by its proof-of-work. Any node can propose a new block and, if they submit it with its proof-of-work, it gets added to the blockchain. The node that gets to add a block receives a reward in return for their effort.[4] Nodes that fulfill this role in the network are called *miners*,[5] and whenever a new block is added, they all race to try and add the next to capture the corresponding reward.

Note   The mechanism for these proofs is actually quite simple. The identifier for every block in the chain is a hash that includes the identifier of the previous block, all transactions in the block, and a *nonce*. By changing the nonce, the calculated block's digest will be completely different. In order to add a new block to the chain, this identifier must have a certain structure (begin with N zeros). Since it is not possible to predict what a digest will look like, a miner can only try calculating the block hash repeatedly while changing the nonce until he hits a digest that matches the requirements. This requires many attempts and is hence considered a proof-of-work.

---

[3]This is commonly known as a *double-spend*.

[4]The reward is often composed of a fixed amount that is created out of thin air when the block is created, as well as all the transaction fees included in the block.

[5]The difficulty of the proof-of-work increases the more miners are in the network. Today, it is impossible to mine neither bitcoin nor ether on a regular computer, as the difficulty is so high that it requires large farms of dedicated hardware pooled together.

Remember that the entire infrastructure runs over a peer-to-peer decentralized network. This allows nodes to join and leave the network as they wish without requiring a centralized server. Here, the proof-of-work algorithm provides a way for new nodes to know which is the actual chain: they just need to look for the chain with the largest accumulated computing power invested.

This also prevents a malicious actor from just altering a record on the chain and recomputing all subsequent block hashes, as we were discussing in the previous section. In order to do this, the attacker would need to solve all proof-of-works from the block he changed onward, which requires more computing power than the rest of the miners in the network.

Note   There are other mechanisms for consensus besides proof-of-work. In Chapter 8, we will review with proof-of-authority and proof-of-stake as alternatives for building faster and smaller chains.

The consensus algorithm is closely tied to the *finality* of the network. We say a transaction is *final* when we know it has been included in the blockchain and will not change. A transaction added in the most recent block is far from being considered final: if a miner manages to mine two blocks on a row starting from the next to last, they may generate a new chain that replaces the latest block and does not include that transaction.

This is called a *reorganization*, and it is not uncommon in proof-of-work chains. To know that a transaction is final, we need to wait for several blocks to be mined on top of the one in which it was included, to ensure it will not change. The number of blocks will depend on the particular chain and how much confidence we need.

On Throughput

Solving a proof-of-work is computationally expensive by design. This by itself enforces a limit on the throughput of a blockchain, by forcing to solve a difficult puzzle every time a batch of transactions is to be added.

However, there is another reason for limiting the number and complexity of transactions per second added to the chain: verifiability. In order to keep the blockchain decentralized, every node in the network needs to be able to verify that every transaction was legitimate and was carried out according to the established rules. If the network accepts a very large number of transactions per second, then only powerful devices would be able to verify the chain, leaving out of the network to any user that cannot access the necessary hardware. Thus, low throughput is related to guaranteeing public access to the blockchain.

In particular, Ethereum is designed to handle about 15 transactions per second. Note that transactions can be more or less complex in Ethereum, since they may execute arbitrary computations, so this cap is actually related to how much effort is required to run and verify each of block's transactions.

Note that these few transactions per second are shared among all users and applications in the network, which is a very low limit even for a single traditional web application. We will see some approaches around this limitation in Chapter 8.

From Bitcoin to Ethereum

We have so far defined a blockchain as a public database, but we have not gone into *what* that database may contain. The first famous blockchain is used to track ownership of a digital currency, the bitcoin.

Most of what we understand as a blockchain today was introduced in 2008 by Satoshi Nakamoto[6] in his "Bitcoin: A Peer-to-Peer Electronic Cash System" paper.[7] The paper is short and easy to read, and it packs most of the blockchain concepts used today. It introduces a "purely peer-to-peer version of electronic cash", without any centralized owner or issuer.

All in all, the Bitcoin blockchain is a public decentralized database that keeps track of the balance in bitcoin of its users and supports transactions for moving funds from one address to another. It is an implementation of a decentralized electronic payments platform.

It's worth mentioning that, besides plain transfers, Bitcoin also supports a limited scripting language. This language allows for constructs such as timelocks, which restrict a transfer from being executed until a certain time in the future, or multisignature transactions, which require multiple accounts to be in agreement to move an asset. However, what can be built with this language is still limited.

It is with the goal to support arbitrary computation in the network that Ethereum came up.

---

[6]Satoshi Nakamoto is the pseudonym of the author. To this day, it is still unknown who is the mastermind behind Bitcoin.

[7]https://bitcoin.org/bitcoin.pdf

Smart Contracts

Ethereum was introduced by Vitalik Buterin in 2013, and first launched in 2015.[8] Its main differentiator was the concept of arbitrary code that could be executed in the blockchain in the form of smart contracts. A smart contract is a short program uploaded to the blockchain, which can react to transactions sent to it by executing arbitrary logic. Each smart contract has its own arbitrary state as well, which can be updated on any transaction and can keep any data whatsoever. And of course, a smart contract can also hold ETH, the native currency of the Ethereum network.

In other words, the Ethereum network holds both a digital currency (the ether) and executable code (the smart contracts) with their own state.

This flexibility allows Ethereum to implement many different constructs. For instance, a whole new coin can be easily implemented as a smart contract. The contract only needs to keep track of the balance of each user, and provide methods for securely transferring them. This allows new cryptocurrencies to be created on top of Ethereum with little effort.[9]

However, remember that all transactions are re-executed by all nodes in the network in order to be verified. This means that, while smart contracts may execute arbitrary code, this code must be *deterministic*. It must always yield the same result, no matter when or where it is run. It also cannot depend on any sources external to the blockchain; otherwise, the validity of the blockchain becomes dependent on those external sources. A smart contract may only query or interact with other smart contracts within the Ethereum network.

Gas Fees

Allowing any user to send a transaction with arbitrary code that will be executed on every single node in the network is potentially dangerous. A malicious user could submit a piece of code extremely expensive to execute or one that never finishes.

To guard against this, Ethereum introduces a concept called *gas*. Think of gas as the measure of the computing power required to process a transaction. In a transaction,

---

[8]https://vitalik.ca/general/2017/09/14/prehistory.html

[9]The effort was so little that led to the ICO craze of 2017, where many projects would spawn their own cryptocurrency (or token) just to raise funds, taking advantage of the hype around blockchain technology.

complex operations will consume more gas than simpler ones. For instance, altering the storage of the contract is much more expensive than a simple arithmetic expression.

A transaction sent to the network requires a gas allocation in order to be sent. This gas is paid for using ETH. Every line of code executed by the transaction consumes a bit of its gas, and if it drops to zero, the processing is immediately stopped, and the transaction fails. Nevertheless, its sender is still charged for the hassle of processing such a long-running process.

The sender of a transaction can also set the gas price, indicating that they are willing to pay more (or less) than other users for the execution of their transaction. This is a way to get their transaction included in the blockchain faster (or cheaper) than other users, by making it more (or less) attractive to miners.

Decentralized Applications

Smart contracts allow the building of *decentralized applications*, which will be our main focus throughout this book. Decentralized applications, or DApps, are client-side single-page web applications backed not by a server, but by a set of smart contracts on the blockchain. Instead of sending HTTP requests to a web server, users of the application send transactions to a smart contract on the Ethereum network. It is even possible to host the web application itself on a decentralized file storage system,[10] making the application completely independent of any centralized infrastructure.

Instead of querying data from a centralized data store, decentralized applications use the blockchain as the source of truth. Data used to populate the app is either stored on the blockchain or on a remote storage location that is referred to from the blockchain. Likewise, the business logic of the application is encoded in a set of smart contracts. Users perform persistent actions on the app by sending transactions to its smart contracts.

User Experience

How does a DApp look and feel to a user? Some DApps will favor decentralization over ease of use and require users to access them with a specialized browser or browser

---

[10]Contrary to a traditional file storage service, in decentralized storage networks, you upload your content and it is distributed across a peer-to-peer network – similar to how BitTorrent works. For more info, see Chapter 6 on IPFS, the InterPlanetary File System, and how to host a web application on it.

extension. These extensions act as wallets, holding the user's keys, and also as a gateway to the blockchain by providing a connection to an Ethereum node. Under the hood, they inject a javascript object that provides low-level methods for accessing blockchain data and sending transactions on behalf of the user. Whenever the application requests to send a transaction, the user is presented with a pop-up to approve it. This moves much complexity from the DApp onto the extension, but also requires a large effort from the user to get set up, by installing the extension, creating and backing up an account, and purchasing ETH to begin operating. We will use this approach to build our first DApp in Chapter 2 and revisit it more in-depth in Chapter 5 as we see the details of sending transactions.

Other DApps have a more user-friendly approach, managing the keys on behalf of the user. It's even possible for a user to be using a DApp without even noticing, if all its complexity is handled behind the scenes. However, this also means that the user is no longer in control of their own keys, but delegates this on the app. Also, if each app manages its own set of keys, interoperability is much more difficult, since the user will have a different identity on each service. We will explore user-friendly approaches, along with the challenges they pose, in Chapter 6. All in all, good apps offer different experiences to different users, depending on how familiar they are with Ethereum.

Regardless of key management, all DApps need to account for the long confirmation times of the network. In traditional web apps, an action in the form of an HTTP request takes a few milliseconds to get to the web server and back. However, in Ethereum, a transaction may take several seconds to be mined, and even more to be confirmed. DApps need to take this into account when designing their interfaces and be prepared to handle reorganizations as well. We will learn more about these challenges in Chapters 4 and mostly 5.

Degrees of Decentralization

As we mentioned, a DApp can be fully decentralized: it can be hosted on a decentralized storage location, load its data from the blockchain, and rely on smart contracts for any business logic. Once launched, there is no centralized party that can stop or alter the application and no service that could go down preventing access to it. These applications are even resistant to censorship by any agent.

However, this comes at a cost. Decentralized storage may be slow or occasionally unavailable if there are not enough replicas of the content. Running queries on the Ethereum network can be too slow for some use cases. And in some scenarios, even the hurdle of setting up an Ethereum account can be a show-stopper for our users. Fortunately, we can trade in some degrees of decentralization in exchange for improving the user experience.

For instance, instead of loading data from the blockchain itself, we can set up a centralized server that acts as a cache, providing much faster access to the data we need on the client. The web application can still fall back to the chain itself if this server goes down or even validate the data it provides against the blockchain when needed for a critical operation. We will explore these solutions in Chapter 6.

Another example is relaying our users' transactions to the network, so they do not need to set up an account, purchase ETH to pay for gas fees, or even interact with the Ethereum network at all. We can create an ephemeral key for the client-side and use it to sign transactions that we submit to the blockchain on their behalf from a dedicated server. This alleviates many of the pains around user onboarding. We will explore this and other alternatives in Chapter 8.

We can even build fully centralized applications that interact with a decentralized protocol powered by smart contracts on the Ethereum blockchain. The value of the blockchain here is not on the application layer, but on the protocol. By managing our users' assets on a decentralized layer, we guarantee that their data is safe, and they can at any time transparently migrate to another application on top of the same trustless[11] protocol.

All in all, the takeaway is that decentralization is not all or nothing. We can and have to choose the appropriate degree of decentralization to implement in our applications, knowing that it comes at a trade-off with its ease of use.

---

[11]In this context, we say a protocol or application is *trustless* when its users do not need to trust in a third party who run it. For example, Bitcoin is a trustless protocol for transferring value, because there is no centralized entity who manages it you need to trust. On the contrary, the App Store is a centralized protocol for distributing Apps, as you have to trust Apple in operating it, while you keep your fingers crossed in hope that it will not change the rules of the store.

Why Blockchain?

The first question you should ask yourself when implementing a blockchain-based system is *whether you actually need a blockchain.*[12]

It is easy in technology to get carried away by hype cycles: you may be using a Kubernetes cluster to horizontally scale the load over your web application that would perfectly run on a single box, or you may be using state-of-the-art machine learning algorithms to infer trends from your dataset with less than 100 entries that would better be visualized in an Excel spreadsheet. Millions have been spent in developing native mobile apps for presenting static info, since it was cooler than *just* a plain responsive web site.

Blockchain is no exception to hype, with the aggravating factor that it can be used as an instrument for financial speculators as well. Always remember that just because you have a shiny new hammer on your hands, not everything becomes a nail. You should not try to hammer a blockchain into every system, but rather design a solution and then consider whether it would actually benefit from a blockchain.

Advantages and Use Cases

After the preceding disclaimer, we can now focus on where blockchains do shine and some suitable use cases for public blockchains or Ethereum in particular.[13]

Decentralized finance is one of the most popular use cases.[14] The first blockchain, Bitcoin, was built as a decentralized payments platform, but financial applications of a blockchain can go much further. Smart contracts can be used to support many kinds of financial workflows, such as decentralized exchanges, derivatives, margin trading, insurance, credits, lending, investing, prediction markets, and so on. These `artifacts` traditionally required users to place their trust and their assets in a centralized institution – this increased the barrier of entry, and the institution often took a hefty fee

---

[12]Refer to the "Do you need a Blockchain?" paper by Karl Wurst and Arthur Gervais (`https://eprint.iacr.org/2017/375.pdf`) for a very critical analysis on blockchain use cases. The site `http://doyouneedablockchain.com/` takes this one step further, greeting you with a "most probably not" response to this question as soon as the page loads.

[13]Many examples listed here are derived from a list shared by Vitalik Buterin at `https://twitter.com/VitalikButerin/status/1072158957999771648`

[14]The site `https://defiprime.com/` keeps a categorized list of the best decentralized finance products if you want to go deeper into it.

for their services. Now, a smart contract in a public auditable blockchain can act as the institution supporting these financial services, acting on cryptocurrencies within the chain.

In general, blockchains shine in scenarios where there was a need for a *trusted third party*, since they act as a credible neutral platform for several participants to interact securely. This holds not just on financial applications but also whenever there is a need to publicly verify the transparency of a process. For instance, in an online auction, it is possible to verify that bids from all participants are processed by having them submitted (encrypted) to the blockchain. If a participant sees that their bid was not considered, they can just show proof of their bid on the blockchain.

By removing the need for a trusted third party, smart contracts can be used to create trustless *platforms* or *protocols*. Instead of building on top of a proprietary layer, where the rules of the game may be changed unilaterally by the owner, you could build on top of a decentralized platform. A good example is a marketplace: traditional big companies that operate application and services marketplaces can alter their terms and conditions (and their cut!) at any time. On the other hand, a marketplace coordinated by a smart contract is immutable and run by no one but the blockchain itself.

Blockchains can also be used to prove existence of a piece of data.[15] By submitting a signed digest of a document to the blockchain, anyone can then prove that certain data was published by a certain date. But, more interestingly, blockchains also allow to verify that a certain piece of data was *not* published. For instance, if a blockchain is used to store certificate revocations, then anyone can easily prove that a certificate was *not* revoked by just showing that the revocation was never uploaded to the chain, which acts as a neutral global database.

Another advantage of a blockchain is that of *permanence*. If you, as a user, hold something of value on a digital system and the maintainer of such system disappears, along goes your stuff. This can be true not just for currencies but also for digital assets, such as collectibles or online achievements. Having digital assets registered on a blockchain guarantees that they are maintained independently of the organization that created them. It can even enable trading of those assets across the boundaries of the system where it was originally created.

Some groups are also exploring new governance mechanisms by building *decentralized autonomous organizations* (DAOs) on Ethereum. In a DAO, a set of

---

[15]www.proofofexistence.com/ was originally developed by Manuel Araoz on the Bitcoin network, as a way to upload a digest of a document to the chain.

participants hold some form of voting power and can submit proposals which are then decided via a mechanism coded into the DAO smart contract.[16] The blockchain ensures the absolute transparency of the process and allows for rapidly experimenting with new ways of organizing groups around a common purpose.

However, for all the advantages that come from a public blockchain, there are also major limitations imposed on what can be built.

Limitations

One of the major limitations imposed by a public blockchain, as we already mentioned, is *transaction throughput*. Processing a dozen transactions per second is often not enough for a single application, much less for all applications built on the same chain to share. This is, however, the cost of decentralization. As Vitalik Buterin himself puts it: "Blockchains are NOT about cutting computational costs (at least relative to centralized servers). Blockchains are about incurring a sacrifice in the form of increased computational costs to achieve a decrease in social costs."[17]

Nevertheless, there is much work toward scaling public blockchains. If a dozen transactions per second is too few to share among all applications in a blockchain, then we can build more blockchains and interconnect them. Or we can process batches of transactions outside the blockchain and then settle them all together in a single transaction. We will explore more about these approaches in Chapter 8, regarding scaling.

Another major challenge for blockchains is that of *user onboarding*. While decentralization offers many benefits in terms of decreasing social costs, removing third parties, and providing privacy, it also makes approaching the platform more difficult. There is no central authority to hold your hand as you jump onto the platform and no one to ask for your help if you misplaced your private keys and lost all your funds. Furthermore, in order to interact with the Ethereum network, you first need to have ether in your possession, not to mention a wallet to hold them, which makes the setup process longer and more cumbersome than most users are willing to accept.

Onboarding is being tackled as one of the major pain points in the usage of cryptocurrencies in applications, with many companies offering centralized solutions

---

[16]As an example, Moloch (`https://github.com/MolochVentures/moloch`) is a DAO used to distribute grants to projects building shared Ethereum infrastructure and tools.

[17]`https://twitter.com/VitalikButerin/status/1072162427045736449`

or acting as custodians for end users' assets. Decentralized applications are also experimenting with smoother user onboarding flows, so users do not fall out of the funnel when asked to download a dedicated browser extension to interact with the app. We will go through many of these techniques to ease user onboarding in Chapter 7.

Note that the limitations and use cases we have defined so far apply to blockchains that are public in nature, that is, networks where any participant can join to verify history, submit transactions, query the current data, or even act as a miner. However, there is another set of blockchains we have not explored so far.

Non-public Blockchains

When we first defined a blockchain, we described it as a *public* digital ledger. However, ever since Bitcoin appeared, there has been extensive work on *permissioned* blockchains, which challenge our preceding definition by removing the public nature of the chain. These blockchains limit which nodes are allowed to join the network or which are allowed to act as miners or send transactions.

For instance, a growing pattern in the enterprise world is that of *federated* or *consortium* blockchains. These blockchains are managed by a group (consortium) of different institutions. Each member of the consortium controls a node in the network that acts as a whitelisted *validator* node and participates in a vote-based consensus algorithm for adding new blocks.[18] This removes the need of a proof-of-work, since consensus is reached by voting among a predefined set of nodes.

These permissioned blockchains may also limit not only the nodes that act as miners but also which nodes join the network and are able to verify the transactions, or which accounts are able to submit transactions for processing.

Note Some companies are taking this one step further and go with fully *private blockchains*, which are internal to the company, and only a single node has the permission to add new blocks. These chains are used mostly for auditability and tracing purposes.

---

[18]This scheme is usually called proof-of-authority, and we will review it in Chapter 8 as a scalability solution for Ethereum.

These changes allow federated blockchains to have a much higher transaction throughput than public blockchains. Also, by restricting the set of nodes that can participate in the network, they are automatically protected against spam, and can drop the requirement of paying for transaction fees.

This allows permissioned blockchains to cater for a different set of use cases. For instance, federated chains are often used to settle global transactions among the different companies that form the consortium, without the restrictions on the number of transactions per second imposed by public blockchains. Here, the value of the blockchain lies in its auditability, and in removing the need of a *single* trusted party to hold the data shared among the consortium.

While there are some disagreements on whether these permissioned chains can be considered *true blockchains* or not, the fact is that blockchain technology is making its way to the enterprise world. However, throughout this book we will focus on public blockchains only, specifically Ethereum. Nevertheless, much of the learning from public blockchains can be applied to the permissioned space as well.[19]

Summary

Hopefully, this chapter served as an introduction to the world of blockchain and Ethereum. You should now have a basic understanding on what a blockchain is, when it makes sense to use one, and what are its limitations.

We introduced basic concepts to which we will constantly return throughout the book, such as smart contracts, transactions, blocks, reorganizations, consensus, and nodes. We went from Bitcoin onto Ethereum and briefly mentioned permissioned blockchains as an alternative to the public chains.

After all this theory, in the next chapter we will go fully hands-on, by implementing our first Ethereum DApp. This will give you a better understanding of the concept of a decentralized application that we presented in this chapter, and we will then go in-depth on its different aspects in the entire book.

---

[19]As an example, Quorum (one of the most popular permissioned blockchain engines, developed by JPMorgan) is built as a variant of Ethereum itself. This allows many of the tools and libraries used in Ethereum today to be ported almost directly to Quorum.

CHAPTER 2

A Sample DApp

In this chapter, we will build a full DApp from scratch. While we will not be going in-depth on the steps involved, this chapter will help you identify all the components involved in the construction of a decentralized application. In the upcoming chapters, we will focus on each of the different parts, but you can always refer back to these pages to understand how each section fits within the bigger picture.

About Our DApp

We will be creating a global **counter** implemented as a DApp. Users should be able to view the value of the counter and increase it by sending a transaction to it. Even though this application has no practical uses, it will be of help to go through each of the components of a DApp.

Our Requirements

Our application will hold a single counter as its state, and allow any Ethereum user to increase it through a transaction. At the same time, any user accessing the DApp should be able to see real-time updates to the counter's value.

The application will not manage any ETH at all and will not have any kind of access control. As long as a user can reach the DApp, they should be able to freely interact with it.

The Smart Contract

Ethereum smart contracts are small programs deployed in the Ethereum blockchain. Every contract has its own code and internal state. In this application, we will store the counter's value in the contract's state. The contract will also provide a getter for any client to easily query its value, as well as a method to increase it by sending a transaction to the contract (Listing 2-1).

17

© Santiago Palladino 2019
S. Palladino, *Ethereum for Web Developers*, https://doi.org/10.1007/978-1-4842-5278-9_2

Listing 2-1. Initial implementation of the smart contract backing our sample DApp

```solidity
pragma solidity ^0.5.0;

contract Counter {
    uint256 public value;

    function increase() public {
        value = value + 1;
    }
}
```

The smart contract should also provide an *event* for clients to listen for real-time updates to its state (Listing 2-2). Every transaction in Ethereum may optionally fire one or more events, and a client can subscribe to a particular set of them, as a means to be notified of any changes to a contract.

Listing 2-2. Updated implementation to emit an event every time the increase method is invoked

```solidity
pragma solidity ^0.5.0;

contract Counter {
    uint256 public value;

    event Increased(uint256 newValue);

    function increase() public {
        value = value + 1;
        emit Increased(value);
    }
}
```

Now, this implementation shows all the basic ways in which a smart contract provides an interface for a client to interact with it:

- A getter to query the internal state of the contract, `value`. It is autogenerated by the use of the `public` keyword when declaring the field. Querying a contract is fast and does not involve sending a transaction, and so it does not require gas or even having an Ethereum account.

- A function to modify the state of the contract, `increase`. These functions require a transaction to be sent, which require ETH to be executed. As such, they require having a funded account.

- The `Increased` event, to listen for updates to the contract state. Any client can request to subscribe to a set of events from a contract, to get notifications of any changes to it.

We will go into detail on smart contracts in the next chapter. For now, these concepts will do in order to build our DApp.

The Architecture

We will build a traditional DApp for this example. The application will be backed by a smart contract in the Ethereum network, which will act as a distributed database for the Dapp's users. The front-end will be set up as a regular client-side javascript application.

For the glue between the javascript front-end and the Ethereum network, we will rely on a web3-enabled web browser. This is a kind of browser that allows the user to connect not only to the Internet but also to the Ethereum network via a node of their own choice. It also manages the user's private keys and transaction signing.

The most popular web3-enabled browser is MetaMask,[1] which is not a browser per se but a plugin, that provides all the required features. MetaMask keeps track of the user private keys, allows connections to a list of predefined nodes or to a custom one, and prompts the user to accept any transaction that the current page is trying to send on their behalf.

From the developer's perspective, MetaMask injects a global connection provider to an Ethereum node, and intercepts all transactions for signing them with its own keys.

Setting Up the Environment

Before we start building the DApp, we will set up our development environment, as well as the required tools for interacting with and testing our DApp.

---

[1]See `https://metamask.io/`

Development Toolchain

The basic setup for our development environment will be the one required to build a simple client-side-only javascript application. Make sure to have nodejs and npm installed[2] on your development machine to get started.

We will jumpstart our application by relying on the `create-react-app` package. This is a package, provided by the Facebook development team, that initializes a new preconfigured React web application. This will allow us to save most of the setup time and focus on building the DApp.

```
npm init react-app counter-app
```

As for the Ethereum-specific libraries, while there are many development frameworks available, we will stick to the bare minimum for this example. The only Ethereum-related javascript library we will be using is `web3.js`.[3] This is a library whose development is backed by the Ethereum foundation and is regarded by many as the de facto canonical library.

```
npm install web3@1.2.0
```

Regarding the Ethereum build toolchain, we will again focus on the minimum set of tools needed. First we will install the Solidity compiler, in order to compile the smart contracts.[4] Make sure you install version 0.5.0 or above.

```
$ solc --version
solc, the solidity compiler commandline interface
Version: ...
```

Then, in order to set up automated tests for our application, we will install ganache. Ganache is a process that exposes a similar interface to an Ethereum node and simulates an entire Ethereum blockchain by itself. It is particularly useful in development environments or for running unit tests.

```
npm install -g ganache-cli
```

---

[2]Node and npm are usually installed together, head over to `https://nodejs.org/` for installation instructions.

[3]See `https://github.com/ethereum/web3.js/`

[4]Download instructions for different platforms are available at `https://solidity.readthedocs.io/en/v0.5.1/installing-solidity.html`

By default, ganache immediately mines a new block for every transaction sent, eliminating the time to wait until a transaction is confirmed. This makes it easy for using it as a back end while coding, but keep in mind that a ganache environment will be drastically different, especially in terms of user experience, to a real one.

Web3 Browser

We will now set up a web3-enabled browser, using MetaMask. Remember that there are other web3-ready browsers, but at the time of this writing, MetaMask is the most popular way to interact with DApps.

Start out by installing the MetaMask plugin[5] for your browser – it supports Chrome, Firefox, Opera, and Brave. After installation, MetaMask will prompt you to create a password to encrypt your accounts and will present you with the secret backup phrase. Make sure to write down this phrase: in the event that you lose your MetaMask wallet, you can regenerate it using this phrase. Otherwise, all funds contained in it will be irremediably lost.

Warning   Be extra careful when installing MetaMask. Most software related to managing user keys or transactions is prone to be subject to phishing attacks. Always ensure you are accessing the official MetaMask site when downloading.

Next step is to actually fund your account in order to interact with smart contracts. For the examples throughout this book, we will be using the Rinkeby test network (or testnet). Ethereum has several testnets (Ropsten, Rinkeby, Kovan, and Goerli), each with its own characteristics and identified by a unique numeric ID:

- Ropsten (id 3) is the only proof-of-work-based testnet, which makes it the most similar one to mainnet, but is also very unreliable. As there is not much actual *work* being done on the network, block times are unpredictable, and the network is highly susceptible to attacks.

- Rinkeby (id 4) is a proof-of-authority-based testnet, which means that there are a set of trusted nodes which have the *authority* to add new blocks to the blockchain. This makes it much more stable and reliable than Ropsten. However, due to limitations of the consensus algorithm used, only Geth clients can connect to Rinkeby.

---

[5]Download from `https://metamask.io/`

- Kovan (id 42) is similar to Rinkeby, in that it is a proof-of-authority-based testnet, but its consensus algorithm is compatible with Parity clients instead of Geth.

- Goerli (id 6) is the most recent testnet set up. It uses proof-of-authority as well, with the advantage that it is compatible with both Geth and Parity clients.

There are several online faucets[6] to obtain testnet ETH to play around. Use one of them to request funds for one of the accounts you have just created on MetaMask.

Note   How did you find the onboarding process on MetaMask? If you think it was complicated or a bit long, now think of your users. All first-time users to Ethereum need to go through a similar process, with the additional burden of having to sign up in an exchange to purchase real mainnet ETH to interact with your app, which often requires a full KYC process. This is why user onboarding is such a challenge on Ethereum. There are techniques to mitigate this issue, such as not requiring your users to have an Ethereum account until it is absolutely needed, or alternative onboarding flows built on meta transactions. More on this later in Chapter 7!

Building Our Application

We will start building from the create-react-app template. Make sure to have run all the steps on the *"Setting up the environment"* section, and you should have a simple javascript app with a handful of files under the src folder, built around index.js. To verify that everything is running smoothly, run npm run start and open your browser in localhost:3000. You should see the default initial screen of the create-react-app package, including a rotating React logo.

Compiling the Smart Contract

Our DApp will be backed by a single smart contract, Counter. Create a contracts folder in the root of your project, and add a Counter.sol file (Listing 2-3).

---

[6]Check out https://faucet.rinkeby.io/ for Rinkeby.

Listing 2-3. Smart contract implementation in Solidity that we will use in our application

```
// contracts/Counter.sol
pragma solidity ^0.5.0;

contract Counter {
    uint256 public value;

    event Increased(uint256 newValue);

    function increase() public {
        value = value + 1;
        emit Increased(value);
    }
}
```

We will go more in-depth on smart contracts in the next chapter, but for now you can start identifying the important pieces of the contract:

- The contract's state, value, defined as an unsigned integer of 256 bits, the default size in Solidity

- The getter to access value, generated by the use of the public keyword in the declaration of the field

- The increase function to increment value via a transaction

- The Increased event used to signal when a modification of value has occurred

You can test that the contract is fine by running the solidity compiler on it:

```
$ solc contracts/Counter.sol
Compiler run successful, no output requested.
```

We need to specify the format in which we want to output the compilation. We are interested especially in the specification of the public interface of the contract, or ABI (Application Binary Interface), which is how our javascript application will communicate with the contract. We also want the binary code, so we can deploy the contract to the network if we need to do so. We can request the Solidity compiler to output these two in a single JSON file we can then use:

```
solc --pretty-json --combined-json=abi,bin --overwrite \
-o ./build/contracts contracts/Counter.sol
```

Note   The flags needed to output this information from the compiler may change depending on the version you are working with. The preceding code works for Solidity 0.5.1.

The preceding command will generate a file build/contracts/combined.json with all the compilation output. Take a look at it, and we will soon use it to interact with our contract.

Connecting to the Network Via Web3

As mentioned before, we will be using web3.js to connect to the Ethereum network. This requires a web3 *provider*, which is a small object that knows which node to connect to in order to place calls to smart contracts and send transactions to the network. In other words, as its name implies, the provider *provides* a connection to an Ethereum node and, from it, to the entire network.

Depending on the library you are working with, the provider is sometimes conflated with the *signer*. The signer is another component that has the responsibility of signing transactions with the user's keys, in the case that the keys are not managed by a local node. This is the case for most Dapps, since your average user will not have a node running, but depend on a public one. Because of this, the web3 provider injected by MetaMask acts both as a provider and as a signer. We will review these differences in depth later in the book.

The web3 provider injected by MetaMask can be conveniently accessed from code via Web3.givenProvider. You can check this property to know if MetaMask is enabled in your users' browser, and to create a new web3 object if available. We can keep this logic in a network.js file in our application (Listing 2-4).

Listing 2-4. Snippet for creating a web3 object using the MetaMask provider. Note that this code will not work if the user does not have MetaMask installed.

```
// src/eth/network.js
import Web3 from 'web3';

let web3;
export function getWeb3() {
```

```
  if (!web3) {
    web3 = new Web3(Web3.givenProvider);
  }
  return web3;
}
```

The web3 object created has a large number of methods available, most of them under the `web3.eth` namespace. For instance, we can query the list of the user's accounts (Listing 2-5) and retrieve the default one in use – which is the first one from the list.

Listing 2-5. Function for retrieving the user's current default account

```
// src/eth/network.js
export async function getAccount() {
  const web3 = getWeb3();
  const accounts = await web3.eth.getAccounts();
  return accounts[0];
}
```

However, this method will not work for browsers that run in *privacy mode*. Privacy mode restricts accessing to user accounts until the user approves the application to retrieve the accounts held in MetaMask. To unlock this, we must work with a global `ethereum` object and enable it (Listing 2-6).

Listing 2-6. Function updated to handle Ethereum browsers' privacy mode

```
export async function getAccount() {
  const accounts = await window.ethereum.enable();
  return accounts[0];
}
```

The async call to `ethereum.enable` will return once the user has granted their approval on MetaMask. Note that MetaMask will remember the user's approval, so they are prompted to answer only the first time (Figure 2-1).

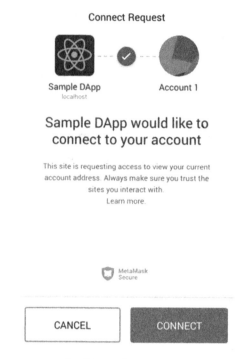

Figure 2-1. *Users must accept the Dapp's connection request in MetaMask*

Now that we have a web3 object set up, as well as access to the user's accounts, we will use them to build our interface to the Counter smart contract deployed on the Ethereum network.

The Contract Interface

In order to interact with our contract from the application, we need three things:

- A connection to the Ethereum network where our contract is deployed

- The address of the contract in the network

- The specification of the contract's public functions, also known as the ABI (Application Binary Interface)

The first item is covered in the previous section, and is encapsulated by the web3 object we provisioned. As for the second item, we will use an already deployed instance in the Rinkeby network at the following address:

0x1D2561D18dD2fc204CcC8831026d28375065ed53

Remember that everything in the blockchain is public and indeleble, so once a contract is deployed, it becomes publicly available for all users to interact with and cannot be deleted. This means we can freely use this instance for testing the DApp.

Note   If you do not want to work with that particular contract instance or prefer to work on a different network, there is a deploy script on the code repository that you can use to set up your own instance.

As for the ABI, we will make use of the output generated by the compiler previously. Copy the output json file into an `Artifacts.json` file in a new `contracts` folder in your application `src`. We can now parse it to obtain the ABI, and create a new web3 contract instance (Listing 2-7).

Listing 2-7. Function to create a `Counter` web3 contract object. Note that the function does not deploy a new contract, it just creates a javascript object that acts as a wrapper to a contract previously deployed at a specified address

```
// src/contracts/Counter.js
import Artifacts from './Artifacts.json';

export default function Counter(web3, address, options = {}) {
  const name = "contracts/Counter.sol:Counter";
  const artifact = Artifacts.contracts[name];
  const abi = JSON.parse(artifact.abi);
  return new web3.eth.Contract(abi, address, options);
}
```

The web3 Contract abstraction is an object that acts as a facade for the actual Ethereum contract. It exposes javascript methods for all its public functions, which get translated into calls and transactions to the network under the hood. We will be using it in the following section to actually interact with the contract.

Now that we have our factory-like function that can create new `Counter` contract abstractions given an address, we will use it to retrieve the deployed contract (Listing 2-8).

Listing 2-8. Code for obtaining a web3 contract instance of the `Counter` contract deployed on the Rinkeby network. Note that, to avoid hard-coding the address, you can also store the address as an environment variable, and retrieve it from `process.env`[7]

```
// src/contracts/Counter.js
import { getWeb3, getAccount } from '../eth/network.js';

export async function getDeployed() {
  const web3 = getWeb3();
  const from = await getAccount();
  const addr = "0x1D2561D18dD2fc204CcC8831026d28375065ed53";
  return Counter(web3, addr, { from });
}
```

Now that we have the means to interact with the deployed contract, we can build the React visual component for our user interface.

Interacting with Our Smart Contract

We will now progressively build our `Counter` visual component to allow the users of our DApp to interact with it. We will begin by retrieving the current value of the counter, then provide a means to send a transaction to modify its state, and then subscribe to real-time updates to it.

Wiring Our Component

Let's start by creating a file `components/Counter.js` (Listing 2-9). This will be an empty React component[8] for now.

---

[7]See `https://facebook.github.io/create-react-app/docs/adding-custom-environment-variables` for more info on how react-app handles environment vars.

[8]React applications are split into multiple components, each representing a section of the application. Components need to implement, at the very least, a `render` function that specifies what they should display (text, HTML, or other components), based on their state and properties. React takes care of re-rendering whenever needed.

Listing 2-9. Empty React component for rendering the `Counter` contract and interacting with it. We will be iteratively adding features to it

```
// src/components/Counter.js
import React, { Component } from 'react';
class Counter extends Component {
  render() {
    return (
      <div>Counter be here</div>
    );
  }
}
```

This component will receive from the `App.js` root component the `Counter` contract instance. It will be the App's responsibility to retrieve such instance and inject into the `Counter` visual component once ready. Let's modify the `src/App.js` file that was autogenerated by create-react-app to load the contract instance (Listing 2-10).

Listing 2-10. Code for the App root component. We use the root App state to store the contract instance, and pass it to the child component as a property

```
import './App.css';
import React, { Component } from 'react';
import Counter from './components/Counter';
import { getDeployed } from './contracts/Counter';

class App extends Component {
  state = { counter: null };

  async componentDidMount() {
    const counter = await getDeployed();
    this.setState({ counter });
  }
```

```
  render() {
    const { counter } = this.state;
    return (
      <div className="App">
        { counter && <Counter contract={counter} /> }
      </div>
    );
  }
}

export default App;
```

We are relying on the `componentDidMount` React event to load the Counter contract instance[9] and storing it in the component's state. Only when this instance is available we render the `Counter` visual component.

Note   By now, you may have realized that we are missing error management in this DApp. For instance, we are not handling the case where the user does not have MetaMask, or if the contract's address is incorrect, or if the connection to the network is lost. This is a deliberate decision, as the goal is to focus on the happy path and provide a quick overview of what constitutes a DApp. In the upcoming chapters, as we go deeper into each subject, we will also cover everything that can potentially go wrong.

At this point, you should be able to run your application via `npm start` and check that everything is rendering correctly. Make sure to have MetaMask installed, unlocked, and connected to the Rinkeby network.

Now that we have all of our application wired, it's time to focus on the `Counter` visual component itself.

---

[9]React components have several hooks associated to their lifecycle, such as when they are mounted on the page DOM. Of course, instead of relying on this hook, you can use whichever async state management solution you prefer for your React application (redux, thunks, sagas, etc.), but we will keep it simple and unopinionated throughout this book.

Querying the Contract's State

We will begin by displaying the value of the Counter contract on our component (Listing 2-11). Since we will not be changing the Counter instance during the lifetime of our component, we can simply retrieve that value when the React component is mounted.[10]

Listing 2-11. Retrieving the initial value of the Counter when the component is mounted

```
// src/components/Counter.js
async componentDidMount() {
  const counter = this.props.contract;
  const initialValue = await counter.methods.value().call();
  this.setState({ value: initialValue });
}
```

Note the call to the counter contract instance to retrieve the initial value. The web3js API for the call may seem awkward, but it has a rationale behind it:

- The methods property grants access to all the public methods defined in the contract's ABI. They are not set at the contract instance itself, to prevent clashing with other methods specific to the web3 contract object.

- The value() call does not actually query the network, but simply builds a method call. If the function required any parameters, they would have to be supplied here.

- The call() invocation finally issues the query to the blockchain. We will review in the next chapter the difference between querying a method and issuing a transaction, but for now, all we need to know is that call() is used when we want to *retrieve* data from a contract.

Once we have set the initial value in the component's state, we can finally render it to our users (Listing 2-12).

---

[10]If we needed to support a scenario in which the component could receive different contracts throughout its lifetime, we could use getDerivedStateFromProps instead or apply a key equal to the contract's address to force re-creating a new instance of the component. These are patterns very specific to React itself and fall out of our scope.

Listing 2-12. Render method to display the counter's value. Note that the value is only available after the initial query to the contract returns, so we need to handle the case where the value is not yet at our disposal

```
render() {
  const { value } = this.state;
  if (!value) return "Loading";

  return (
    <div>
      <div>Counter value: { value.toString() }</div>
    </div>
  );
}
```

By this point, you should be able to reload your application in your browser and see the value of the Counter instance on the Rinkeby network.

Tip   You can double-check the value displayed against the one reported by a blockchain explorer, such as Etherscan.[11] Etherscan is a blockchain explorer, a web site that provides a visual interface to addresses and transactions, and is available for mainnet and most test networks. Look for the address of the contract, and under the Read Contract tab, you will be able to check the value of the counter.

Our next step will be to allow the user to increase the value of the counter, by issuing a transaction.

---

[11]See https://rinkeby.etherscan.io/address/0x1D2561D18dD2fc204CcC8831026d28375065ed5
3#readContract

Sending a Transaction

Let's start by writing a function to send a transaction to call the `increase` function on the Counter contract.

```
increaseCounter() {
  const counter = this.props.contract;
  return counter.methods.increase().send();
}
```

After the previous section, the call to send the transaction should be more familiar. Note that in this case we are using `send()` instead of `call()`. This is because we need to actually send a transaction to affect the contract's state, instead of just querying data from the network.

We can now wire this method to a button in our interface (Listing 2-13), and test it.

Listing 2-13. Updated render method to display a button that increases the counter

```
render() {
  const { value } = this.state;
  if (!value) return "Loading";

  return (
    <div>
      <div>Counter value: { value.toString() }</div>
      <button onClick={() => this.increaseCounter()}>
        Increase counter
      </button>
    </div>
  );
}
```

If you try this, you will be greeted with Metamask's dialog to confirm a transaction, which should look more or less like Figure 2-2.

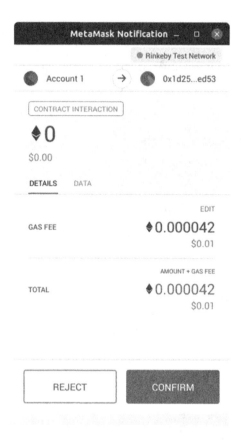

Figure 2-2. *Metamask confirmation dialog to accept a transaction issued by the application. Your users will be shown this dialog every time you try to send a transaction on their behalf*

If you refresh the page a few seconds after confirming the transaction, you should see the new value of the counter. However, to avoid requiring a page reload to update the value, we will query the value again after the transaction is confirmed (Listing 2-14).

Listing 2-14. Query the counter's value after the transaction is mined

```
increaseCounter() {
  const counter = this.props.contract;
  return counter.methods.increase().send()
    .on('receipt', async () => {
      const value = await counter.methods.value().call();
      this.setState({ value });
    });
}
```

The send() method returns an event emitter, which allows us to listen for different events in the lifetime of a transaction. For now, we are interested only on the event when the transaction is mined, that is, included in a block in the chain. This event is referred to as receipt, since it corresponds to when the transaction receipt object is available. If we wanted, we could also check when the transaction was actually sent to a node, or when it has reached a reasonable number of confirmations.

Now, even if the updated code does refresh the counter's value, we need to let the user know what is going on. The transaction's confirmation takes several seconds, which is definitely more than what a regular web 2.0 application usually takes.

We will track the transaction state (Listing 2-15) to show a simple "Awaiting transaction" message to let the user know what is going on, and disable the button in the meantime (Listing 2-16). We will also handle the case in which the transaction fails, so we don't disable the button permanently. Of course, in a real DApp, you may want to provide better visual cues.

Listing 2-15. Updated increaseCounter function to keep track of a flag to identify pending transactions and any error returned

```
increaseCounter() {
  const counter  = this.props.contract;
  this.setState({ increasing: true, error: null });
  return counter.methods.increase().send()
    .on('receipt', async () => {
      const value = await counter.methods.value().call();
      this.setState({ value, increasing: false });
    })
    .on('error', (error) => {
      this.setState({ error, increasing: false })
    });
}
```

Listing 2-16. Updated render method to display a notification when a transaction is pending or has failed, and disable the button until the transaction is finished

```
render() {
  const { value, increasing, error } = this.state;
  if (!value) return "Loading";

  return (
    <div className="Counter">
      <div>Counter value: { value.toString() }</div>
      <button
        disabled={!!increasing}
        onClick={() => this.increaseCounter()}>
          Increase counter
      </button>
      <div>{ increasing && "Awaiting transaction" }</div>
      <div>{ error && error.message }</div>
    </div>
  );
}
```

Note   As an alternative to waiting for the transaction to be mined, we could also *optimistically update* the value. An optimistic update is a technique, used in many asynchronous applications beyond DApps, that consists in assuming that a transaction performed by the user will succeed and immediately updating the value client-side. This way, the user perceives that the application reacts almost instantly and can keep interacting with it and has immediate feedback on the result of their actions.

While this solution is good enough for a single user interacting with a contract, it falls short when there are multiple users involved. You can try this out by opening the web site from two different browser windows: any changes made in one window will not affect the other, unless the contract is queried again by reloading the page. To solve this issue, we will rely on the last concept we introduced in the contract's interface: events.

Monitoring Updates Via Events

A contract's public interface is not just composed of public functions. A contract may also emit custom *events* upon certain transactions. Our Counter contract emits an event named Increased every time the increase function is called, and includes the new value of the counter as an argument.

To monitor all instances of this event, we will subscribe to it when the component mounts and update the component state accordingly (Listing 2-17).

Listing 2-17. Subscription to the Increased event, which updates the component's state whenever a new instance of the event is emitted

```
async componentDidMount() {
  const counter = this.props.contract;
  const initialValue = await counter.methods.value().call();
  this.setState({ value: initialValue });

  counter.events.Increased()
    .on('data', (event) => {
      const value = event.returnValues.newValue;
      this.setState({ value });
    });
}
```

Note that here we are referring to the counter.events property instead of to the counter.methods like we did before. Here, the event emitter fires a data event every time a new event is found, and includes the arguments of the event.

Also, by updating the component's state on every event, we no longer need to query the contract state whenever a transaction is confirmed. The receipt event handler on the increaseCounter function can be simplified to the following.

```
  .on('receipt', async () => {
    this.setState({ increasing: false });
  })
```

With this new setup, you can now receive real-time updates on a contract, regardless of where the state change originated from. Try again opening two browser windows and increasing the counter from one of them, and see how the change is reflected on both of them once the transaction is confirmed. And if you are lucky, you may even stumble upon a change issued by another reader of this book on the same contract instance.

Deploying the Application

As you may have noticed, our sample application runs exclusively client-side. All logic takes place on the browser, and the blockchain is used as a back end to perform simple computations and persist a shared state among all users, acting as a consensus layer on the state of the counter. This makes deployment straightforward, since the DApp needs only to be hosted as a static site.

Summary

In this chapter, we have gone through the process of developing a simple DApp, providing our users with a basic web-based interface for a single smart contract. We have explored how to read state from a contract and send transactions to it and how to monitor events for real-time updates.

We have built our entire application relying on just two libraries: web3js for interacting with the Ethereum network and React as a presentation framework. Given the pace at which libraries and frameworks change in both the javascript and the Ethereum ecosystems, the goal has been (and will be throughout this book) to use as few dependencies as possible and focus on the concepts behind building a DApp instead of on the specific APIs of the tools of the moment. Of course, this does not mean that you should not rely on such tools when building your own DApp, since they may be of great help. Make sure to check out OpenZeppelin, Truffle, Buidler, Etherlime, Embark, Clevis, and whatever is available by the time this book reaches your hands.

All in all, this chapter should have helped as an overview to the entire development process and components of a DApp. We have glossed over the deployments of the contracts themselves, as well as account and ETH management in general. We have not covered many edge cases or error situations that arise when dealing with a blockchain-based back end. Nevertheless, throughout the book, we will go in-depth in all these topics, plus new and more advanced ones, and revisit each step the building of a DApp on more interesting examples.

CHAPTER 3

A Crash Course on Smart Contracts

Smart contracts are the key component in Ethereum. They hold the logic to be executed on the network, keep track of their own state, and can interact with other smart contracts as well. However, they have some limitations, such as restricted computation per transaction and expensive storage costs. They also cannot initiate new transactions – they depend on external accounts to trigger them. And since they run on the Ethereum network, they cannot directly interact with anything outside it. In this chapter, we will

- Define Ethereum smart contracts, as opposed to externally owned accounts

- Identify the components of a transaction, such as data, gas limit, and price

- Learn how to write a contract in Solidity

- Go through Solidity modifiers, data types, and events

- Review how inheritance works in Solidity

- Present the ERC20 and ERC721 widely used token standards

What is a Smart Contract?

The concept of smart contract was coined by Nick Szabo in the 1990s,[1] referring to self-executing code in a public network that could capture the concept of a real-life contract and enforce it via code.

---

[1]Nick Szabo, "Formalizing and Securing Relationships on Public Networks," 1997.

© Santiago Palladino 2019
S. Palladino, *Ethereum for Web Developers*, https://doi.org/10.1007/978-1-4842-5278-9_3

The basic idea behind smart contracts is that many kinds of contractual clauses (such as collateral, bonding, delineation of property rights, etc.) can be embedded in the hardware and software we deal with, in such a way as to make breach of contract expensive (if desired, sometimes prohibitively so) for the breacher.

—Nick Szabo

In the Ethereum network, a smart contract is represented as code, deployed at an address, with its own state. The code is executed on every transaction sent to it and can perform arbitrary computation, read and write to its own storage, and potentially call other contracts in the network. A smart contract can also hold and transfer ETH, just like any other Ethereum address.

Note   Since smart contracts are powered by code that can execute any computation, they are not actually limited to financial contractual clauses. For instance, they can be used to express different kinds of agreement or consensus, or even governance mechanisms.

A good analogy for a smart contract in software is an *actor*. In the actor model, a system is composed of stand-alone units called actors that receive messages and execute code in response to it, modifying their own internal state and potentially interacting with other actors in the system. Smart contracts can also be thought of as *reducer functions* in functional terms: given a transaction and the contract's state, the smart contract returns an updated state.

External Accounts vs. Smart Contracts

When a smart contract is deployed on the Ethereum network, it is created at a new *address*. This address acts as an identifier for a smart contract: whenever a user (or another contract) wants to interact with it, they send a *transaction* to that particular address.

Externally owned accounts (often abbreviated EOAs), on the other hand, are accounts owned by real-life users – or by any agent outside the network. They are also represented by addresses, which use the exact same format as the ones that identify smart contracts. As such, references to a user or a smart contract are equal in Ethereum: they are just addresses. This allows sending ETH to a recipient, without needing to differentiate whether it is an address backed by a smart contract or managed by an end user.

However, there are a few differences between smart contract and externally owned accounts that are worth mentioning:

- First and foremost, a smart contract account has *code* that is executed on every transaction. Sending a transaction to an externally owned account does not trigger any execution on the network.

- Smart contract accounts cannot initiate transactions. A smart contract can only react to an incoming message, and potentially call into other contracts in the process, but they cannot start a new transaction by themselves. A contract that needs to execute on a timely basis (similar to a cron job) or upon an event (such as balance being moved between certain addresses) needs an EOA to call into it to trigger the operation.

- Only externally owned accounts have a corresponding *private key*. Private keys are used for signing new transactions sent to the network as a means of authentication. Smart contracts cannot initiate new transactions, so there is need for them to sign any operation.

Note   An implication of this last difference is that only externally owned accounts can *sign* arbitrary messages. A private key can be used not only to sign Ethereum transactions but also plain text messages with any information. For example, a user may sign a message attesting his identity (such as "I am spalladino on Github"), and anyone (even a contract) can recover the Ethereum address that corresponds to that signature. This allows them to verify that the owner of that account is who wrote that message.[2] The fact that a smart contract does not have a private key means that it is not possible for it to sign a message.

---

[2]In Chapters 7 and 8, we will review advanced techniques, such as meta transactions and state channels, that rely on message signatures.

Code and State

A smart contract has two main properties: its code and its state. A contract's state is composed of its ETH balance (since all Ethereum addresses have an associated balance) and its storage (where the value of its variables is persisted).

Code in a smart contract is typically short, since its execution "time" has a tight upper bound, defined by the Ethereum network. The code is run every time a transaction is received by the contract, and has access to the contract's local storage, and the transaction's context.

Note   The code of a smart contract is immutable. This means that once deployed, a smart contract cannot be changed. While this is in line with the original concept of real-life contracts made software, it poses some challenges around development. It makes iterative development particularly difficult, and the contract must also be bug-free before being pushed to the production network. This is why security in smart contracts is such a critical issue: not only are smart contracts sitting in a public network where any attacker can freely interact with them, but if a vulnerability is found, there is no way for the original developer to patch it. If the prospect of this limitation seems daunting, fear not, for there are workarounds[3] that can be used for upgrading smart contracts even if their code is immutable.

All Ethereum code is not run natively, but executed by Ethereum nodes on the Ethereum Virtual Machine, or EVM. The EVM executes a low-level stack-based assembly that operates with 32-byte words, typically referred to as *EVM assembly*. This assembly has opcodes for traditional arithmetic and logic operations, basic control flow, and some Ethereum-specific operations such as accessing storage and memory, or querying and managing ETH balance. There are also primitives for computing hashes or working with elliptic curve signatures.[4] It is worth mentioning that the EVM has no support for floating-point arithmetic, and all operations are done on 256-bit integers used as fixed point decimals, to minimize the risk of numerical errors.

---

[3]See https://github.com/OpenZeppelin/openzeppelin-sdk for a development framework that provides out-of-the-box upgradeability for smart contracts. We will also briefly touch contract upgrades in Chapter 7.

[4]Technically, these functions are not implemented as assembly opcodes, but as precompiled contracts with reduced execution cost.

Note   At the time of this writing, a second back end based on WebAssembly, named eWASM, is under development, as an alternative environment for executing Ethereum code. Since it is based on existing WebAssembly technology, it will be possible to leverage the toolchain and optimizations already available instead of having to reimplement them from scratch. Ethereum nodes will be expected to accept and execute smart contract code in either format.

The execution model of the EVM is designed to favor simplicity over performance. All transactions are executed in a serial fashion (i.e. one after the other) and always in a single execution thread. This makes reasoning on smart contracts much easier: while a contract is executing a piece of code in response to a transaction, you can be sure that it will not receive a simultaneous transaction that could affect the current thread.

However, since contracts can call other contracts, the EVM does allow *reentrant calls*. For instance, if contract A calls contract B, nothing prevents B to call back into A during the same transaction. Reentrancy can be tricky to reason about and has been the source of some major hacks in the ecosystem. The famous DAO hack in 2016, which prompted the chain to fork into Ethereum and Ethereum Classic when it was decided to return the funds to the hacked users, was possible due to a reentrancy bug:

> *Special care is required in reviews of Ethereum code to make sure that any functions moving value occur after any state updates whatsoever, otherwise these state values will be necessarily vulnerable to reentrancy.*

> –Phil Daian, "Analysis of the DAO exploit"[5]

Note   As in most platforms, it is rare that you will find yourself coding smart contracts directly in assembly, unless you are working in some particularly obscure feature. There are several high-level languages, built specifically for smart contracts, that compile to EVM code. The most popular of them is Solidity, which we will review in the upcoming sections.

---

[5]http://hackingdistributed.com/2016/06/18/analysis-of-the-dao-exploit/

State in a smart contract is comprised of its storage and balance. The latter is the most straightforward of the two: all address types in Ethereum, regardless of being externally owned accounts or smart contracts, have an associated balance in ETH. Ethereum provides primitives for querying such balances (both from within a smart contract and from outside the network), and for easily transferring it.

As for the storage space in a smart contract, it is extremely large: it is an addressable space of 2^256 slots of 32 bytes each. However, writing to storage in the EVM is very costly, so it should always be used with care.

Since storage usage is expensive, the EVM also provides another 256-bit-addressable transient space called the *memory*, which is equivalent to a memory heap in other environments, and is guaranteed to be cleared in-between transactions.

Gas Usage

Executing code in the Ethereum network costs *gas*. Every operation run by a smart contract consumes a predefined amount of gas, where more complex operations consume more gas than simpler ones. All in all, gas is just a measure of execution cost, designed to prevent excessively complex computations on Ethereum. Since every transaction needs to be executed by every full node on the network to verify it, it is critical to keep them as simple as possible. This is also why operations that create new data on the blockchain, such as writing to storage or creating a new contract, are among the most costly ones in terms of gas.

How is gas obtained? The process is handled automatically on every transaction. Whenever a user sends a new transaction, they specify a *gas price*, which is the conversion rate between ETH and gas. After the transaction is run, the total amount of gas used is calculated, which gets converted to ETH using this gas price, and then deducted from the sender's balance. Note that there are no requirements on gas price, and it can be nearly arbitrarily high or low. However, transactions with a very high gas price will be extremely costly to send; on the other hand, transactions with a very low gas price will be unattractive to miners, and will most likely never be included in the blockchain.

Note There are some services, such as the ETH gas station,[6] which provide real-time statistics on gas price costs for the Ethereum network. This provides you with info on the average gas price to use to send a transaction.

Additionally to the gas price, the transaction sender must specify a maximum gas allowance to be used during execution. If the transaction reaches a point where it has used all the gas allowed, it stops running and reports an out-of-gas error. This allows a user to control up to how much they are willing to spend on a transaction. Conversely, this also allows the network to check that a user has enough ETH for paying forexecution before actually running the code by checking that the sender's balance is at least the maximum gas allowance times the specified gas price.

Note that Ethereum nodes can be used to query an estimation of the gas required to run a transaction, assuming the context where it runs does not change. This allows dynamic calculation of how much gas should be attached to a transaction instead of needing to hard-code it for every call issues by your system.

However, since the amount of gas used depends on which operations were executed, which in turn depend on the context where the transaction is run, the estimation performed by a node may not always be representative. For example, given the following pseudocode for a smart contract:

```
if balance > 1ETH:
    run_expensive_operation
else:
    return true
```

If the estimation is run when the contract's balance is below 1 ETH, then the gas estimation will be low, and the user may send the transaction to the network using that value. However, before the transaction is actually picked up by a miner, another transaction may front-run the original one and increase the contract's balance to be over 1 ETH. This would cause the original transaction to actually require a much higher amount of gas, and end up failing with an out-of-gas error. You should be aware of these situations when coding interactions with the network by always adding a reasonable buffer to the gas allowance on top of the estimated amounts and retrying transactions with updated estimations if needed.

---

[6]https://ethgasstation.info/

Transactions

To recap, in order to interact with a smart contract, an external account must sign and broadcast a transaction directed to the contract's address. The network then executes the smart contract's code, with all data contained in the transaction (and the contract's state) as context.

A transaction is a message with the following properties:

- A sender address, which is always an externally owned account

- A destination address

- An amount of ETH to transfer, which can be zero

- A binary data field, which packs the arguments for the smart contract to execute

- A nonce

- Maximum gas allowance

- Gas price, for converting between gas and ETH

Transactions can also be sent to another externally owned account. In these cases, data is typically left empty, as the purpose is only to transfer ETH between accounts. However, they also consume gas, albeit a small amount compared to those sent to smart contracts.

Note   At the lowest level, the transaction does not actually include the sender address as a property. It is retrieved from the transaction's signature.

The only field in a transaction that we have not yet reviewed is the *nonce*. This is an incremental integer value that ensures that all transactions sent from an account are processed in order: a nonce cannot skip a value and is always equal to the number of executed plus pending transactions sent from the address. It is also part of the network's replay protection. Typically, you will not need to deal with nonces explicitly.

The lifecycle of a transaction is a bit complex, since transactions need to be picked up by a miner and confirmed in order to be considered final (Figure 3-1).

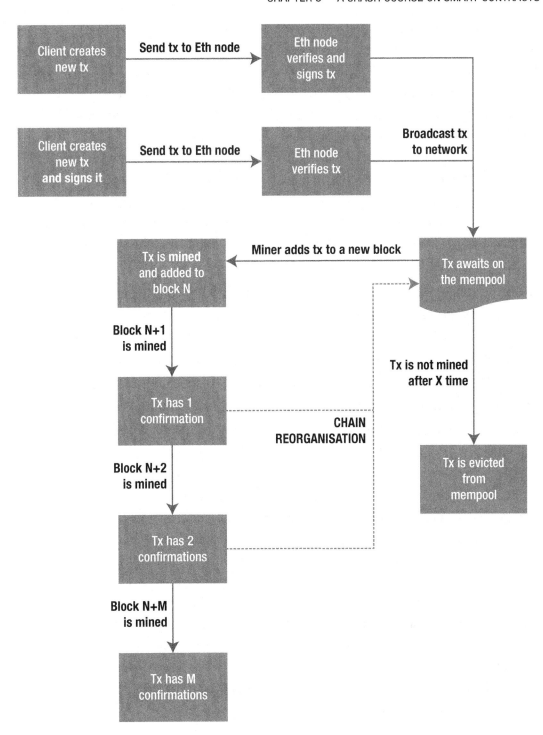

Figure 3-1. *Lifecycle of an Ethereum transaction*

The first step in a transaction's lifecycle is to be sent to an Ethereum node. This could be a private node owned by the user or a public node with no accounts associated. On the former, signing is typically handled by the node, which holds the user's private keys; on the latter, transactions are signed by client software and then sent to the node. In either case, the node checks that the transaction is valid by trying to execute it locally, and if it is, it broadcasts it to the network.

Broadcasted transactions are said to be *pending*, since they have not yet been included in a block, but are waiting on what is called the *mempool*. The time until the transaction is processed by a miner and added to the blockchain will typically depend on network congestion and the gas price of the transaction itself – as we mentioned before, higher gas prices lead to more attractive transactions which are mined faster.

Note   Pending transactions can be *replaced* before they are mined. After a transaction is broadcasted, and before it is picked up by a miner, you may send another transaction with the same nonce and a higher gas price. Upon seeing both pending transactions, miners will prefer the new one, which will render the original one invalid since it has an outdated nonce. Replacing transactions is used to correct a mistake or to increase the gas price of the same transaction to speed up its confirmation, but it is not a technique very widely used. We will review this in Chapter 5.

Eventually, the transaction is *mined* and included in a block. However, due to how the consensus algorithm in Ethereum works, it is still possible that a chain *reorganization* occurs, and the block that included this transaction is replaced by a different one. This is only likely to occur in very recently mined blocks. With every new block mined on top of it, the chance of a block being plucked out of the chain gets slimmer. A dozen confirmations (i.e., new blocks mined) is good enough for most scenarios, but you may want to wait for even more depending on your use case.

It is possible for a single account to have multiple pending transactions, since it is not required by the protocol to wait for a transaction to be mined or confirmed before sending the next one. The nonce ensures that all pending transactions will be processed by miners in the correct order.

Transactions in Ethereum may not always be successful. A transaction can fail due to a variety of reasons, such as running out of gas during execution, or because of a failed precondition check in the smart contract code. Smart contracts can enforce checks on the parameters with which they are called, which may cause a transaction to fail if it does not pass all preconditions. Transactions are atomic, meaning that they are all or nothing in terms of changes to state. In other words, a failing transaction will not persist any changes to the blockchain, except for the deduction of the gas execution fee from the sender's balance. As such, when a transaction you sent fails, you can be confident that the state of your contracts on-chain was not altered in any way.

Note   Failed transactions are either ABORT'ed or REVERT'ed. The difference between the two is that the former will consume all gas up to the maximum allowance of the transaction, whereas the latter only consumes the gas used up to the point where the transaction failed. Smart contracts usually fire a REVERT when a precondition check fails, so as not to waste user's gas.

During execution, a transaction may *log* arbitrary information. These logs cannot be accessed from another smart contract and are only visible from outside the Ethereum network itself, such as from a front-end interface. Logged data may be structured and even *indexed*, allowing clients to search for specific events. We will work with logs more in-depth when we tackle Solidity's *events*.

Calls

While transactions are the only way to perform a change in the Ethereum blockchain, they are not the only way to interact with smart contracts. Any off-chain client can perform a query on a smart contract by making a static *call* to it.

Calls are different from transactions in that they do not need to be signed and are not broadcasted to the Ethereum network, and thus cannot make any changes to the blockchain state and do not cost any gas. Calls are always resolved by the node that receives them and are only used for querying data from a smart contract.

A call executes smart contract code just like a transaction does, the only difference is that any changes performed during a call are not persisted, and the return value of a call is sent back to the sender (unlike transactions, where the sender has no way to get a return value back). If transactions can be thought of as setters that change the state of a smart contract, calls would be the getters.

Calls can even be issued on older blocks. Since all data in the blockchain is persisted, the state of the chain on every block,[7] so a call to a smart contract can be made in the context of an older block. This feature is not used very often, but can be used to reconstruct the history of a contract, although *logs* are the preferred method to do this.

Solidity

Solidity is an object-oriented statically typed language, with curly-braced syntax inspired in Javascript, and support for multiple inheritance. It is the most popular language for smart contract development. At the time of this writing, the latest minor version available is 0.5, which we will be using throughout the book.

The basic unit of Solidity code is a `contract`, which is similar to a class, but compiles to code that spawns a new smart contract. Solidity contracts can have state variables, which are persisted in the contract's storage, and can define functions that are executed upon a call or a transaction. The language also supports modifiers, events, libraries, complex data types, and other concepts that we will explore in this section.

We will only be making an overview of Solidity, covering the required features to be able to understand and make small changes to a smart contract system. It is strongly suggested that you go through the Solidity documentation[8] to learn more in-depth about the language, and it is also a good idea to review security best practices before rolling out your contracts.[9]

---

[7]However, as we will see later, not all nodes actually persist all historical data, so this feature may not always be available.

[8]https://solidity.readthedocs.io/

[9]https://consensys.github.io/smart-contract-best-practices/

Remix

Before going into Solidity itself, we will introduce Remix,[10] a tool for quickly prototyping Solidity code (Figure 3-2). Remix is a full in-browser IDE for Solidity development. It bundles a Solidity code editor, a compiler, and an EVM runtime. The EVM runtime allows you to locally deploy and test your smart contracts in a mock environment. Remix can also be connected to any Ethereum node, allowing you to manage your smart contract on any network, whether it is a local development network or the main Ethereum network (also referred to as *mainnet*).

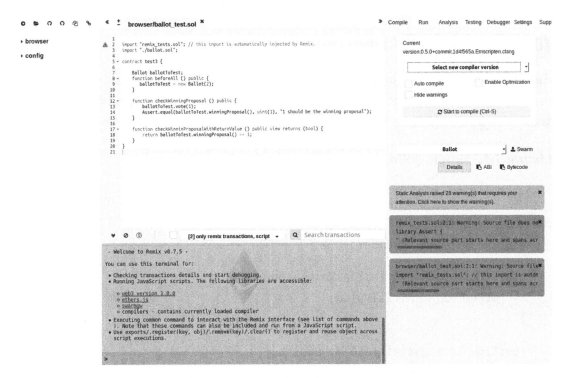

Figure 3-2. *Screenshot of remix IDE at remix.ethereum.org*

Remix has several features for developing, analyzing, deploying, interacting with, and debugging smart contracts. We will focus on the most fundamental ones, but feel free to play around with the tool.

---

[10]https://remix.ethereum.org/

To start, add a new file by clicking the plus sign on the top left of the IDE, and create a new MyContract.sol file. On the right side of the screen, in the *Compile tab*, make sure you are using the compiler version 0.5.0, and choose to *auto-compile* your contracts. We will use this to test our first Solidity contract.

Note   The Solidity compiler, written in C++, is not only compiled to native code but also to javascript using Emscripten. This allows you to compile a Solidity smart contract directly in your browser.

Your First Solidity Contract

We will start with a very simple Solidity contract (Listing 3-1). This contract will hold a single integer value myNumber and provide a constructor to set its initial value, a public function to increase it by a certain amount, and a public getter to retrieve it.

Listing 3-1. Simple Solidity contract, implementing a counter

```
pragma solidity ^0.5.0;

contract MyContract {
    uint256 private myNumber;

    constructor(uint256 initialValue) public {
        myNumber = initialValue;
    }

    function increase(uint256 x) public {
        require(x > 0);
        myNumber = myNumber + x;
    }

    function getValue() public view returns (uint256) {
        return myNumber;
    }
}
```

Let's go through this contract. First thing to notice is the `pragma` directive to set a required Solidity compiler version that corresponds to the code. A compiler that does not match the required version will refuse to compile the file. In particular, `^0.5.0` indicates any version that starts with `0.5`.[11]

Next is a `contract` block, which defines a smart contract to be deployed. The contract can define several state variables, such as `myNumber` in the example, which will be saved to storage in the EVM.

Note   Storage is always initialized to zero in the EVM. This means that all state variables in Solidity are zero by default. To prevent any billion-dollar mistakes, Solidity does not have `null` values.[12]

A contract can define multiple functions that will be executed in its context and will have access to its storage. Functions must always define the type of their arguments and their return type, if any. Also, functions can have different visibilities, depending on whether they can only be called internally within the contract or from outside, and can be restricted to not modify the contract's storage, like `getValue` in the example. A `constructor` can be optionally defined and is run when the contract is deployed.

Note   Solidity supports function overloading; this means having two functions in the same contract with the same name but different arguments. While useful for certain scenarios, several client-side libraries, especially those in javascript, do not always have good support for them. Furthermore, it can be argued that overloaded functions make code more difficult to follow, and other smart contract languages have even made the explicit design decision to not support function overloading.

Another interesting keyword in this sample contract is `require`. It allows you to check for a condition and throw an error (an EVM revert) if it doesn't hold. It is commonly used to check for preconditions in functions.

---

[11]Solidity uses the same notation as npm for specifying version restrictions. See `https://docs.npmjs.com/misc/semver` for more info.

[12]"I call it my billion-dollar mistake. It was the invention of the null reference in 1965." –Tony Hoare, QCon London, 2009.

Remember that your contract is exposed to everyone on the blockchain. This means that any attacker can send a transaction to any public function with any parameters they wish. This makes a very compelling case for adding as many `require` statements as you need to always validate the inputs to your functions.

Before delving deeper into Solidity code, let's try out our first contract in Remix. Copy the code for `MyContract` into the newly created `MyContract.sol` file tab in Remix, and wait for it to auto-compile. Then open the *Run* tab on the right side of the IDE (Figure 3-3). This will allow you to configure the environment where you want to deploy your contract: choose *JavaScript VM* to run the code in a simulated blockchain in your browser, and pick any of the provided *Accounts*.

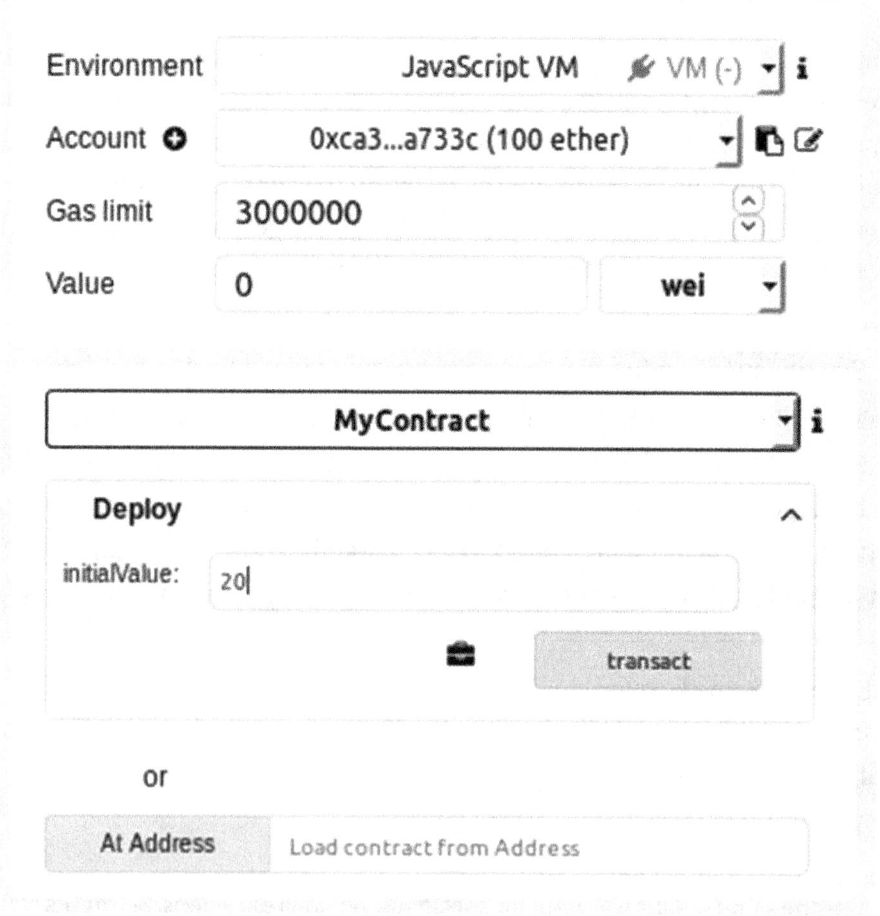

Figure 3-3. *Deploying a contract via Remix*

To deploy your contract, choose MyContract from the contracts drop-down, enter an initial value to be used for the constructor we had defined, and accept the transaction. This will deploy the contract to your in-browser environment, which will execute almost instantly. Remember that when working in a real blockchain, the deployment will actually take several seconds.

You will notice that a new log entry showed up at in the middle-bottom panel (Figure 3-4). This has detailed information on the transaction executed. Take some time to go through it and understand all the info listed, referring back to the "Transactions" section in this chapter.

[vm] from:0xca3...a733c to:MyContract.(constructor) value:0 wei data:0x608...00014 logs:0 hash:0x98c...e74c3	
status	0x1 Transaction mined and execution succeed
transaction hash	0x98cd7f526ba5fb46c37fc313c2f53bc6b615e1f06b36402ca70dc2b5250e74c3
contract address	0x692a70d2e424a56d2c6c27aa97d1a86395877b3a
from	0xca35b7d915458ef540ade6068dfe2f44e8fa733c
to	MyContract.(constructor)
gas	3000000 gas
transaction cost	140709 gas
execution cost	68225 gas
hash	0x98cd7f526ba5fb46c37fc313c2f53bc6b615e1f06b36402ca70dc2b5250e74c3
input	0x608...00014

decoded input	{
	        "uint256 initialValue": "20"
	}

decoded output	-
logs	[]
value	0 wei

Figure 3-4. *Details of a transaction as shown in Remix's console*

Also, on the bottom of the right sidebar of the IDE, you will now see that an instance of `MyContract` is listed under the *Deployed Contracts* section, including the address at which it was deployed. Expanding it will give you access to the public functions of the contract: `increase` and `getValue`. Try calling both of them, using different values for `increase`, to play around with the contract and check out the transactions generated.

Remember the distinction we made earlier between transactions and calls to contracts: the former broadcasts a transaction to the entire network that may change the state of a contract or the balance of an address, while the latter simply queries a single node to retrieve a value. Since `getValue` is flagged as a method that does not modify the contract (via the `view` keyword), Remix automatically issues a call to the contract when you execute it instead of a transaction. On the other hand, since `increase` does alter the contract's state, it spawns a new transaction every time you call it.

We will now go more in depth into Solidity. Feel free to copy the code samples into Remix, deploy them, and interact with them. Remember that if you change the code of a contract, you will need to deploy a new instance of it in order to interact with the new version, since already deployed contracts cannot be changed. Also, refer to the Solidity documentation if you want to explore a particular topic in detail.

What's in a Function?

A function definition in Solidity has the following structure:

- A function name
- A set of typed parameters
- A visibility modifier
- A pay-ability modifier
- A set of custom modifiers
- A set of return values

A function may then look like the following. Note that a function may return more than a single value, expressed as a tuple.

```
function myFunction(uint256 param1, bool param2)
  public payable onlyOwner
  returns (uint256, bool);
```

Visibility Modifiers

As in most object-oriented languages, functions in Solidity can specify different visibility or access modifiers, that control whether a function can be called from outside the contract or not. Solidity provides the following four access levels:

- External

- Public

- Internal

- Private

Private functions can only be called from within the same contract. Under the hood, they are implemented as a `jump` to another part of the contract's code. This means that a call to a private function does not create a new scope, with associated call data, value, gas, and so on. Instead, it executes within the same scope of the caller, what makes the call itself cheap in terms of gas usage. **Internal** functions work exactly the same, only that they allow derived contracts to call them (equivalent to `protected` in other languages).

On the other hand, **external** functions can only be called from an external account or from another contract. External functions are used to define the exposed surface of a contract and are usually where most input argument checks are made. When a contract calls into another, it does by making an EVM `call`, which creates a new scope, with its own call data, transferred value, gas, and so on. This is more expensive than a jump to an internal or private function, but it is required by the EVM. Note that it is possible to call an external function from the same contract where it is defined, but this requires an EVM call as well.

If you have an external function that you would also need to call from within your contract, you would label it as a **public** function. Public functions are a mix between external and internal: they support being called from both outside the contract and from within. The compiler is smart enough to use an internal cheap jump if the function is called from within the same contract, but creates a new EVM call if calling a public function from another contract.

Note that state variables also have their own set of visibility modifiers, which are `public`, `internal`, and `private`, though they have slightly different semantics. A private state variable can only be accessed from within the same contract and an internal one from the same contract and from any derived contract as well (as is the case with functions). However, the public modifier, when applied to a state variable, acts as an internal modifier and defines an implicit getter function with the same name as the state variable (Listing 3-2).

Listing 3-2. Example of using a getter function vs. the public state variable modifier. Both contracts are equivalent in terms of the getter. There is one caveat though: implicit getters cannot be overridden by derived contracts

```
contract ExplicitGetter {
  uint256 internal _value;

  function value() public returns (uint256) {
    return _value;
  }
}
contract ImplicitGetter {
  uint256 public value;
}
```

Payability Modifiers

A function may optionally be defined as payable (Listing 3-3). This tells Solidity that the function can accept ETH when called. The compiler will throw an error if you try to send ETH to a function not defined as payable. This prevents from accidentally sending balance to a contract that is not prepared to handle it, potentially locking ETH in it.

Listing 3-3. Payable vs. non-payable functions in Solidity

```
contract Payable {
  function canPay() public payable {  }
  function cannotPay() public { }
}

contract Payer {
  function pay(Payable p, uint256 eth) public {
    // this syntax is used for sending eth
    // along with a function call
    p.canPay.value(eth)();
```

```
    // this fails to compile
    p.cannotPay.value(eth)();
  }
}
```

Solidity also adds runtime checks to ensure that no balance is sent to non-payable functions. For instance, if you try to send ETH to a non-payable function of a contract from an external account, you will get a `revert` error.

Custom Modifiers

Solidity allows you to define your own function modifiers. These are code blocks that can execute as a filter before and after a function and can even call into other contract functions, manage storage, or react based on the current message.

Information on the current call is available via a context variable named `msg` and includes the ETH `value` received, the `sender` address of the call, the gas provided, the gas price, and more.

A typical use case for modifiers is access control (Listing 3-4). By defining who can call into a function in a modifier, you can then easily reuse that logic across multiple functions via the usage of modifiers.

Listing 3-4. Using custom modifiers for access control

```
contract OwnerDepositable {
  address public owner;

  constructor(address _owner) public {
    owner = _owner;
  }

  modifier onlyOwner {
    require(msg.sender == owner);
    _;
  }

  modifier minDeposit(uint256 value) {
    require(msg.value > 0);
    _;
  }
```

```
function ownerDeposits()
  onlyOwner minDeposit(1 ether) payable public {
  // here we know that the sender is the owner,
  // and has transferred at least 1 ETH
  }
}
```

Modifiers are defined with the `modifier` keyword and yield the call to the original function via an underscore. They are then applied to a function by listing them by name in the function's definition. Modifiers can even accept arguments, which must be provided when applied to a function.

Fallback Function

A contract may define a function without a name. This function is referred to as the *fallback function* and is invoked if the contract receives a call that does not match any other function.

Even though they can be used as catch-all functions in contracts, the main use case of fallback functions is handling plain ETH transfers (Listing 3-5). When you transfer funds to a contract address, you typically do not include anything in the transaction's data. Fallback functions allow contracts to do something in response to that transfer, or perform checks on the transfer itself.

Listing 3-5. Using a fallback function to prevent a contract from accepting transfers that are below 1 ETH

```
contract NotCheap {
  function() external payable {
    require(msg.value >= 1 ether);
  }
}
```

Note that when transferring ETH from Solidity code using the `transfer` method, only a very small gas stipend will be allocated. This is due to security reasons in order to prevent reentrancy attacks when transferring funds. What this means is that the fallback function should only perform very simple checks or operations, or risk running out of gas when receiving ETH, thus reverting the transfer transaction. Even a write to storage is more expensive than the gas stipend available in a plain transfer.

Warning   Fallback functions are also required to signal whether a contract can receive ETH. If a contract does not define a payable fallback function, then no plain ETH transfers can be sent to it. This prevents from accidentally sending funds to a contract that cannot handle them, thus locking the funds.

Value Data Types

Solidity supports the traditional basic data types, such as `bool` or `uint`, plus some more complex data types such as `array`, `mapping`, or `struct`. We will start with the most simple data types: value types (Listing 3-6).

Listing 3-6. Overview of value data types in a contract

```
pragma solidity ^0.5.0;

contract MyContract {
  bool private myFlag;
  uint256 private myUnsignedNumber;
  int256 private mySignedNumber;
  address private myAddress;
}
```

Booleans and Equality

Boolean literals are denoted by the keywords `true` and `false`. The usual logical operations are available, using the same symbols, and with the same short-circuit semantics as in javascript:

- Negation `!x`
- Conjunction `x && y`
- Disjunction `x || y`

On the other hand, equality comparison operators `==` and `!=` actually behave as javascript's `===` and `!==`. Solidity will not coerce types when comparing and will throw a compiler error when attempting to compare objects of two different types. This holds for all data types, not just booleans.

Integers and Arithmetic

Integer types can be both signed and unsigned, and can be defined of different sizes – from 8 to 256 bits in steps of 8. The usual arithmetic, shifting, and bitwise operations are available, as well as comparison operators:

- uint8, uint16, uint24, ..., uint256 are unsigned integer types.

- int8, int16, int24, ..., int256 are signed integer types.

Since integer types are often used to represent *value* in smart contracts, unsigned integers are much more common than signed. Also, since fixed or floating-point values are not (fully) supported, it is common to represent all values using integers with a fixed amount of decimals. This is especially true of ETH balances, which are always expressed in *wei*, the smallest divisible unit of ETH: 1e18 wei are equal to 1 ETH. Solidity even provides suffixes for working with these units: the literal 1 ether is actually the integer value 1e18. There are also suffixes for working with time values, such as minutes, hours, days, and weeks. In these cases, the base unit is the second, so 3 minutes is compiled to the integer value 180.

A word of warning: all integer arithmetic operations in Solidity are unchecked; this means that it is possible to silently overflow. This is especially risky when dealing with unsigned numbers associated to value. For instance, accidentally decreasing a variable that represents someone's balance below zero would actually turn that value into nearly 2^255. For this reason it is strongly suggested to always use SafeMath[13] (Listing 3-7), a library provided by the OpenZeppelin framework that adds overflow checks to every arithmetic operation (more on imports and libraries later).

Listing 3-7. Example of SafeMath usage for arithmetic operations

```
import "openzeppelin-solidity/contracts/math/SafeMath.sol";

contract MyContract {
  using SafeMath for uint256;

  uint256 private myNumber;
```

---

[13]https://github.com/OpenZeppelin/openzeppelin-solidity/blob/v2.0.0/contracts/math/
SafeMath.sol

```
function unsafeDecrease(uint256 x) {
  // if x > myNumber, myNumber will silently wrap around
  myNumber = myNumber - x;
}

function safeDecrease(uint256 x) {
  // if x > myNumber, this will throw an error
  myNumber = myNumber.sub(x);
}
}
```

We will review how to use imports and libraries later in this chapter. For now, keep in mind that directly using arithmetic operators in Solidity, without going through SafeMath, is a potential security risk.

Fixed Size Bytes

Solidity also provides fixed size byte strings of up to 32 bytes, in the form of the bytes1, bytes2, ..., bytes32 data types. Since these all fit within an EVM word, they are all handled as value types as well, and behave similarly to integer types, only that they do not provide any arithmetic functions. They do support comparison, bitwise, and shift operators, plus an index access operator to retrieve a single byte from the array.

```
bytes32 data;
uint8 index;
byte firstByte = data[0];
```

These types are often used to store hashes or identifiers, where the numeric value itself is not relevant. For instance, precompiled hashing functions like sha256 or ripemd160 return bytes32 and bytes20, respectively.

Addresses, Contracts, and Transfers

The address data type represents any Ethereum address. While any integer or byte type of at least 160 bits could be used to store addresses, Solidity specifically provides this type to handle them. Addresses also have specific properties for checking ETH balances, as well as for transferring funds.

Solidity differentiates addresses into two separate types: address and address payable. The underlying representation for both is the same, and the difference is that only the latter provides the transfer method for sending ETH to it. This allows you rely on the type system to decide which addresses should be allowed to receive funds from your contracts. A non-payable address only provides a balance property to query its ETH balance.

The following quite uninteresting contract (Listing 3-8) keeps track of an owner who created the contract and provides a single function to forward funds to them.

Listing 3-8. Sample contract using address data types

```
contract MyContract {
  address payable private owner;
  address private lastContributor;

  constructor(address payable _owner) public {
    owner = _owner;
  }

  function forward() public payable {
    uint256 ethReceived = msg.value;
    require(ethReceived > 0);
    lastContributor = msg.sender;
    owner.transfer(ethReceived);
  }
}
```

Note that the owner address needs to be stored as an address payable type; otherwise, the compiler will throw an error when attempting to compile owner. transfer(ethReceived). On the other hand, lastContributor can be a plain address, since it will never receive ETH from the contract.

Note   Solidity provides another function for sending ETH, which is send. The difference between the two is that send returns a boolean value indicating whether the ETH transfer was successful, and transfer throws a REVERT on failure. To avoid errors caused by forgetting checking send return values, it is recommended to always use transfer.

Any contract defined in Solidity can also be used as a type (Listing 3-9). A contract instance has all the public functions defined in the contract.

Listing 3-9. Calling a contract public function from Solidity

```
contract Provider {
  function answer() public pure returns (uint256) {
    return 42;
  }
}

contract Caller {
  function fetchAnswer(Provider provider) public {
    uint256 answer = provider.answer();
    // do something with the answer
  }
}
```

Internally, a contract instance is stored as its address, so contracts can be casted to and from the address type. This is useful when attempting to check the balance of a contract or transfer funds to it, since only the address type provides the balance and transfer methods.

```
function sendFunds(MyContract recipient) {
  recipient.transfer(1 eth); // compile error
  address(recipient).transfer(1 eth); // ok!
}
```

Contract types can also be used to deploy a new instance of a contract (Listing 3-10). You can leverage this to create factory-like contracts that are used to set up and create other contracts.

Listing 3-10. Creating a contract from Solidity

```
contract Box {
  uint256 public value;
  constructor (uint256 _value) public {
    value = _value;
  }
}
```

```
contract Factory {
  function create(uint256 _value) public returns (Box) {
    return new Box(_value);
  }
}
```

Also, like many other languages, Solidity also provides a this keyword that represents the current contract. The type of this is the contract itself.

```
function forward(address payable beneficiary) public {
  uint256 myBalance = address(this).balance;
  beneficiary.transfer(myBalance);
}
```

Reference Types

Reference types in Solidity include arrays, strings, mappings, and structs. Unlike value types, which are always handled by copy when assigning them or passing them as a parameter, reference types usually pass a handle to an object that can be aliased or modified from another function. We will review how this works with the most common reference type: the array.

Arrays, Bytes, and Strings

Solidity supports both fixed size and dynamic arrays. Array types are parametric, which means they are defined as an array of a base type. This allows you to define dynamic integer arrays like uint256[], or fixed size address arrays like address[4]. You can even work with arrays of arrays, but keep in mind that in Solidity the notation is reversed as compared to other languages: bool[][4] is an fixed size array of four dynamic arrays. Furthermore, you cannot return arrays of arrays in an external function call.

Arrays have a length method to query their size and provide an indexing operator to access or modify a position in the array. Dynamic arrays also have push and pop methods to add or remove elements. Arrays are typically iterated using a for-loop in Solidity (Listing 3-11).

Listing 3-11. Sample code for appending elements to an array and iterating them. Note that this example is subject to arithmetic overflow, since it is not using SafeMath for computing the sum over the array

```
contract ArrayTest {
  uint256[] array;

  function sum() public view returns (uint256) {
    uint256 total = 0;
    for (uint256 i = 0; i < array.length; i++) {
      total += array[i];
    }
    return total;
  }

  function add(uint256 value) public {
    array.push(value);
  }
}
```

Warning   Using a for-loop over an unbounded array is risky, since it may consume an arbitrarily high amount of gas, potentially more that fits in a single block, rendering the function impossible to call. Always avoid looping over an array that can grow out of control, or at least provide methods for iterating it by batches of controllable size.

Remember that arrays are reference types instead of value types. Reference types contain, as their name indicates, a reference to an object instead of the actual value. This means that, depending on the context, assigning an array variable to another will not create a copy but hand over a reference to the same array.

Whether the array is copied or a reference is passed depends on the *data location*. Data location may be a confusing concept, since it does not have a direct equivalent in other languages, and is an abstraction leakage from the EVM. Instead of trying to hide it and lead to potentially surprising results, Solidity opts for surfacing this distinction and forcing the programmer to be conscious about this important implementation detail.

As we mentioned before, every contract has access to an internal storage that can be used to persist data. And since this space is very expensive to use, the EVM provides access to a memory heap for transient operations. These are precisely the two main data locations that Solidity defines: `storage` and `memory`. The third location is `calldata`, which refers to the space where data is supplied in a transaction. For all practical purposes, `calldata` works just like memory, only that it is immutable.

Data locations need to be specified for every local variable or function parameter of a reference type. The only case where data location is unneeded is when declaring contract state variables, since these are always kept in storage. Note that when specifying locations for function arguments, you need to adhere to the following rules:

- External functions can only accept `calldata` reference types.

- Public functions can only accept memory reference types.

- Internal or private functions can only accept memory or storage reference types.

Assignment semantics then depend on the location of a reference type (Listing 3-12). An assignment from a memory reference to another will just pass a reference to the same object, and the same happens when assigning from a storage reference to another. However, when assigning from a memory reference to a storage one, Solidity will **copy** the entire memory array into storage.

Listing 3-12. Demo of how the memory and storage location modifiers work in Solidity

```
contract DataLocations {
  uint256[] public storageArray;

  function test(uint256[] memory memoryArray) public {
    // We alias memoryArray to localMemory
    uint256[] memory localMemory = memoryArray;
    localMemory[0] = 42;
    require(localMemory[0] == memoryArray[0]);

    // We copy memoryArray into storageArray
    storageArray = memoryArray;
    require(storageArray[0] == 42);
```

```solidity
    // We alias storageArray to localStorage
    uint256[] storage localStorage = storageArray;
    localStorage[0] = 21;
    require(localStorage[0] == storageArray[0]);

    // And changes to storageArray don't affect
    // the original memoryArray
    require(storageArray[0] != memoryArray[0]);
  }
}
```

A special case of an array is bytes, which behaves exactly as a byte[] (i.e., a dynamic array of byte). However, this type is optimized and tightly packed in memory or storage, so it should always be preferred over byte[].

Another special case are strings. A string is an immutable UTF-8-encoded byte array, which doesn't allow indexed access. String literals are defined using double quotes. Keep in mind that Solidity ships with almost no string manipulation functions, so strings are mostly stored as immutable identifiers or descriptions.

```solidity
string myString = "foo";
```

Unlike value types, when an array state variable is defined as public, the implicit getter generated by Solidity accepts an index parameter, to identify which item in the array is to be retrieved. This only holds for regular dynamic arrays: bytes and strings are returned in a single call.

As an example, given the following contract with a public dynamic array, string, and bytes, the following getters (Figure 3-5) are available:

```solidity
contract PublicArrays {
    uint256[] public numbers = [20,30,40];
    string public text = "foo";
    bytes public data = hex"20";
}
```

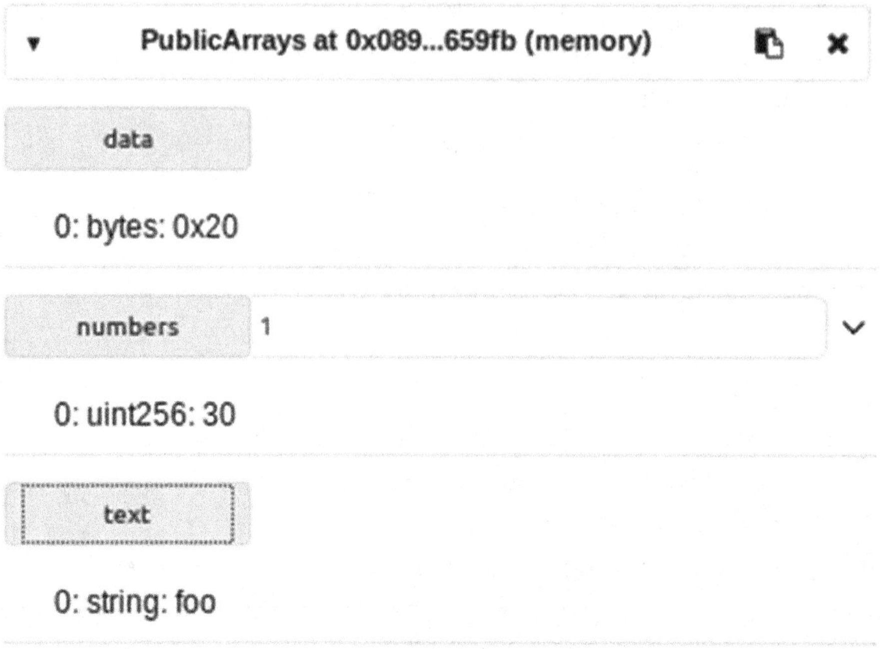

Figure 3-5. *Accessing a public dynamic array with a getter that requires an index vs. getting a string or bytes variable*

Mappings

Mappings, also referred to as hashes or dictionaries in other languages, are an associative reference type in Solidity.

Like arrays, they are parametric, in that they contain elements from other types. Mappings go from keys to values, and they accept any value type (plus bytes or strings) as keys, and can handle any type whatsoever (including other mappings) as values. Unlike arrays, however, the only valid location for mappings is storage, not memory or calldata.

Note   Under the hood, mappings are hash tables that rely on the fact that the storage space of a contract is large enough to ensure there will be no collisions for two different keys, so they guarantee that access to a value is always in constant time.

Autogenerated public getters for mappings (Listing 3-13) are similar to those of arrays, only that instead of accepting an index, they accept a key (Figure 3-6). In the case of nested mappings, a getter for a nested mapping will require a parameter for each key in each nesting level and only return the innermost value.

Listing 3-13. Sample contract with autogenerated getters for two mappings: a simple one and a nested one

```
contract PublicMappings {
  mapping(uint256 => string)
    public num2str;
  mapping(uint256 => mapping(uint256 => string))
    public num2num2str;

  constructor() public {
    num2str[10] = "foo";
    num2num2str[10][20] = "bar";
  }
}
```

Figure 3-6. *Getting a value from a nested mapping requires providing a value for each key in each nesting level*

An important caveat about mappings in Solidity is that, unlike other languages, there is no way to iterate the keys or values present in the mapping. This is related to how mappings are implemented. If you do need to keep track of the keys inserted into a mapping, you will need to keep a separate array to store them.

Structs

The last reference type in Solidity are structs (Listing 3-14). As in C, structs act as a named set of fields of other types.

Listing 3-14. Sample usage of structs in a Solidity contract

```
contract HasStruct {
  struct MyStruct {
    uint256 number;
    string text;
  }

  mapping(uint256 => MyStruct) structs;

  constructor() public {
    structs[10] = MyStruct(20, "foo");
  }

  function getStruct(
    uint256 key
  ) public view returns (uint256, string memory) {
    MyStruct storage s = structs[key];
    return (s.number, s.text);
  }
}
```

Structs are mutable and can be stored in a mapping or array, and they can contain other structs or reference types as their own fields. Remember that, as with any other Solidity types, structs are initialized with zeroes, so an empty struct is one where every field is zero.

Emitting Events

Solidity provides an abstraction over transaction logs named *events*. A Solidity event is identified by a name and can have several arguments to provide additional data (Listing 3-15). Since they are implemented as logs, a Solidity event can only be emitted, but not observed from a smart contract. We will later learn how to monitor or query events from a client.

Listing 3-15. A smart contract that emits an event every time an `increase` function is called

```
contract EmitsEvents {
  mapping(string => uint256) private counters;

  event CounterIncreased
    (string indexed key, uint256 newValue);

  function increase(string memory key) public {
    counters[key] += 1;
    emit CounterIncreased(key, counters[key]);
  }
}
```

The event is declared using the `event` keyword and fired using `emit`. Note that, in the event declaration, some of its arguments can be flagged as `indexed`. These allow watching or querying events that have a certain value for that parameter. Whether to flag an argument as indexed or not will depend strictly on your use case.

Note   Due to EVM restrictions, indexed variable length arguments are not stored using their actual value, but with the hash of the value. This means that, in the example, you will be able to search for a particular key among all `CounterIncreased` events, but you will not be able to retrieve the actual key from a given event.

Events are useful not just for monitoring a contract for changes but also as a replacement for return values in a transaction. Since it is not possible for a client to retrieve a return value from a method called in a transaction, it is common to emit an event with the value that needs to be obtained. The client then retrieves the events attached to the transaction receipt and extracts the value from there.

Imports, Inheritance, and Libraries

Solidity files can import other files (Listing 3-16). The import statement is similar to javascript's require, in that it pulls to the current file declarations from another. In Solidity, since the only top-level objects are contracts (plus libraries and interfaces, as we will see in a minute), an import allows you to refer to contracts defined in another file.

Listing 3-16. Sample usage of the import statement to load a contract defined in another file

```
// Callee.sol
contract Callee {
  function f() external;
}

// MyContract.sol
import "./Callee.sol";
contract MyContract {
  function call(Callee c) public {
    c.f();
  }
}
```

In the preceding example, MyContract pulls the definition of Callee by importing the file in which it is defined. Note that Callee does not define the implementation of the function f, so it is actually an abstract contract. Since this is enough for MyContract to know how to call into an instance of Callee, these files compile successfully. Moreover, since we are using Callee just as an interface definition, we can redefine the contract using the interface keyword:

```
// Callee.sol
interface Callee {
  function f() external;
}
```

Note   When importing code from a dependency, typically as an npm package, the import statement refers to the package name. The exact syntax varies depending on the build tool in use, but it commonly follows the pattern `import "package-name/contracts/Contract.sol"`.

A file can be imported not only to refer to another contract but also to extend from it. Solidity has support for multiple inheritance. This makes inheritance the default mechanism to extend functionality, or to pull in features from another contract, using base contracts as if they were mixins (Listing 3-17).

Derived contracts can access internal and public methods from the base contracts, as well as all struct, modifier, and event definitions. They can also override methods from base contracts.

Listing 3-17. Typical pattern of base contracts that provide behaviors or aspects to be included similar to mixins in a contract. These base contracts define their own state, and provide modifiers or internal functions to be leveraged by the derived contract

```
contract Timelocked {
  uint256 internal locktime;
  modifier whenNotLocked() {
    require(now > locktime);
    _;
  }
}

contract Ownable {
  address internal owner;
  modifier onlyOwner() {
    require(msg.sender == owner);
    _;
  }
}
```

```
contract MyContract is Timelocked, Ownable {
  constructor(uint256 _locktime) public {
    locktime = _locktime;
    owner = msg.sender;
  }

  function f() whenNotLocked onlyOwner public {
    // only reachable when called by the owner
    // and the contract is not locked
  }
}
```

Last but not least, Solidity allows to define *libraries*, which are modules of helper functions, that may optionally be applied over a specific data type (Listing 3-18). Depending on whether their functions are defined as internal or not, libraries are actually inlined in the contract that includes them or deployed separately and linked. A good example of a library is the previously mentioned SafeMath, which defines simple arithmetic operations with overflow checks.

Listing 3-18. Sample usage of SafeMath in a contract

```
// Snip of the code of openzeppelin-solidity SafeMath.sol
library SafeMath {
  function add(uint256 a, uint256 b)
    internal pure returns (uint256) {
      uint256 c = a + b;
      require(c >= a);
      return c;
  }
}

// MyContract.sol
import "openzeppelin-solidity/contracts/math/SafeMath.sol";
contract MyContract {
    uint256 value;
```

```
function increase(uint256 x) public {
    value = SafeMath.add(value, x);
}
}
```

Since it is frequent for libraries to define functions on a certain data type, such as uint256 in the case of SafeMath, Solidity provides a convenience using statement (Listing 3-19) that adds all methods of the library to all variables of a specified type. This is particularly powerful when combined with structs, since it allows us to define custom datatypes with their own set of functions.

Listing 3-19. Previous example rewritten with the using statement, which adds all methods in a library to a type in the scope of the contract

```
contract MyContract {
    using SafeMath for uint256;
    uint256 value;
    function increase(uint256 x) public {
        value = value.add(x);
    }
}
```

Well-known Smart Contracts

To wrap up this chapter on smart contracts, we will review two of the most well-known contract standards, which are ERC20 and ERC721. These correspond to fungible and non-fungible tokens, respectively. However, before diving into them, we will first introduce a concept that goes beyond the Solidity language: the ABI.

Application Binary Interface

The Application Binary Interface (ABI) of a contract is the set of public methods exposed by a contract. Think of it as its public API that can be called from an external account or another contract.

The key concept behind the ABI is that it is language independent. It is a specification on how function calls, arguments, and return values should be encoded. This allows a contract written in Solidity to seamlessly interact with a contract written in another high-level language, such as Vyper.

The ABI has a set of data types fairly close to those of Solidity, including addresses, integers (signed and unsigned), booleans, strings, arrays, and so on. The main exceptions are contract types, which are handled as plain addresses, and structs, which are encoded as tuples with all their fields.

EIPs and ERCs

Being a decentralized protocol, all improvements to Ethereum often start as a proposal (or EIP, Ethereum Improvement Proposal) to be discussed by the community. These proposals encompass from changes to the core protocol itself to application-level standards defined for compatibility.

The latter are referred to as Ethereum Request for Comments (or ERC, following the RFC nomenclature used by the Internet Engineering Task Force). These are of particular importance, since they define the common ABIs and semantics of contracts to be used. They act as building blocks for larger applications and foster reusability by setting a common interface agreed upon by the community.

Two of the most popular smart contract standards, fungible and non-fungible tokens, are defined as ERCs – ERC20 and ERC721, respectively.

ERC20 Tokens

Tokens, defined in the ERC20 standard,[14] are probably the most common building block of Ethereum applications. In its core, an ERC20 contract keeps track of a balance for every token holder address and provides methods for querying and managing such balances (Listing 3-20).

A token can act as a decentralized currency for any project. As such, any team can easily roll out their own cryptocurrency on top of the Ethereum network, without needing to set up their own blockchain.

---

[14]https://eips.ethereum.org/EIPS/eip-20

Nevertheless, tokens have more uses besides currency. The purpose of the token is given to it by the protocol in which it is used: it can be used to signal vouching for a particular item, or voting power in a decentralized organization. Many projects nowadays rely on one (or sometimes more) ERC20 token.

Listing 3-20. Complete interface of the ERC20 standard

```
interface ERC20 {
  function totalSupply()
    external view returns (uint256);

  function balanceOf(address who)
    external view returns (uint256);

  function allowance(address owner, address spender)
    external view returns (uint256);

  function transfer(address to, uint256 value)
    external returns (bool);

  function approve(address spender, uint256 value)
    external returns (bool);

  function transferFrom(
    address from, address to, uint256 value
  ) external returns (bool);

  event Transfer(
    address indexed from,
    address indexed to,
    uint256 value
  );

  event Approval(
    address indexed owner,
    address indexed spender,
    uint256 value
  );
}
```

The first step to understand an ERC20 token is to glimpse its state. A fungible token is backed by a mapping from a user to a balance, which is exposed by the `balanceOf` getter.

```
function balanceOf(address who)
  external view returns (uint256);
```

Balances are modified via invocations to `transfer`. A user can choose to transfer a certain amount of their tokens to another address – either a contract or an external account. Whenever this method is invoked, the `Transfer` event is emitted to log the action.

```
function transfer(address to, uint256 value)
  external returns (bool);
```

An addition to this basic behavior of balance transfer is the concept of *allowances*. A user can approve any address to manage up to a certain number tokens on their behalf. The state of the token allowances can be queried via the `allowance` getter.

```
function allowance(address owner, address spender)
  external view returns (uint256);
```

To set an allowance for an address, the contract provides the `approve` method, which is required to emit an `Approval` event when called. Note that a user may set an approval for an arbitrarily high number of tokens – regardless of whether they own them or not.

```
function approve(address spender, uint256 value)
  external returns (bool);
```

Allowances are consumed as the spender account transfers tokens of the owner. If address A has allowed B to spend up to 20 tokens on their behalf, after B transfers 5 of A's tokens, the remaining allowance will be 15. Transferring on behalf of another user is done via the `transferFrom` method, which will affect both balances and allowances.

```
function transferFrom(
  address from, address to, uint256 value
) external returns (bool);
```

Additionally, the standard includes three optional getters: `name`, `symbol`, and `decimals`. These are often used by wallets or other client software to display information about a token given its address.

The standard does not specify how tokens are initially distributed or how their total supply evolves over time. Certain tokens have a fixed supply set when created and assigned to a single address which manually distributes them. Others can be minted over time and distributed based on certain rules.

Tip   A canonical and audited implementation of the ERC20 standard can be obtained from the OpenZeppelin contracts package,[15] so you don't need to implement your own.

ERC721 Non-fungible Tokens

The ERC721 standard (Listing 3-21) defines the specification for digital collectibles, also called non-fungible tokens (often abbreviated NFTs). NFTs are different from the traditional ERC20 token in that each token is identifiable and different from the other. As such, a user no longer has a number of tokens, but has a particular set of unique identifiable tokens, each with its own metadata associated to it. As an analogy, if ERC20 tokens can be used to represent a currency, ERC721 tokens can be used to represent collectible cards.

The interface for ERC721 is heavily inspired from ERC20, with the difference that all operations act on identifiable tokens and not on a balance. ERC721 also introduces a few additions over ERC20 which we will now review.

Listing 3-21.   Interface of the ERC721 standard

```
contract ERC721 is IERC165 {

  function balanceOf(address owner)
    public view returns (uint256 balance);

  function ownerOf(uint256 tokenId)
    public view returns (address owner);

  function approve(address to, uint256 tokenId)
    public;
```

---
[15]https://github.com/OpenZeppelin/openzeppelin-solidity

```solidity
  function getApproved(uint256 tokenId)
    public view returns (address operator);

  function setApprovalForAll
    (address operator, bool _approved)
    public;

  function isApprovedForAll
    (address owner, address operator)
    public view returns (bool);

  function transferFrom
    (address from, address to, uint256 tokenId)
    public;

  function safeTransferFrom
    (address from, address to, uint256 tokenId)
    public;

  function safeTransferFrom
    (address from, address to, uint256 tokenId, bytes data)
    public;

  event Transfer(
    address indexed from,
    address indexed to,
    uint256 indexed tokenId
  );

  event Approval(
    address indexed owner,
    address indexed approved,
    uint256 indexed tokenId
  );
  event ApprovalForAll(
    address indexed owner,
    address indexed operator,
    bool approved
  );
}
```

The first methods for querying the number of tokens held by an address, as well as for querying whether a particular token belongs to an address, are quite straightforward.

```
function balanceOf(address owner)
  public view returns (uint256 balance);
```

```
function ownerOf(uint256 tokenId)
  public view returns (address owner);
```

Throughout the standard, tokens are identified by an opaque uint256 value. While some implementations use incremental numbers for IDs, this is not required at all.

Note that the standard does not provide any way of actually listing the existing tokens or the tokens that belong to a user. To solve this, there is an optional extension (Listing 3-22) that provides methods for enumerating all the tokens in existence, as well as the tokens of a particular user.

Listing 3-22. ERC721Enumerable optional extension

```
function totalSupply()
  public view returns (uint256);
```

```
function tokenOfOwnerByIndex
  (address owner, uint256 index)
  public view returns (uint256 tokenId);
```

```
function tokenByIndex(uint256 index)
  public view returns (uint256);
```

To avoid returning an arbitrarily large array with all the tokens created, or all the tokens that belong to a user, this Enumerable extension provides means to know the total number of tokens (or the number of tokens that belong to a user) and to iterate through them via an index.

Like ERC20, ERC721 has the concept of allowances, though managed slightly different. ERC721 allows an owner to designate one or more spenders for each of their tokens individually and at the same time to designate one or more addresses to manage all of their tokens on their behalf. The latter are sometimes called *operators*. These two concepts – approval for a particular token or for all tokens – are queried and set via the following methods, and reflected by the Approval and ApprovalForAll events.

```
function approve(address to, uint256 tokenId)
  public;

function getApproved(uint256 tokenId)
  public view returns (address operator);

function setApprovalForAll
  (address operator, bool _approved)
  public;

function isApprovedForAll
  (address owner, address operator)
  public view returns (bool);
```

ERC721 does not include a transfer method. Instead, all token transfers are to be handled via transferFrom, which requires the spender to specify not only the token to transfer and the destination but also the current owner. If the current owner does not match the from parameter, the transfer is rejected.

```
function transferFrom
  (address from, address to, uint256 tokenId)
  public;
```

This standard includes two other methods for managing transfers:

```
function safeTransferFrom
  (address from, address to, uint256 tokenId)
  public;

function safeTransferFrom
  (address from, address to, uint256 tokenId, bytes data)
  public;
```

The safe transfer methods check that the recipient of the token can actually manage them, by calling into a specified onERC721Received method in the recipient (Figure 3-7). If the recipient does not implement this method, the transfer is aborted. This prevents tokens from being accidentally lost by sending to contracts that cannot manage them, thus locking them forever, which is a common problem in ERC20. As such, it is recommended to always prefer this method over the plain transferFrom.

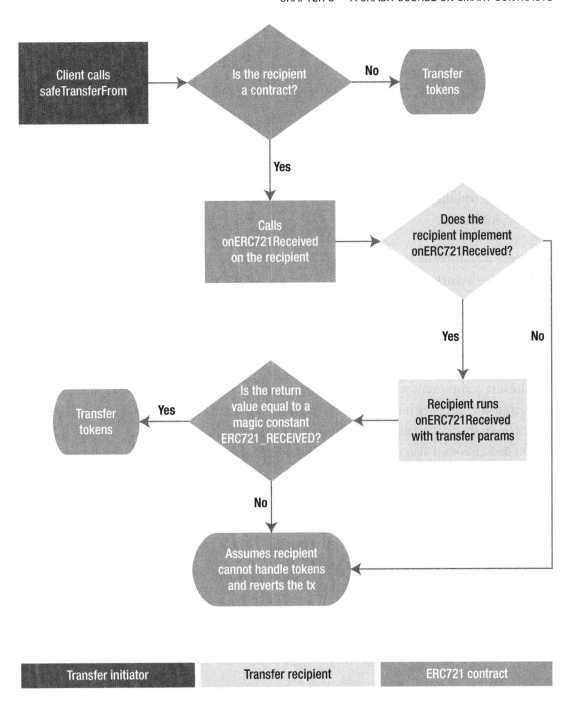

Figure 3-7. *Execution flow of an ERC721 safe transfer*

An overload of this method includes an extra data parameter. This data is forwarded on the onERC721Received call and can be used by the recipient to decide whether to accept the token to be transferred.

Another part of ERC721 is the requirement to implement ERC165 (Listing 3-23). ERC165 provides a standard way to query whether a contract implements an interface or not. This allows users or other contracts to actually check if any given address responds to a method before attempting to call into it. In the context of ERC721, this means that you can actually *ask* an address whether it is an ERC721 contract or not. However, keep in mind that whether the actual implementation is correct or malicious is an entirely different subject.

Listing 3-23. Interface of ERC165. The interfaceId is a well-known identifier set for every standard and is often composed of the hash of the public function signatures

```
function supportsInterface(bytes4 interfaceId)
  external view returns (bool);
```

The last component of ERC721 is an optional extension for metadata (Listing 3-24). This extension not only includes the name and symbol getters that were also present in ERC20 (note that decimals do not make sense in this context, since non-fungible tokens are not divisible) but also a way to fetch metadata information for any given token.

Listing 3-24. Metadata optional extension for ERC721

```
function name() external view returns (string);
function symbol() external view returns (string);
function tokenURI(uint256 tokenId)
  public view returns (string);
```

While the format of tokenURI is not defined and is left for implementers to choose,[16] it provides a standard way to obtain information on a particular token instance, such as an image or a blurb of text that describes it. Token URI often points to an off-chain[17] resource that contains a manifest for the token.

Summary

Throughout this chapter, we have presented what a smart contract is and how it is composed of code and state, differentiating it from an externally owned account. We have reviewed what a transaction is, its lifecycle, and how it interacts with a smart contract, potentially modifying its state – in opposition to static calls, used to query contracts without changing them. We have also presented some concepts such as gas usage and price, which are of particular importance to clients issuing transactions to the network.

We have also studied Solidity as a high-level programming language for coding smart contracts. Solidity's basic unit is a contract, which is composed of state variables and functions, which can be decorated with modifiers and potentially emit events. Solidity contracts can extend from multiple other contracts, or include libraries, as a means to modularizing code. This introduction was far from covering all Solidity concepts and left out several security insights that are vital when developing production-level smart contract code, but is enough for you to understand smart contracts and be able to code small systems.

Last, we reviewed two of the most widely used building blocks in smart contracts – tokens, defined in ERC20 and ERC721. These cover fungible tokens and digital collectibles, respectively, and most applications operate on either (or both) of the two.

Overall, the main goal of this chapter is not for you to become an expert in smart contract development, but to understand key concepts that will be useful when developing web applications backed by these contracts.

---

[16]At the time of this writing, EIP 1047 is in draft state, and includes a proposal for JSON metadata to be associated with a token.

[17]We typically use the term off-chain to refer to actions that occur outside the Ethereum network. This is not inside a smart contract or as part of a transaction, but in a front-end application or a script interacting with the blockchain.

CHAPTER 4

Querying the Network

After a not-so-brief interlude on writing smart contracts, we will review the different ways to connect to the Ethereum network to retrieve data. We will cover different connection methods, as well as patterns for listening to changes, and put it all together in a sample application for monitoring transfers of an ERC20 token.

Connecting to the Network

The first step in retrieving data from the network is to actually connect to an Ethereum node. Since web applications do not connect directly to the network, they depend on a node to answer any queries on the blockchain state. We will start by reviewing node types, connection methods, and the provider object.

About Full and Light Nodes

A typical Ethereum node is a Geth or Parity instance[1] that has its own copy (partial or full) of the blockchain, can answer queries from clients (such as a DApp), and relays transactions (more on this in the next chapter). A node with a full copy of the blockchain is called a *full node*. These nodes either have or can recompute any data from the blockchain history. Most clients run in this mode by default.

Full nodes may also store all historical data. These nodes are called *archive nodes*, and they are much more infrequent, due to the large amount of disk size needed to support them – nearly 2TB at the time of this writing. They are required in case you want to query particular information from older blocks, such as the state of a contract or a balance of an account from a year ago.

---

[1]While there are other Ethereum client implementations, Geth and Parity are the most popular ones.

© Santiago Palladino 2019

S. Palladino, *Ethereum for Web Developers*, https://doi.org/10.1007/978-1-4842-5278-9_4

As an alternative to full nodes, some nodes may run in *light client* mode. These nodes keep only the block headers, and request information from the network as needed. They are much lighter to run than full nodes, which make them suitable for mobile devices, but make a poor choice for the back end of a DApp, since queries take longer to resolve.

Infura and Public Nodes

The next question about nodes is which ones are available for our applications. In an ideal decentralized scenario, every user should be running their own full Ethereum node, in order to validate all transactions themselves, and avoid trusting a third party. Users on mobile or IOT devices may choose to run light nodes instead, which would trust other nodes to relay the information but nevertheless verify it.

In the current landscape, a small fraction of our users will actually be running an Ethereum node. Most of them will be just learning what Ethereum is about, and wondering how to buy their first ETH to pay for the gas to fuel their initial transactions. Having them running their own nodes is still out of the question.

As such, and in order to help the Ethereum adoption process easier, there are a number of *public nodes* available. An Ethereum node is said to be a public node when it holds no private keys, is available to the public, and is used to answer blockchain queries and relay pre-signed transactions.

In particular, **Infura** (Japanese for "infrastructure") is a service that provides HTTP and websocket endpoints to public full nodes for the Ethereum Mainnet, as well as for the Kovan, Ropsten, and Rinkeby testnets. Due to its reliability, and to the fact that it is free to use, it is widely used by many decentralized apps and wallets.

The JSON-RPC Interface

All Ethereum nodes, regardless of the particular implementation, expose a set of well-known methods, which compose the *JSON-RPC interface*. As the name implies, this is a JSON-based API for executing remote procedure calls, and constitutes the low-level interface for a client to interact with a node. Common methods include call, sendTransaction, getBlockByNumber, accounts, or getBalance. There are even methods for querying the state of the node itself, such as whether its syncing or how many peers it is connected to.

Note   Given it is a low-level interface, it is odd that you will find yourself building JSON-RPC calls manually. Most libraries (such as web3.js or ethers.js) will take care of generating the calls on your behalf and provide you with the responses. Nevertheless, it is always useful to understand what is going on under the hood in case you stumble upon a dreadful abstraction leakage.

It is worth mentioning that certain nodes may not implement all methods. For instance, the Infura HTTP endpoint does not offer costly operations such as `newFilter` (more on filters later in this chapter). This will be important to keep in mind when we discuss how to connect our app to the Ethereum network.

Connection Protocols

There are three different protocols that can be used as a transport for interchanging JSON-RPC messages. Nodes can be configured to handle any of them.

The **HTTP** protocol is the simplest one. It provides a simple HTTP-based interface for POSTing JSON messages. Certain nodes may be set up behind HTTPS-encrypted connections, and may require basic authentication to access them. A simple HTTPS connection string looks like the following:

```
"https://user:password@example.com:8545/"
```

A more interesting alternative is the **websocket** protocol. A websocket connection is a persistent two-way connection between a client and a server. This allows a client to not only perform all the available JSON-RPC calls but also to subscribe to changes that are pushed from the node to the client (more on this later). Like HTTP connections, websockets may also be established over SSL, and potentially include basic authentication:

```
"wss://user:password@example.com:8545/ws"
```

Finally, the **IPC** (inter-process communication) protocol is based on a local UNIX domain socket created by the node. Clients with access to the socket may connect to it via its filename. These connections are meant to be used by processes with access to the same filesystem as the node, and as such are not used on web apps.

```
"ipc://home/ubuntu/.ethereum/geth.ipc"
```

Alternative APIs

As an alternative to establishing a connection to the JSON-RPC interface of a node, you may opt to query blockchain data from a different source.

Etherscan (etherscan.io) is a centralized service that provides not only a web-based blockchain explorer where you can visually check all transactions sent to and from an account but also a plain HTTP API (Listing 4-1) that implements many of the methods present in the JSON-RPC interface.

Listing 4-1. Example of executing a getTransactionCount call to the etherscan API (preceding) vs. the standard JSON-RPC call (following). Both return the same JSON object as a response

```
# Etherscan API
curl "https://api.etherscan.io/api
?module=proxy
&action=eth_getTransactionCount
&address=$ADDRESS
&tag=latest
&apikey=YourApiKeyToken"

# Regular JSON-RPC call
{"jsonrpc":"2.0"
,"method":"eth_getTransactionCount"
,"params":["$ADDRESS","latest"]
,"id":1}
```

Certain javascript libraries, such as ethers.js, even include *provider* objects that abstract a connection to the Etherscan API, so it can be used seamlessly as any other standard JSON-RPC connection. Let's now go into the role of the provider.

Note   We are not dwelling into domain-specific APIs at this point. A project may decide to offer an API to query relevant data from its domain. You may also choose to set up a centralized server that aggregates blockchain data from your protocol, and relays it to client-side apps.

The Provider Object

As we briefly saw in Chapter 2 while building our first sample DApp, the connection to a node is managed by a *provider* javascript object. It is the provider's responsibility to abstract the connection protocol being used and offer a minimal interface for sending JSON-RPC messages and subscribing to notifications.

Note   At the moment of this writing, providers from different libraries have slightly different APIs. There is an effort to standardize the minimal provider as EIP 1193, but is still a draft.

For example, the web3 javascript library[2] offers the following providers for connecting to HTTP, websocket, or IPC interfaces (Listing 4-2). The provider is then used to initialize an instance of the full web3 object.

Listing 4-2.   Example web3@1.2.0 code for creating a provider and initializing a web3 instance

```
const Web3 = require('web3');

const httpProvider = new
Web3.providers.HttpProvider("https://example.com");

const wsProvider = new
Web3.providers.WebsocketProvider("wss://example.com");

const ipcProvider = new
Web3.providers.IpcProvider("/home/ubuntu/.ethereum/geth.ipc");

const web3 = new Web3(provider);
```

You will only need to create a provider instance if you have to manually set up a connection to a node. In most scenarios, you will actually delegate this responsibility to the user's web3-enabled browser.

---

[2]www.npmjs.com/package/web3

Metamask and Web3-enabled Browsers

After Chapter 2, you should now be familiar with Metamask, the browser extension that acts as a bridge for a web application and the Ethereum network. There are other options as well, such as the Cipher or the Opera browsers for Android, though we will focus on Metamask throughout the book, as it is the most widespread tool at the moment.

Web3-enabled browsers work by injecting a *provider* instance in the global scope. How this provider works or how it is backed should not be of importance for your DApp. The DApp should be able to query whichever information it needs and let the provider resolve it.

Note that this provider may need to be *enabled* in order to gain access to the user's accounts or request to sign transactions (Listing 4-3), which will prompt the user to accept a request from the DApp to access his accounts information.

Listing 4-3. Snippet for instantiating a web3 object using a provider injected by Metamask

```
// Metamask injects the web3 provider as window.ethereum
const Web3 = require('web3');
const provider = window.ethereum;

if (provider) {
  try {
    // Request access to querying the accounts of the user
    await provider.enable();
  } catch (error) {
    // User denied account access, but we can still
    // run queries to the network
  }
  const web3 = new Web3(provider);
}
```

Metamask connects by default to the Infura public servers via HTTPS. This allows any user who has downloaded the extension to have a connection to the Ethereum network up and running right away, without needing to maintain and sync their own nodes. Nevertheless, Metamask also allows advanced users to set up their own custom connections to other nodes, such as their own (Figures 4-1 and 4-2).

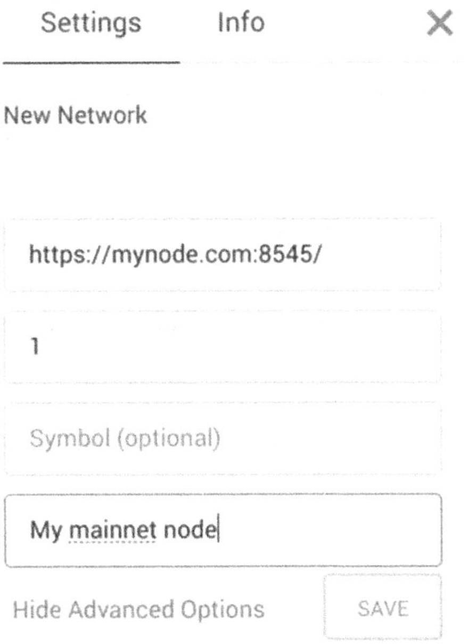

Settings   Info   ✕
_____

New Network

https://mynode.com:8545/

1

Symbol (optional)

My mainnet node|

Hide Advanced Options   SAVE

Figure 4-1. *Metamask settings tab allows a user to configure their own connection to a node*

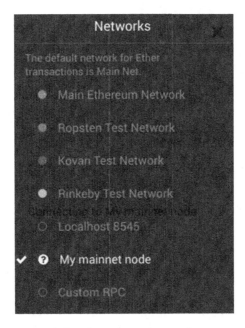

Figure 4-2. *Metamask control for choosing the node to connect to, displayed when clicking the network drop-down at the top of the extension dialog. The first four are connections to public nodes hosted by Infura*

Subproviders

Certain web3 providers may also be composed of *subproviders*. A subprovider is a non-standard object that intercepts calls made via the provider. Among other uses, subproviders help provide a common interface by filling in any gaps in the feature set of the Ethereum node being used. In this sense, subproviders act as polyfills hidden within the provider.

As an example, a provider that connects to a node that does not offer the *filters* API (used for polling for specific changes) may include a *filter subprovider* that emulates that feature client-side. Such is the case with the web3 provider injected by Metamask: since Infura does not offer the filters API, Metamask adds that feature at the provider level via a custom subprovider. This way, you as a developer do not need to worry about which APIs are supported, and are given a consistent interface regardless of the node answering your queries.

We will revisit subproviders in the next chapter, where we discuss about providers and signers, since Metamask implements its signer as another subprovider.

Choosing the Right Connection

Up to this point, we have reviewed different kinds of nodes (full and light, public and private), as well as different connection protocols (ipc, http, and websockets). We have also learned how to set up a provider object and how to enable the one injected by a web3-enabled browser. Given all these options, it begs the question of which connection we should choose for *querying information from a DApp*.

Respecting the Choice of the User

First and foremost, if our user is using a web3-enabled browser, our DApp should rely on the provider injected by it. A web3-enabled browser means the user is already part of the Ethereum ecosystem, and could be potentially running a node of their own. As such, we need to provide them with the means to choose which node they want to use when browsing our DApp.

While we could reimplement Metamask's interface for choosing a network connection, it makes little sense to do so. A user who wishes to connect to an alternative node will already be running Metamask or another web3-enabled browser, and have already preconfigured their own nodes. Therefore, an injected web3 provider should always be our first choice for connecting to the network.

Keep in mind that providers need to be enabled in order to access the list of accounts of the user. Nevertheless, if the application does not need this information, this step can be skipped.

Using a Public Node

The next option is simple: connect to a public node. You can either set up your own for your DApp or use one from Infura. Going with your own node has all the benefits and drawbacks of rolling out your own infrastructure: you do not depend on a third party, but you need to watch out for the health of your nodes. Remember that nothing prevents an arbitrary number of users from connecting to your node, so you should be prepared for surges in traffic. Because of this, it may be easier to just rely on an external infrastructure provider.

As an alternative to Infura, you can also rely on a public API such as that of Etherscan. Ethers.js, an alternative to web3.js, connects by default to Infura, and falls back to Etherscan if the connection fails.

Note that in all cases where your DApp relies on a third party, it is relying on a foreign centralized service for fetching data from the blockchain. Since one of the strong points of DApps is precisely decentralization, adding a component that needs to be trusted may be a step backward in this direction. It is up to you to decide on the trade-off between convenience and decentralization for the users of your DApp. As such, a good rule of thumb is to use an injected provider if found, and fall back to a centralized service otherwise.

Putting it all Together

The code in Listing 4-4 attempts to load the injected provider from a web3 browser, both modern and legacy ones. If it fails, it falls back to using an Infura secure websocket endpoint. The provider is used to create a web3.js instance, but the same code can be repurposed for other libraries.

Listing 4-4. Code snippet for initializing a web3 connection for a DApp, based on the code provided by metamask.io

```
async function getWeb3() {
  // Modern web3 browsers
  if (window.ethereum) {
    const web3 = new Web3(window.ethereum);
```

```
    // Only if we need access to user accounts
    try {
      await window.ethereum.enable();
    } catch (error) {
      console.error("No access to user accounts");
    }
    return web3;
  }
  // Legacy web3 browsers
  else if (window.web3) {
    return new Web3(window.web3.currentProvider);
  }
  // Standard browser
  else {
    return new Web3("wss://mainnet.infura.io/ws/v3/TOKEN");
  }
}
```

Retrieving Data

Now that we know how to connect to the network, we can start actually retrieving data. We will review how to access network information, account balances, perform static calls, and subscribe to events. As before, we will be using web3@1.2.0 as a library to interact with the Ethereum network, but other libraries should provide similar features.

Network Information

We can start out by querying general network information. To begin with, it is a good practice to always check that you are connected to the expected network. If your application is meant to be used on the Rinkeby test network, you do not want a user to be accidentally using a connection to Mainnet. To do this, you can get the identifier of the network you are connected to and compare it to the identifier of the expected network.

```
> await web3.eth.net.getId()
1
```

Networks are identified by a numeric identifier. Mainnet is 1, Ropsten is 3, Rinkeby is 4, and Kovan is 42. Ephemeral development networks are typically set up with higher IDs.

Note   Like most requests to an external data source in javascript, calls to the Ethereum network are asynchronous operations. Different libraries may have different ways to handle this, either by using callbacks or returning promises. In particular, web3.js supports traditional error-first callbacks as well as promi-events. Promi-events are promise objects which double as an event emitter, allowing you to listen to different stages of the asynchronous operation. They will become more relevant in the next chapter. For now, we will simply use the async-await syntax for working with promises.

Another piece of information we can get from the network is the current block number. Polling this value can let us know when a new block was added to the chain, potentially including transactions that have modified the state of the contracts we are working with, thus triggering a re-read in our app.

```
> await web3.eth.getBlockNumber()
7059809[3]
```

We can also get detailed information from a block, such as its hash, the total gas used, its miner, and a list of all the transactions included in it. Note that we can refer to a block either by number, hash, or the string latest to signal that we want the latest block on the chain.

```
> await web3.eth.getBlock('latest')
{ author: '0xea674fdde...',
  gasLimit: 8000029,
  gasUsed: 1808896,
  hash: '0xcdb2699b240ece675611aa...',
  number: 7059810,
```

---

[3]You can find out exactly when this code sample was written by checking that particular block's timestamp using getBlock.

```
transactions:
 [ '0xca7d315abc76988ddcfa49...',
   '0x9b72090bbabe017d4bcf5b...',
   '0xa50150e448a0cc40a29986...',
   ... ],
... }
```

We can also get information not on the network but on the node itself. For instance, we can query the software version that a node is running, and even warn our users if there is a known issue on that release.

```
> await web3.eth.getNodeInfo()
'Parity-Ethereum//v2.1.11-stable-e9194b0-20190107/x86_64-linux-gnu/
rustc1.31.1'
```

Another potentially useful check is whether the node is up to date with the rest of the chain. Nodes that have been just set up may not have synced yet, so they will not be able to return recent information from the network. If a node is no longer syncing, you can safely rely on it.

```
> await web3.eth.isSyncing()
false
```

There is more information you can query from a node. Make sure to check out the web3.js reference[4] for additional methods.

Account Balances and Code

Given an address, you can query the ETH stored by that account, regardless of it being an externally owned account or a contract. Furthermore, since blockchain history is indelible, you can even query the balance of the account in an earlier point in time (Listing 4-5). The number of blocks you can go back will depend on whether you are working with an archive or a regular node.

---

[4]https://web3js.readthedocs.io/en/v1.2.0/index.html

Listing 4-5. Querying the balance of an address from ten blocks ago

```
> const addr = '0xcafE1A77e84698c83CA8931F54A755176eF75f2C';
> const block = await web3.eth.getBlockNumber() - 10;
> await web3.eth.getBalance(addr, block);
'180300794957635301822239'
```

Note that ETH balances are **always** expressed in Wei, which is the smallest unit in which an ETH can be subdivided. One ETH is equivalent to 1e18 Wei (i.e., 1 followed by 18 zeros). You can use the web3 utils module (Listing 4-6) to convert between them.

Listing 4-6. Using `web3.utils.fromWei` for converting from Wei to ETH. The reverse method is `toWei`

```
> const balance = await web3.eth.getBalance(addr, block)
> web3.utils.fromWei(balance)
'180300.794957635301822239'
```

You may have noted from the preceding snippets that ETH balance is returned not as a number but as a **string**. This is meant to avoid losing precision when dealing with very large numbers, since javascript numbers cannot deal with very large magnitudes. As an example, 1822239 wei are lost in the conversion to integer in the following code.

```
> parseInt(balance).toLocaleString();
'180,300,794,957,635,300,000,000'
```

This decision is specific to the web3.js library. Other libraries rely on javascript bignumber implementations, such as bignumber.js[5] or bn.js[6]. It is most likely that once support for native bignumbers[7] is stabilized in the language, libraries will switch to it. Either way, what is important is that you keep in mind that most numbers in Ethereum cannot be handled using regular javascript numbers, or you risk losing precision.

---

[5]http://mikemcl.github.io/bignumber.js/

[6]https://github.com/indutny/bn.js/

[7]https://developer.mozilla.org/en-US/docs/Web/JavaScript/Reference/Global_Objects/BigInt

Besides balances, you can also get the code at an address, and use it to check whether an address is a contract or an externally owned account. You can also check the code itself to see if it matches the binary from a known contract.

```
> await web3.eth.getCode(addr);
'0x6060604052361561011...'
```

Keep in mind that this method for checking whether an account is a contract or not is far from robust. If you get no code from an address, it does not necessarily mean it is externally owned: a contract may be deployed to that address later, or a contract may have been deployed there but was eventually self-destructed. All in all, you should avoid relying on whether an arbitrary address is externally owned or not for particularly sensitive operations.

Calling into a Contract

As we saw in Chapter 2, you can call into a contract to query information from it by issuing a JSON-RPC call to its address. Most contracts expose getter functions that return information on their current state or perform pure calculations; these functions can be identified as they are tagged with the view or pure modifiers in Solidity. Like all the functions listed in this chapter, calling into them does not cost any gas, since the call can be answered by any node in the network, and does not need to introduce a change on the blockchain.

These calls can be executed at a low level using the call function from web3.js, which requires manually providing the target address and the raw data to send to the target contract. As an example, 0x18160ddd is the function selector[8] for accessing the totalSupply of an ERC20 token contract, so we can test it against an existing contract on mainnet, such as the BAT token on mainnet, which returns the hexadecimal representation of 1.5e27.

```
> const addr = '0x0d8775f648430679a709e98d2b0cb6250d2887ef';
> await web3.eth.call({ to: addr, data: '0x18160ddd' });
'0x00000000...0004d8c55aefb8c05b5c000000'
```

---

[8]Function names are not stored in smart contracts. Instead, the first bytes of the hash of the function name and signature are kept. This is referred to as the selector, and it is provided as the data in a call or transaction to tell the contract which function to run.

However, we will typically rely on the web3 Contract abstraction for interacting with a contract (Listing 4-7). Creating one of these, as we saw before, requires the contract's ABI and its address. We will replicate the preceding example using the ABI for the ERC20.[9]

Listing 4-7. Accessing the same token's total supply via the web3 Contract object. Note how the output is formatted based on its type instead of returned as a raw hexadecimal value

```
> const abi = [
  {
    "constant": true,
    "inputs": [],
    "name": "totalSupply",
    "outputs": [{"name": "", "type": "uint256"}],
    "payable": false,
    "stateMutability": "view",
    "type": "function"
  }, ...
];

> const erc20 = new web3.eth.Contract(abi, addr);
> await erc20.methods.totalSupply().call()
'1500000000000000000000000000000'
```

> **Note** Like getBalance, all calls to a contract can also include an optional
> block parameter, in case you want to query a contract's state at a previous point
> in time. Remember that requesting changes for a block too long ago in the chain
> requires a connection to an archive node, which is not always available. Also
> keep in mind that, depending on your use case, it may be prudent to only display
> information from a dozen blocks ago, to shield yourself against possible chain
> reorgs. Data this recent is usually always available, regardless of the node keeping
> an archive or not.

---

[9]Full ABI available at https://github.com/ethereum/wiki/wiki/Contract-ERC20-ABI

The Contract object can also be used to obtain the function selectors that can be plugged into low-level calls or raw transactions. In the following line, the encodeABI method returns the data selector that we used at the beginning of this section.

```
> await erc20.methods.totalSupply().encodeABI()
'0x18160ddd'
```

Contracts also expose a handy interface to all events declared on the ABI (Listing 4-8), making it easy to query all events in a block range.

Listing 4-8. Obtaining the transfer events on the BAT token on mainnet that occurred in the past 100 blocks. In this example, the address starting with 0xAAAAA6 transferred 1.9e21 tokens to address 0x664753

```
> const block = await web3.eth.getBlockNumber();
> const opts = { fromBlock: block - 100, toBlock: block };
> await erc20.getPastEvents('Transfer', opts);

[{address: '0x0D8775F648430679A709E98d2b0Cb6250d2887EF',
  blockNumber: 7060651,
  logIndex: 91,
  removed: false,
  transactionHash: '0x3bd37...',
  transactionIndex: 96,
  transactionLogIndex: '0x0',
  type: 'mined',
  returnValues:
    Result {
      '0': '0xAAAAA6...',
      '1': '0x664753...',
      '2': '1905510325611397921584',
      from: '0xAAAAA6...',
      to: '0x664753...',
      value: '1905510325611397921584' },
  event: 'Transfer'
}, ... ]
```

Each log object informs of the block and the transaction where it occurred, as well as the name of the event (in this case, `Transfer`), and includes the parameters with which it was emitted.

Detecting Changes

We will now go deeper into events. Even though we now know how to query past events, listening to new events is a useful method to detect changes to a contract in our application in real time. We will see three different ways for monitoring changes.

Polling for New Blocks

Polling is a simple yet effective method for reacting to changes (Listing 4-9). Given that any change in the Ethereum network needs to be introduced via a new block in the chain, a perfectly valid approach is to just poll for new blocks, and re-read the contract state that you are interested in whenever a new block is mined. Since Ethereum blocks are generated every few seconds, a 1-second interval can be good enough.

Listing 4-9. Polling for new blocks to update the `totalSupply` of an ERC20 contract. Though we could directly poll for the total supply, this approach is more efficient if there is more data that we need to update on every block

```
let block = null,
    totalSupply = null;

const interval = setInterval(async function() {
  const newBlock = await web3.eth.getBlockNumber();
  if (newBlock !== block) {
    // update block number
    block = newBlock;
    // re-read relevant data from contract
    totalSupply = await erc20.methods.totalSupply().call();
  }
}, 1000);
```

Whenever a new block is spotted, you can query the contract your app is interacting with to retrieve its latest state and update your app accordingly if there were any changes. An alternative would be to run `getPastEvents` on the new block and only react if there were any events that affect your contract.

Installing Event Filters

Event filters are a mechanism provided by Ethereum nodes for retrieving new events that match a specified set of conditions. It works by allowing you to install an event filter **on a node** and then polling for any new events that match that filter. At a JSON-RPC level, this pattern is supported mainly by the following methods:

- `newFilter` to install a new event filter on a node, which returns a filter ID

- `getFilterChanges` that returns all new logs for a given filter ID since the last time this method was called

- `uninstallFilter` to remove a filter given its ID

Event filters still rely on polling a node for new changes, but they are more convenient to use, since it is now the node that keeps track of exactly what new events need to be sent to the client. This saves the client from needing to issue regular `getPastLogs` calls to check for new events and allows the node to precalculate the data to send if needed. It is also possible to install filters for new blocks and pending transactions that are sent to the node.

Warning   Some public nodes, such as the ones offered by Infura, may not support installing event filters. To work around this, Metamask ships with a web3 subprovider to fake the behavior of filters completely on the client side. This allows you to code your application using event filters without needing to worry about whether the node you are connecting to actually supports them. However, keep in mind that the performance gain you could get by using filters is completely lost in this scenario.

At this point, it is worth going into what options can be specified for retrieving and polling events. These options can be used both when creating new filters and when getting past logs:

- **Block ranges** can be used to specify which blocks to monitor for events. By default, filters are created to monitor the latest block mined.

- One or more **addresses** where the logs originate from. Retrieving events from a web3 Contract object will automatically restrict the logs to the address of the contract instance.

- The **topics** used to filter the events. Remember from Chapter 3 that EVM logs can have up to four indexed topics – these are used for filtering them during queries. The first topic is always the event selector, while the remaining topics are the indexed arguments from Solidity. A filter can impose restrictions on any of the topics, requesting a topic to optionally match a set of values.

As an example, the following filter object can be used to retrieve all transfers of an ERC20 token sent to a group of three token holders during the last 1000 blocks.

```
> const block = await web3.eth.getBlockNumber();
> const filter = { to: [holder1, holder2, holder3] };
> const opts = { fromBlock: block - 1000, filter: filter };
> await erc20.getPastEvents('Transfer', opts);
```

The web3 library has no support for event filters. Instead, monitoring for events is done via the third and last mechanism for listening to changes: subscriptions.

Creating Subscriptions

A more advanced option to monitor events is to create a subscription. Event subscriptions work similar to event filters in that they are created in a node from a set of filters (block range, addresses, and topics) to indicate which events are of interest to the client. However, subscriptions do not require the client to poll for changes, but rely on two-way connections to directly push new events to the client. For this reason, subscriptions are only available on websockets or IPC connections and not on HTTP ones.

Note   Unlike event filters, Infura does support websocket connections, via the URL `wss://mainnet.infura.io/ws/v3/PROJECTID`. Still, in the event that the user chooses a custom node via a regular HTTP connection, Metamask also ships with a subprovider to fake subscriptions client-side by relying on polling. Again, this allows you to transparently use event subscriptions on your app, having a subprovider polyfill the feature if the connection or node does not support it.

Under the hood, web3 uses subscriptions when you listen to an event (Listing 4-10). This means that you will only be able to rely on events if you are running on a websocket or IPC connection, or you have a subprovider to polyfill for subscriptions. The web3 event emitter will report whenever a new event that matches the filter is available, when an error occurs, and when an event is removed from the blockchain due to a reorganization.

Listing 4-10. Setting up a subscription to monitor `Transfer` events on an ERC20 token contract. The `data` handler fires on every new event, while `error` fires upon an error in the subscription. Events removed from the chain due to a reorganization are fired in `changed`.

```
> const filter = { to: [holder1, holder2, holder3] };
> const sub = erc20.events.Transfer({ filter })
  .on('data', (evt) =>
    console.log(`New tx from ${evt.returnValues.from}`)
  )
  .on('error', (err) =>
    console.error(err)
  )
  .on('changed', (evt) =>
    console.log(`Removed tx from ${evt.returnValues.from}`)
  )
```

Subscriptions are automatically cleared when the connection to the server is closed. Alternatively, they can be removed via the `unsubscribe()` method on the subscription object, or by using `web3.eth.clearSubscriptions()`, which removes all active subscriptions.

As with event filters, it is possible to set up subscriptions for events from multiple addresses, as well as for new pending transactions or new blocks. Using the latter, a similar pattern to polling can be implemented, in which a subscription is installed to monitor for new blocks, and upon every block the state of the contract is re-read. Nevertheless, if the contract emits events for all state changes, monitoring them is much more efficient.

Example Application

We will now put together everything we learned in this chapter and build a web application for monitoring transfers on an ERC20 token. This application will just retrieve data from the token and not provide any interface for actually sending transactions.

Setup

We will once again use the `create-react-app` package to bootstrap our application. Needless to say, using this package is not required, but will simplify our setup and let us focus on building the app itself.

```
npm init react-app erc20-app
```

Dependencies

Besides web3, we will install the `openzeppelin-solidity` package as a dependency. OpenZeppelin is an open source library of secure reusable smart contracts, and includes vetted implementations for some standards. We will use it to obtain the ABI of the ERC20 contract that we need to create the web3 Contract instance. We will also add `bignumber.js` for manipulating a few numeric values throughout the app.

```
npm install web3@1.2.0 openzeppelin-solidity@2.1 bignumber.js@8.0
```

As before, try running `npm start` to make sure that the sample react-app runs successfully. We can now start coding.

Initializing Web3

We will create a `network.js` file as before to manage a web3 object to connect to the network. We will rely on the injected web3 provider, falling back to a websocket connection to Infura. Note that since we will not request access to user accounts, we can skip the `ethereum.enable()` call.

```
// src/eth/network.js
import Web3 from 'web3';

let web3;
export function getWeb3() {
  if (!web3) {
    web3 = new Web3(window.ethereum
              || (window.web3 && window.web3.currentProvider)
              || "wss://mainnet.infura.io/ws/v3/PROJECT_ID");
  } return web3;
}
```

Note   Make sure to use a valid URL for the fallback provider, by filling in with your Infura token, in case the user browsing the site does not have Metamask or a web3 compatible browser. Note that it is websocket-based, since we will be using event subscriptions later on the app.

The ERC20 Contract

We will create a small function for initializing new web3 contract objects for ERC20s. Recall that in order to do this, we needed access to the web3 object (which we have already set up), the contract ABI, and the address.

```
// src/contracts/ERC20.js
import ERC20Artifact from 'openzeppelin-solidity/build/contracts/
ERC20Detailed.json';

export default function ERC20(web3, address = null) {
  const { abi } = ERC20Artifact;
  return new web3.eth.Contract(abi, address);
}
```

We retrieve the contract ABI from OpenZeppelin, while we'll leave the address as a parameter for now. Now that we have all basic components set up, we can get started with the application views.

Building the Application

We will start with a main App component that will initialize the connection and set up the ERC20 contract instance that we will be monitoring. Once we have the contract instance ready, we will begin by retrieving some information from it.

Root Component

The App component will be the root of our component tree (Listing 4-11). This component will manage the connection to the network and the ERC20 contract instance, both of which will be set up on the componentDidMount lifecycle method.

Remember that this method is automatically fired by React when the component has mounted, and is the suggested event for retrieving async data. Of course, if you are using a particular state management library (such as Redux), your strategy for loading async data may be different.

Listing 4-11. Initial version of the root App component for our application. Note that the highlighted line in componentDidMount that is setting up the ERC20 contract is using the factory method we built earlier

```
// src/App.js
import React, { Component } from 'react';
import ERC20Contract from './contracts/ERC20';
import { getWeb3 } from './eth/network';

const ERC20_ADDRESS = "0x1985365e9f78359a9B6AD760e32412f4a445E862";

class App extends Component {
  state = { loading: true };

  async componentDidMount() {
    const web3 = getWeb3();
    const erc20 = await ERC20Contract(web3, ERC20_ADDRESS);
    this.setState({ erc20, loading: false });
  }

  render() {
    return (
      <div className="App">
```

```
        { this.getAppContent() }
      </div>
    );
  }

  getAppContent() {
    const { erc20 } = this.state;
    if (!erc20) {
      return (<div>Connecting to network...</div>);
    } else {
      return (<div>ERC20 at {erc20.options.address}</div>);
    }
  }
}
```

Since the address in the preceding example refers to a contract on mainnet, the app will only work if we have a connection to the Ethereum main network. If we are connecting to another network, the contract will probably not exist at the address listed, causing the app to fail.

Note   If you are curious about the ERC20 address chosen, it is the Augur REP token. Augur is a decentralized oracle and prediction market, and its main token is used reporting and disputing the outcome of events. If you want to experiment with other ERC20s, Etherscan provides a handy list of top tokens at etherscan.io/tokens.

To handle this case, we will add a few lines to detect the current network, and validate that we are indeed on mainnet (Listing 4-12). You can play with this by changing the current network on metamask while on the application.

Listing 4-12. Checking that we are currently connected to mainnet. Note that the contract is only instantiated if we are on the correct network

```
async componentDidMount() {
  const web3 = getWeb3();
  const networkId = await web3.eth.net.getId();
  const isMainnet = (networkId === 1);
  this.setState({ isMainnet });
```

```
  if (isMainnet) {
    const erc20 = await ERC20Contract(web3, ERC20_ADDRESS);
    this.setState({ erc20 });
  }

  this.setState({ loading: false });
}
```

The render method needs to be changed accordingly to handle not just the loading and loaded states but also the state where we are not on mainnet.

```
getAppContent() {
  const { loading, isMainnet, erc20 } = this.state;
  if (loading) {
    return (<div>Connecting to network...</div>);
  } else if (!isMainnet) {
    return (<div>Please connect to Mainnet</div>);
  } else {
    return (<div>ERC20 at {erc20.options.address}</div>);
  }
}
```

We still have another issue to tackle: what if the connection just fails? The node we are connecting to may be offline, or the contract address could just be incorrect. We need to add proper error handling when we are retrieving blockchain data (Listing 4-13).

Listing 4-13. Updated `componentDidMount` method to add error handling. Note that the `render` method also needs to be updated accordingly to display the error message if it is present in the component state

```
async componentDidMount() {
  const web3 = getWeb3();
  await this.checkNetwork(web3);
  await this.retrieveContract(web3);
  this.setState({ loading: false });
}
```

```
async checkNetwork(web3) {
  try {
    const networkId = await web3.eth.net.getId();
    const isMainnet = (networkId === 1);
    this.setState({ isMainnet });
  } catch (error) {
    console.error(error);
    this.setState({ error: `Error connecting to network` })
  }
}

async retrieveContract(web3) {
  if (!this.state.isMainnet) return;
  try {
    const erc20 = await ERC20Contract(web3, ERC20_ADDRESS);
    this.setState({ erc20 });
  } catch (error) {
    console.error(error);
    this.setState({ error: `Error retrieving contract` })
  }
}
```

We can now focus on the token itself. Let's create a new component named ERC20, display it instead of the contract's address (Listing 4-14), and start working on it.

Listing 4-14. Updated render helper method to display an ERC20 component, which expects the `erc20` contract instance as a property

```
getAppContent() {
  const { loading, error, isMainnet, erc20 } = this.state;
  if (error) {
    return (<div>{error}</div>);
  } else if (loading) {
    return (<div>Connecting to network...</div>);
  } else if (!isMainnet) {
    return (<div>Please connect to Mainnet</div>);
```

```
    } else {
      return (<ERC20 contract={erc20} />);
    }
  }
}
```

ERC20 Component

This component shall receive the contract instance, knowing that all connection details have been settled by the parent component, and display it. We will start by retrieving some static information, such as the name, symbol, and number of decimals (Listing 4-15). These are optional attributes according to the ERC20 standard, since they are never used as part of the contract's logic; nevertheless, most tokens do implement them.

We will also retrieve the token's total supply. This is the total number of tokens created for this contract. Unlike the name, symbol, and decimals, there is no guarantee that this value will stay constant: some tokens have a continuous issuance model, which causes the total supply to increase on every block, while others may have a deflationary model where certain events actually burn tokens.

For the sake of this app, we will work only with tokens with a fixed supply, so we will not need to refresh the total supply. Nevertheless, you could easily add a polling mechanism for updating the total supply on every call, as we have seen earlier in this chapter.

Listing 4-15. React component for displaying information on the ERC20 token. Once again, we rely on the componentDidMount method to load async information to populate the state. By using Promise.all(), we fire all four requests simultaneously and only set the return values once we have obtained all of them

```
class ERC20 extends Component {
  async componentDidMount() {
    const { contract } = this.props;
    const [name, symbol, decimals, totalSupply] =
      await Promise.all([
        contract.methods.name().call(),
        contract.methods.symbol().call(),
```

```
        contract.methods.decimals().call(),
        contract.methods.totalSupply().call(),
    ]);
    this.setState({ name, symbol, decimals, totalSupply });
  }
}
```

We can now render this information by showing the token name and symbol to our users, as well as the total supply (Listing 4-16). We will rely on the decimals of the token to format all the values we display.

Listing 4-16. Render method to display the static information of an ERC20 token. Note that the `totalSupply` is adjusted by the decimals of the token

```
render() {
  if (!this.state.totalSupply) return "Loading...";
  const { name, totalSupply, decimals, symbol } = this.state;
  const formattedSupply = formatValue(totalSupply, decimals);
  return (<div>
    <h1>{name} Token</h1>
    <div>Total supply of {formattedSupply} {symbol}</div>
  </div>);
}
```

For the auxiliary `formatValue` function (Listing 4-17), we will rely on `bignumber.js`, a library for manipulating and formatting big numbers in javascript. We will convert the total supply value to a bignumber instance, right-shift it (on base 10) by the number of decimals, and format the result as a string.

Listing 4-17. Auxiliary function to format token amounts based on the decimals property of the contract

```
// src/utils/format.js
import BigNumber from 'bignumber.js';
BigNumber.config({ DECIMAL_PLACES: 4 });
```

```
export function formatValue(value, decimals) {
  const bn = new BigNumber(value);
  return bn.shiftedBy(-decimals).toString(10);
}
```

The output so far should look like Figure 4-3, assuming you did not change the token address from the example.

Figure 4-3. *Our sample application displaying the static information of the Augur REP token: name (Reputation), symbol (REP), and total supply (1.1e25) formatted with the token decimals (18)*

Displaying Transfer Events

We will now add the last component of our application that will display the latest transfers of the token and listen for any new ones in real time.

Loading Past Transfers

Let's start by adding a Transfers component to the ERC20 component we already have (Listing 4-18), that will start out by loading past transfers. This component will receive the contract, decimals, and symbol as props from its parent: the first one to monitor for events and the other two to format values.

Listing 4-18. Updated render method from the ERC20 component to include the new `Transfers` component

```
render() {
  if (!this.state.totalSupply) return "Loading...";
  const { name, totalSupply, decimals, symbol } = this.state;
  const { contract } = this.props;
  const formattedSupply = formatValue(totalSupply, decimals);

  return (
    <div className="ERC20">
      <h1>{name} Token</h1>
      <div>Total supply of {formattedSupply} {symbol}</div>
      <div>
        <h2>Transfers</h2>
        <Transfers contract={contract}
          decimals={decimals} symbol={symbol} />
      </div>
    </div>
  );
}
```

We will be loading all transfer events from the past 1000 blocks to seed the component. Attempting to load all transfers in history will probably fail, given that REP has over 75,000 transfers at the time of this writing, which is too large an amount to query from the node in a single request. There are other tokens with even more transfers, such as OMG, which is at over 2 million at the time of this writing.

```
// src/components/Transfers.js
import React, { Component } from 'react';
import { getWeb3 } from '../eth/network';

export default class Transfers extends Component {
  async componentDidMount() {
    const { contract } = this.props;
    const blockNumber = await getWeb3().eth.getBlockNumber();
    const EVENT = 'Transfer';
```

```
  const pastEvents = await contract.getPastEvents(EVENT, {
    fromBlock: blockNumber - 1000,
    toBlock: blockNumber
  });

  this.setState({
    loading: false,
    transfers: pastEvents.reverse()
  });
  }
}
```

Note   For the sake of this application, we are just loading the events from an arbitrary number of blocks ago, in order to seed the component with initial data as it loads. Depending on your use case, you may want to add an option to load more events (for instance, when the user scrolls to the end of the list) by firing subsequent getPastEvents calls.

The render method for this component is straightforward: we will show a pure component to display each transfer in a list (Listing 4-19). We will pass down the symbol and decimals to format the amount of tokens transferred in each event.

Listing 4-19. Displaying each transfer in the collection by using a pure component that simply displays the data received

```
render() {
  const { loading, transfers } = this.state;
  const { decimals, symbol } = this.props;
  if (loading) return "Loading...";

  return (<div className="Transfers">
    { transfers.map(transfer => (
      <Transfer
        key={getLogId(transfer)}
        transfer={transfer}
        decimals={decimals}
```

```
        symbol={symbol} />
    )) }
  </div>)
}
```

Keep in mind that React requires us to assign a unique key to each element in a collection. To generate this key, we are using a `getLogId` helper function (Listing 4-20) that combines the transaction hash in which the event occurred and the log index (i.e., the index of the particular event in the array of all logs emitted in the transaction). This combination is guaranteed to be unique.

Listing 4-20. Simple function for generating a unique identifier for a log. Note that web3.js already assigns an ID to a log entry, calculated as a hash over the same parameters. However, the hash is then truncated to 4 bytes, which may yield collisions if we are dealing with a large number of events

```
function getLogId(log) {
  return `${log.transactionHash}.${log.logIndex}`;
}
```

For the `Transfer` pure component (Listing 4-21), we will just rely on the `formatValue` helper function we used previously and fetch the `from`, `to`, and `value` arguments from the transfer object. As an extra, we will include a link to the transaction on etherscan so our users can review the transaction there, so they can perform an additional check on the data we display on our app.[10]

Listing 4-21. `Transfer` component for displaying a single `Transfer` event loaded from the ERC20 token contract

```
const ETHERSCAN_URL = 'https://etherscan.io/tx/';

export default function Transfer (props) {
  const { decimals, symbol, transfer } = props;
  const { from, to, value } = transfer.returnValues;
```

---

[10]It is a common practice to add links to view a transaction on an explorer, so the users can easily verify that a transaction listed on your app indeed took place. Note that this still is no guarantee, since the blockchain explorer is a centralized service, but this "second confirmation" is valued by most users.

```
  const roundedValue = formatValue(value, decimals);
  const url = ETHERSCAN_URL + transfer.transactionHash;

  return (
    <div>
      <a href={url}>
        {from} to {to} for {roundedValue} {symbol}
      </a>
    </div>
  );
}
```

With this code, every time we reload the page, we will see the transfers from the last 1000 blocks for the token. We can now add support for listening to new transfers as they occur.

Monitoring New Transfers

In order to monitor new transfers, we will install a *subscription* for Transfer events of this contract (Listing 4-22), as we have already seen previously in this chapter. We will listen to all transfers starting from the block right after the one we used for fetching past events and unsubscribe once the component is unmounted (Listing 4-23).

Listing 4-22. Subscription function to listen for new transfer events, to be called from componentDidMount, using erc20 and blockNumber+1 as arguments. Note that we are storing the subscription object in state to be able to unsubscribe later

```
subscribe(contract, fromBlock) {
  const eventSub = contract.events.Transfer({ fromBlock })
    .on('data', (event) => {
      this.setState(state => ({
        ...state,
        transfers: [event, ...state.transfers]
      }));
    });
  this.setState({ eventSub });
}
```

Listing 4-23. Code to stop listening for events when the component is to be unmounted from the tree. Even though we will never unmount the component in this particular application, it is a good practice to always remove the subscriptions when they are no longer used

```
componentWillUnmount() {
  const { eventSub } = this.state;
  if (eventSub) eventSub.unsubscribe();
}
```

Your application should now show new transactions as they occur, without the need for refreshing the page. However, to make sure we properly handle all scenarios, we will add handlers for when a transfer event is removed from the blockchain due to a reorganization and for when the subscription fails (Listing 4-24).

Listing 4-24. Adding handlers for the changed and error events of the subscription. The former fires whenever an event is removed from the blockchain, so we remove it from our state, while the latter fires upon an error, which we add to our state to be displayed to the user

```
subscribe(contract, fromBlock) {
  const eventSub = contract.events.Transfer({ fromBlock })
    .on('data', (event) => {
      this.setState(state => ({
        ...state,
        transfers: [event, ...state.transfers]
      }));
    })
    .on('changed', (event) => {
      this.setState(state => ({
        ...state,
        transfers: state.transfers.filter(t =>
          t.transactionHash !== event.transactionHash
          || t.logIndex !== event.logIndex
      )})))
    })
```

```
    .on('error', (error) => {
      this.setState({ error })
    });

  this.setState({ eventSub });
}
```

Awaiting Confirmations

As the last step in the application, we will avoid displaying unconfirmed transfers to the user. Instead of showing a transfer event as soon as we receive it, we will instead wait for a certain number of blocks to be added to the chain before rendering it in our list.

In order to do this, we first need to monitor the current block number. We will add a subscription specifically for that (Listing 4-25), though we could also poll the getBlockNumber method every second to achieve a similar result.

Listing 4-25. Updated section of componentDidMount to set the initial block number in the component's state, and add a subscription to update it as new blocks are received

```
async componentDidMount() {
  const blockNumber = await getWeb3().eth.getBlockNumber();
  this.setState({ blockNumber });

  const HEADERS = 'newBlockHeaders';
  const blockSub = getWeb3().eth.subscribe(HEADERS)
    .on('data', ({ number }) => {
      if (number) this.setState({ blockNumber: number});
    });
  this.setState({ blockSub });

  // Subscribe to new transfers and load previous ones
  // ...
}
```

Now we can limit our component to just render the transfer events that happened at least a number of blocks ago (Listing 4-26). By checking the block number in which the transaction occurred against current block number, we can easily implement this filter.

Listing 4-26. Updated render method to show only transfers with at least 12 confirmations

```
render() {
  const { transfers, blockNumber } = this.state;
  const confirmed = transfers.filter((transfer) => (
    blockNumber - transfer.blockNumber > 12
  ));

  // Render only confirmed transfers
  // ...
}
```

Note   Different applications will have different requirements for the number of confirmations, some of them going up to hundreds of blocks. This will depend strictly on your use case.

Summary

In this chapter, we have gone in-depth into how to extract data from the Ethereum network and feed it into our app. We started out by reviewing how connections to nodes work, listing the protocols available for the JSON-RPC interface, and looking into the Provider object used by web3 and other libraries to manage the underlying connection. We also learned that there are different types of nodes available and how a Provider, such as the one injected by web3-enabled browsers, may abstract away some of these differences via the usage of subproviders.

Using web3.js as a sample library, we studied what kind of queries we could issue to the blockchain: general network information, address-specific data such as balance and code, and calls to existing contracts. When connecting to an archive node, these queries can be issued to any block in the past, not just the most recent ones.

We also studied different ways for monitoring changes to contracts in real time in our applications. While polling is a classic method that is always available, event filters or subscriptions may be more interesting options due to better performance or faster notification times.

To wrap up the chapter, we built an application for retrieving information from an ERC20 token contract, and monitor all its transfer events using subscriptions. In the next chapter, we will learn how to make changes to the blockchain, going into all the details involved in sending a new transaction to the network.

CHAPTER 5

Sending Transactions

After reviewing in the previous chapter how to read data and monitor changes on the network, we will now go into how to write data by sending transactions. We will start by setting up a development environment for easily playing with smart contracts, then move into a web3-enabled context, and finally go into the details of issuing transactions and monitoring their lifecycle. Once again, we will wrap up with a sample application that puts all the learnings of the chapter together.

Setting Up the Environment

Before going into the details of transactions, we will first set up a development environment for building and testing our applications.

Development Nodes

Instead of using a remote public node for our application, this time we will work with a local private node. Recall from the previous chapter that a node is said to be *private* when it holds a set of accounts and their private keys, so it can be used for signing transactions. This makes them friendlier for scripting and testing, since we do not need to worry about account management on our code and can delegate that responsibility to the node itself.

Running a local node has another benefit, which is that we can create our own network instead of connecting to an existing one. This is useful for development and especially for automated testing, since we do not need to wait for long networking or mining times – we can set up our own network with near-instant mining. Such networks are usually called *development networks*.

© Santiago Palladino 2019
S. Palladino, *Ethereum for Web Developers*, https://doi.org/10.1007/978-1-4842-5278-9_5

The usual workflow when building an application is to rely on a local development node for coding and unit testing, then move to a testnet for a more realistic environment, and eventually go onto mainnet as you deploy to production.

Using Ganache

One of the most widely used client for development is *ganache* (formerly known as *testrpc*). Ganache is a tool exclusively built for development: it does not connect to any Ethereum network – it just starts and runs a new development chain. It also creates a set of random testing accounts, seeded with a bunch of ETH each, and exposes their private key and mnemonic (Listing 5-1).

Listing 5-1. Globally installing and running a local development network using Ganache. Note the -d flag, which stands for deterministic: with this, ganache will always generate the same set of accounts. Otherwise, the accounts and mnemonic change from run to run

```
$ npm install -g ganache-cli@6.4
$ ganache-cli -d

Ganache CLI v6.4.3 (ganache-core: 2.5.5)

Available Accounts
==================
(0) 0x90f8bf6a479f320ead074411a4b0e7944ea8c9c1 (~100 ETH)
(1) 0xffcf8fdee72ac11b5c542428b35eef5769c409f0 (~100 ETH)
...

Private Keys
==================
(0) 0x4f3edf983ac636a65a...
(1) 0x6cbed15c793ce57650...
...

HD Wallet
==================
Mnemonic:      myth like bonus scare over problem client lizard pioneer
submit female collect
```

128

```
Base HD Path:  m/44'/60'/0'/0/{account_index}

...

Listening on 127.0.0.1:8545
```

Note   You may have noted an HD Wallet section on the ganache output, which includes a mnemonic and an HD path. HD stands for hierarchical deterministic, and is a concept borrowed from Bitcoin for creating any number of accounts given an *extended* pair of private/public keys. Without going into technical details, a new pair of private/public keys can be created from the extended pair by providing different *derivation paths* (such as m/44'/60'/0'/0/0, m/44'/60'/0'/0/1, etc., as shown in the ganache output). The extended pair itself can be derived from a *mnemonic*: a set of randomly generated words which are much friendlier to remember or jot down. All in all, this allows an unlimited number of accounts to be securely derived from a single set of words. We will review this in-depth in Chapter 7.

Ganache defaults to instant sealing, meaning that whenever a new transaction is received, a new block is automatically mined on the spot and added to the chain.[1] To test this out, start a new ganache instance via `ganache-cli` (Listing 5-3). On a different terminal, create a new project with `web3@1.2.0` and start a new console[2] (Listing 5-2), where we will execute a transaction.

Listing 5-2. Testing sending 1ETH between two of the accounts generated by ganache. Keep an eye on the ganache log as you send the transaction: you will note that it is processed and mined immediately

```
$ npm init -y
$ npm install web3@1.2.0
$ node --experimental-repl-await
```

---

[1] This makes interactions extremely fast, but at the same time a poor representation of how an actual blockchain works. Keep this in mind when testing your application.

[2] We will use the `--experimental-repl-await` flag when starting the console. This allows us to use top-level `await` in the REPL, which is particularly handy for playing around with promises. Note that more modern versions of node may not require this flag.

```
> // Load web3 and open a connection to the node
> let Web3 = require('web3')
> let web3 = new Web3('http://localhost:8545')

> // Loads first two accounts as alice and bob
> let [alice, bob] = await web3.eth.getAccounts()

> // Checks bob's initial balance (remember 1ETH = 1e18 Wei)
> await web3.eth.getBalance(bob) / 1e18
100

> // Send 1ETH from Alice to Bob
> // Note that the transaction is mined immediately
> web3.eth.sendTransaction({from: alice,to: bob,value: 1e18})

> // Check bob's balance again and see the additional 1ETH
>   await web3.eth.getBalance(bob) / 1e18
101
```

Listing 5-3. Output of the ganache log from the execution listed previously

```
> ganache-cli -d
Listening on 127.0.0.1:8545
eth_gasPrice
eth_getBalance
eth_sendTransaction

   Transaction: 0x6c79e178...
   Gas usage: 21000
   Block Number: 1

eth_getTransactionReceipt
eth_getBalance
```

Instead of having ganache mine a new block on every transaction, you can specify a blockTime (in seconds) which indicates the interval in which new blocks will be generated. While slower than instant seal, this is a better representation of how an actual chain works.

You can also force ganache to mine a new block at any time by sending a special evm_mine instruction via its JSON-RPC interface (Listing 5-4). This instruction is specific to ganache and is not part of the standard JSON-RPC API.

Listing 5-4. Adding a new block to a ganache development blockchain by sending an evm_mine call directly via the provider. Ganache also supports an evm_increaseTime call to fake the passing of time, which is particularly useful for automated tests

```
> // Check the current block number
> await web3.eth.getBlockNumber()
1

> // Force ganache to mine a new block
> let provider = web3.currentProvider
> let send = util.promisify(provider.send).bind(provider)
> await send({ method: 'evm_mine' })

> // Verify that the block number has increased
> await web3.eth.getBlockNumber()
2
```

By default, all chains generated by ganache are ephemeral: they are lost when the ganache process is stopped. This can be changed by starting ganache with a db option to store its state in a local folder, as shown in the following.

```
$ mkdir -p ganachedb
$ ganache-cli -d --db ganachedb
```

Make sure to run --help to check all the available options: ganache is a very flexible tool for testing and allows you to set up whichever accounts you want with arbitrary balances. It can even fork off an existing chain for running dry runs of actions on actual networks.

Geth or Parity Development Mode

An alternative to using ganache for development is to work with a common Ethereum client, such as Geth or Parity, set on development mode. This mode creates a new private blockchain, managed entirely by the node, with optional instant seal. While they offer less flexibility for testing than ganache, they are more representative, since you connect your app to the same clients as you would do in production.

Note   While we will focus the rest of this section on Geth, make sure to check out Parity's documentation as well to review the options available for its dev mode.[3]

To start geth in development mode, install it on your workstation[4] and run the following command. Make sure to first stop the ganache instance we started earlier if it is still running, since both will attempt to use the same port.

```
$ geth --datadir=geth-data --rpc --ws --dev --dev.period=1
```

This will open the HTTP interface in the default 8545 port and the websocket interface in 8546. The dev.period option specifies the interval (in seconds) in which new blocks should be mined – omitting this option toggles instant seal as in ganache. Also, note the datadir option, which will store all blockchain data in the local geth-data directory; if you do not set this flag, geth will store all data in a default location in your home directory.

Upon startup, Geth will create a single account with large amounts of ETH for development. Nevertheless, if you want to generate additional accounts, you may use the account subcommand, setting the same datadir as in the original geth command.

```
$ geth --datadir=geth-data account new
```

```
Your new account is locked with a password. Please give a password. Do not
forget this password.
Passphrase:
Repeat passphrase:
Address: {3975c2...}
```

Geth will ask you for a passphrase to encrypt the account, which you may leave as empty for a development network (but definitely not for a real one!). All Ethereum clients keep user accounts encrypted, until the owner requires to use them. As such, to actually use the account, the owner must first unlock it by providing the passphrase. Let's test this: we will once again start a node console and connect to the node.

---

[3]https://wiki.parity.io/Private-development-chain

[4]See https://github.com/ethereum/go-ethereum/wiki/Building-Ethereum for installation
 instructions. This chapter uses geth version 1.8 for all examples.

```
$ node --experimental-repl-await
> // Load web3 and open a connection to the node
> let Web3 = require('web3')
> let web3 = new Web3('http://localhost:8545')

> // List accounts on the node
> let accounts = await web3.eth.getAccounts()
[ '0xC5A4bA36f7C0B4eD17455C1A578a6ab3Fb738245', ...]

> // Send a transaction from the always-unlocked dev account
> await web3.eth.sendTransaction({ from: accounts[0], to: accounts[1],
  value: 5e18 })
{ transactionHash: '0x18737033...', ... }

> // Try sending a transaction from the newly created account
> await web3.eth.sendTransaction({ from: accounts[1], to: accounts[0],
  value: 1e18 })
Returned error: authentication needed: password or unlock
```

Unlocking an account requires access to the *personal* API, which is disabled by default on the HTTP interface. To avoid going into detail on how to configure API accesses for a node, we will simply restart the geth process supplying an unlock option with the comma-separated list of addresses we want to freely use. Geth will prompt for the account's password upon startup.

```
$ geth --datadir=geth-data --rpc --ws --dev --dev.period=1
--unlock=3975c2...
```

Note   So far, we have only been interacting with the eth API of a node, which is used for regular interaction with the Ethereum network. But nodes also provide other APIs, which are used for managing accounts, administering the node, mining, or even debugging. Startup options control which APIs are offered via which interfaces: by default, sensitive APIs such as personal or management are only exposed locally via the IPC interface.

Keep in mind that a geth node can be used either in development mode, in connection to a testnet, or in direct connection to mainnet. When working on an actual network, you only need to swap out the dev startup option by a `networkid` specifying which Ethereum network you want to connect to.

Remember that, unlike in Bitcoin, Ethereum accounts are valid for any network, so take special care not to mix up your development accounts and your mainnet ones. It is a good practice to use different addresses for different networks. You do not want to burn 10ETH from your default account in development only to realize that you were actually running on mainnet.

Creating Contracts

Now that we have a local node with a development network set up, we will go through the process of compiling and deploying a smart contract to it. Keep in mind that since we are working on a fresh development network, there are no contracts already deployed for us to interact with, so we will need to create all of them.

Compiling

To begin with, in a new project folder, create a new `contracts/Greeter.sol` file with a Greeter contract we will use for testing.

```
// contracts/Greeter.sol
pragma solidity ^0.5.0;

contract Greeter {
  string private greeting;

  constructor(string memory _greeting) public {
    greeting = _greeting;
  }

  function greet() public view returns (string memory) {
    return greeting;
  }
}
```

Install the Solidity compiler[5] version 0.5 or higher, and run the following command in your project root to compile the contract and save the output to a local Artifacts.json file.

```
solc --pretty-json --JSON=abi,bin contracts/*.sol > Artifacts.json
```

This will generate a JSON file with one entry for each Solidity file on your contracts folder, and include both the ABI and the compiled code.

```
{
  "contracts":  {
    "contracts/Greeter.sol:Greeter": {
      "abi" : "[{\"constant\":true,... "
      "bin" : "6080..."
    }
  }
}
```

However, the command-line interface for the Solidity compiler is quite limited. The recommended usage for more complex applications is the standard JSON interface, which accepts a JSON file for configuring the compilation task and outputs one file per contract. The caveat is that this interface is rather complex to use manually.

Nevertheless, there are several wrappers that offer a friendlier interface for the compiler. Here we will use the sol-compiler from the 0x team, which is a thin wrapper over the standard JSON format. Install and run it with the following commands, which will generate one JSON file per contract in an artifacts folder.

```
$ npm install -g @0x/sol-compiler@3.1
$ sol-compiler
```

The output files generated by sol-compiler have the following structure. Note that a compiler.json configuration file can be set up[6] to control which fields are generated, as well as some compiler options, such as the optimizer.

---

[5]See https://solidity.readthedocs.io/en/v0.5.3/installing-solidity.html. You can also just run npm install -g solc@0.5 to install a javascript version via npm.
[6]See https://0x.org/docs/sol-compiler#types-CompilerOptions

```
{
  "contractName": "Greeter",
  "compilerOutput": {
    "abi": [ {"constant": true, ... } ],
    "evm": {
      "bytecode": {
        "object": "0x6080..."
      }
    }
  }
}
```

Abridged sample output of sol-compiler.

Note   While the content is the same as the one generated previously via the JSON option of solc, it is organized differently. From here on, we will use the output from sol-compiler in all examples.

Deploying

Now that we have compiled our Solidity files, we can deploy them to our development network. While there are a number of tools that manage this process for us, we will keep our toolchain as simple as possible and rely just on web3 to do this.

To deploy a contract using web3, we first need to create a web3 contract object, making sure we provide the contract's binary (which we can extract from the compiled artifact). We will leave out the second parameter of the constructor which is the contract's address, since it does not exist yet.

```
Greeter = new web3.eth.Contract(abi, null, { data: binary })
```

Once we have the contract object, we can invoke the deploy method by providing an unlocked sender account and a gas stipend. The returned object is a full web3 contract we can interact with.

```
greeter = await Greeter.deploy().send({ from, gas: 1e6 })
```

Let's put all of this together in a new `scripts/deploy.js` file (Listing 5-5). We will retrieve the ABI and bytecode from the `artifacts` folder and connect to a local node to run the deployment.

Listing 5-5. Deployment script for the `Greeter` contract. Note that the data and abi are fetched from the JSON file generated by sol-compile, and the sender account is set to the first account in the node

```
// scripts/deploy.js
const Web3 = require('web3')
const GreeterJSON = require('../artifacts/Greeter.json')

async function deploy() {
  const web3 = new Web3('http://localhost:8545')
  const [from] = await web3.eth.getAccounts()
  const gas = 1e6
  const arguments = ["Hello world!"]

  const data = GreeterJSON.compilerOutput.evm.bytecode.object
  const abi = GreeterJSON.compilerOutput.abi
  const Greeter = new web3.eth.Contract(abi, null, { data })

  const greeter = await Greeter.deploy({ arguments })
                               .send({ from, gas })
  console.log(greeter.options.address);
}

deploy();
```

To test this, make sure to first start a ganache instance (or a geth in development mode) as shown before, listening to the default port 8545. Then run the preceding script via `node scripts/deploy.js`, which should output the deployment address. We can then start a javascript console to connect to the node and run the contract's `greet` function (Listing 5-6) as a means to verify that everything worked as expected.

Listing 5-6. Script for initializing a greeter contract object at the deployed address and testing the call to the greet function. Make sure to replace the sample address with the actual deployment address

```
$ node --experimental-repl-await

> Web3 = require('web3')
> GreeterJSON = require('../artifacts/Greeter.json')

> let web3 = new Web3('http://localhost:8545')
> let abi = GreeterJSON.compilerOutput.abi

> let greeter = new web3.eth.Contract(abi, '0xa42d93...')
> await greeter.methods.greet().call()
'Hello world!'
```

The deployment script, while simple, can be generalized for any contract in your application and modified to accept command-line options or environment variables to configure the connection to the node, the sender account, or the constructor parameters. It is also a good idea to save the deployment address to a local file, rather than just output it in the console. We will revisit this near the end of the chapter when we build a full application.

Managing Accounts

Our next step will be account management, which includes both creating and seeding accounts in a development environment, as well as accessing them from our web applications.

Revisiting Metamask

As in previous chapters, we will rely on Metamask for connecting to the network from our web application. However, we will now be working not on an actual Ethereum network, but on a local development one. We shall switch to testnets and mainnet at a later stage.

> **Note**   As we have previously pointed out, addresses in Ethereum are valid in all networks. This means that you can use the same private key and address pair throughout testnet, mainnet, and even your local development network. Of course, the fact that you *can* does not mean that you *should*. It is a good idea to use different accounts altogether, since you will want to treat the keys to accounts in *real* networks with special care. Unfortunately, Metamask will use the same set of accounts for all networks, which are all derived from the same mnemonic. To avoid mistaking development and real accounts, some developers opt for running a different browser profile for development, which allows them to have an entirely separate set of accounts.

Your first step will be to connect Metamask to your development network (Figure 5-1). Hit the network drop-down in the extension and choose to connect to *Localhost 8545*, where your development node is running.

Alternatively, if you have set up your development node on a different port, you will need to register it as a new network. To do this, head over to *Settings*, choose to connect to a *New Network*, and enter an HTTP connection to `localhost` at the port where you started ganache, geth, or parity (8545 by default).

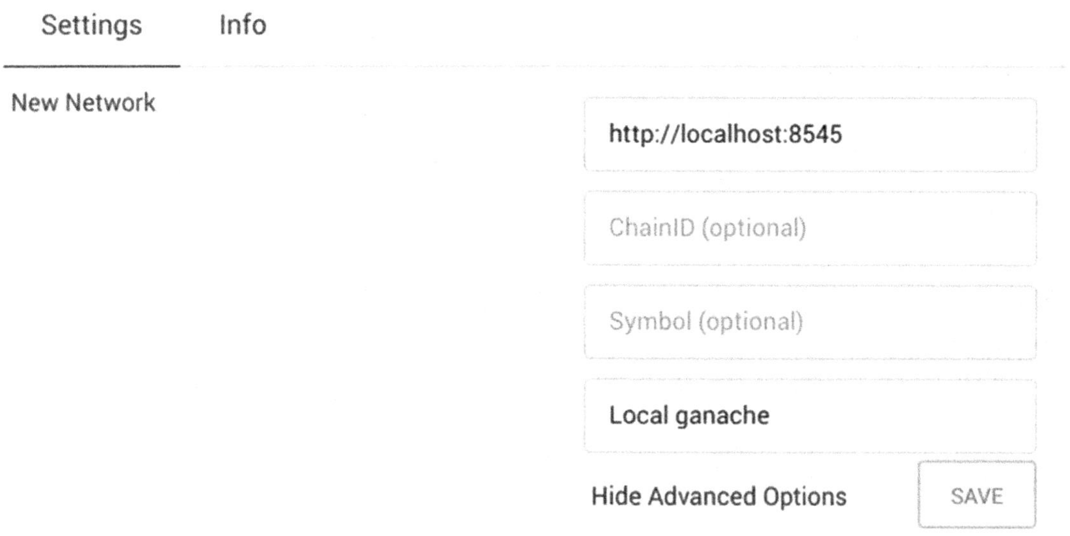

Settings	Info

New Network

http://localhost:8545

ChainID (optional)

Symbol (optional)

Local ganache

Hide Advanced Options   SAVE

Figure 5-1. *Creating a new network connection in Metamask*

Now we need to seed our Metamask account with funds, in order to send transactions with it. Remember that since this is a new account on a new network, it has no balance. Copy your Metamask address(es), and bring up a console as we did before to move funds from your initial accounts to the Metamask ones.

```
$ node --experimental-repl-await
> // Load web3 and open a connection to the node
> let Web3 = require('web3')
> let web3 = new Web3('http://localhost:8545')

> // Get first account on the node
> let [from] = await web3.eth.getAccounts()
[ '0xC5A4bA36f7C0B4eD17455C1A578a6ab3Fb738245', ...

> // Copy here your Metamask address
> let metamask = '0x43a93b...';

> // Seed your Metamask address from your developer one
> await web3.eth.sendTransaction({ from, to: metamask, value: 5e18 })
```

An alternative to having to manually seed your addresses is to have the autogenerated development accounts available on Metamask, which can be easily done if you are using ganache. Since both ganache and Metamask rely on a mnemonic for generating new addresses, you can use the same mnemonic on both of them to ensure the same accounts are used.

To do this, you will need to enter the 12 words displayed by ganache at startup during the Metamask initialization wizard (Figure 5-2), by choosing the option *Import with seed phrase*.

Tip   If you started ganache with the `--deterministic` flag, then that mnemonic should be: `myth like bonus scare over problem client lizard pioneer submit female collect`. Make sure not to use this mnemonic outside a development environment!

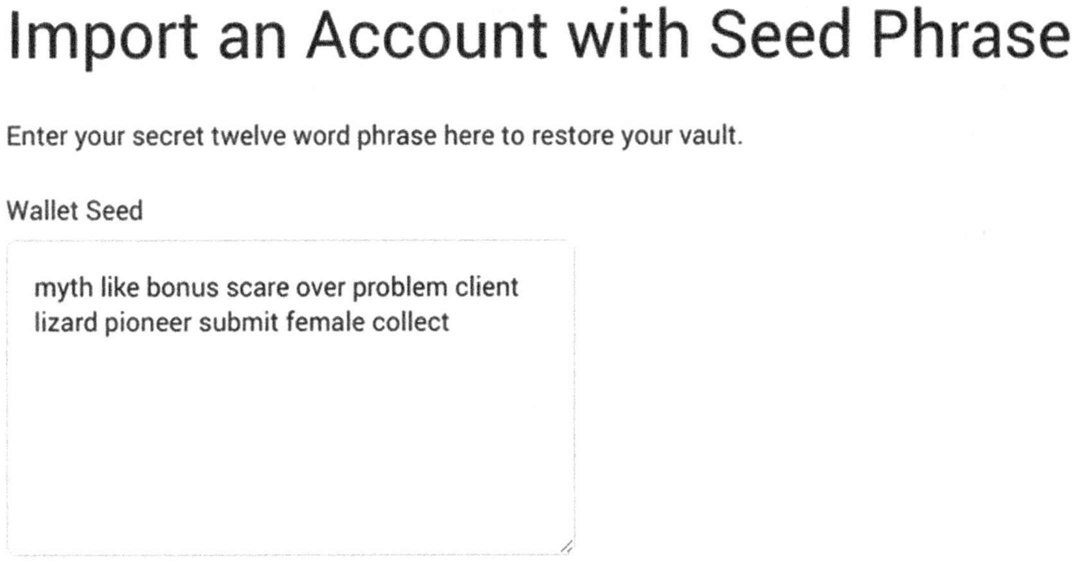

Import an Account with Seed Phrase

Enter your secret twelve word phrase here to restore your vault.

Wallet Seed

myth like bonus scare over problem client
lizard pioneer submit female collect

Figure 5-2. *Entering your ganache mnemonic into Metamask*

The converse is also viable. You can get your Metamask-generated mnemonic and enter it in ganache. This way, all development accounts created by ganache and seeded with funds in the new network will be the same as the ones created by Metamask. If you do not remember your Metamask mnemonic, there is an option *Reveal seed words* under *Settings*.

```
$ ganache-cli --mnemonic="drink focus interest..."
```

Regardless of which of the three options you used, you should now have one or more accounts on Metamask with enough funds to interact with your application in your development network.

Retrieving User Accounts in Our Apps

Remember from the previous chapter the script we were using for connecting to the network from our web application. We will reproduce here just the snippet corresponding to modern web3 browsers.

```
if (window.ethereum) {
  web3 = new Web3(window.ethereum);
  try {
    accounts = await window.ethereum.enable();
  } catch (error) {
    console.error("No access to user accounts");
  }
}
```

The global Ethereum object, injected by the web3 browser (or the Metamask extension in our case), allows us to interact with both the Ethereum network and the user's accounts. The most important method here is enable, which will trigger a prompt to our users asking them if they want to allow our application to list their accounts.

It is important to keep in mind that the list of accounts returned from either ethereum.enable() or web3.eth.getAccounts() is ordered such that the account that the user intends to use is always the first one. Because of this, before sending any transaction, we should first re-retrieve the list of user accounts, and use the first one at that moment, which could have changed since we initialized the web3 instance.

Alternatively, if you want to keep on display the status of the user's current account, you can subscribe to an accountsChanged event on the ethereum object (Listing 5-7), that will fire whenever the user switches to a new account, allowing you to update your interface accordingly.

Listing 5-7. Example code for watching changes on user accounts in Metamask and update UI accordingly

```
ethereum.on('accountsChanged', async function (accounts) {
  currentAccount = accounts[0];
  currentBalance = await web3.eth.getBalance(currentAccount);
  // Show currentBalance in the UI
})
```

Now that we have our local development environment set up, we can finally go into the details of sending transactions in this network.

Issuing Transactions

Even though the gist of sending a transaction is simple, there are several details that you should keep into consideration. We will go through them in this section and then illustrate them in a sample dapp.

Transaction Parameters

We will start by reviewing the parameters available when sending a transaction: data, value, gas, and gas price, as well as the sender and target addresses.

Sending Value or Data

One of the first things to take into consideration is whether your transaction will be sending value, data, or both. By value here we refer to ETH, the currency of the network, and by data we typically refer to executing a function in a contract. In some cases, it may include both: running a function in a contract that requires ETH to be transferred along with it.

Plainly sending ETH to an address is straightforward, as we have seen already in this chapter, by using the `web3.eth.sendTransaction` method. Keep in mind that sending a plain transaction to a contract may still execute code, since a contract can react to an incoming transaction via its fallback function.

On the other hand, invoking a state-changing function in a contract is similar to making a static call: it can be performed at a low level by sending a transaction with a manually crafted data parameter, which indicates which function must be invoked on a target contract and with which arguments, or by interacting with a web3 contract object.

To illustrate this, let's extend our Greeter contract from the *"Creating contracts"* section with an additional `setGreeting` method (Listing 5-8). This method will allow any user to change the current greeting, as long as they pay at least 1 kWei.

Listing 5-8. Sample Greeter contract with a setGreeting function. Note that we are emitting an event with the same data as we return from the function. We will see why later in this chapter.

```solidity
// contracts/Greeter.sol
pragma solidity ^0.5.0;

contract Greeter {
  string private greeting;
  event GreetingSet(string greeting, uint256 balance);

  constructor(string memory _greeting) public {
    greeting = _greeting;
    emit GreetingSet(_greeting, 0);
  }

  function greet() public view returns (string memory) {
    return greeting;
  }

  function setGreeting(string memory _greeting)
    public payable
    returns (string memory, uint256)
  {
    require(msg.value >= 1000);
    greeting = _greeting;
    emit GreetingSet(_greeting, address(this).balance);
    return (_greeting, address(this).balance);
  }
}
```

Compile and deploy this contract to your local network using sol-compile, along with the deployment script we wrote before. We can now interact with the contract from a node console as shown in the following.

```
$ node --experimental-repl-await
> Web3 = require('web3')
> GreeterJSON = require('./artifacts/Greeter.json')
```

```
> let web3 = new Web3('http://localhost:8545')
> let abi = GreeterJSON.compilerOutput.abi
> let greeter = new web3.eth.Contract(abi, ADDRESS)
```

We can test the setGreeting function by invoking the method in the greeter instance (Listing 5-9). Note that, unlike in the previous chapter, we are using send instead of call – this will trigger a new transaction instead of a static call. We also need to specify a sender account that will have the gas fees deducted from its balance. And since the setGreeting method requires us to send some ETH along with the transaction, we include a value option as well.

Listing 5-9. Sending a transaction to alter the greeting of our contract

```
> let [from] = await web3.eth.getAccounts()
> let value = 1000
> greeter.methods.setGreeting('Hi there!').send({from, value})
> await greeter.methods.greet().call()
'Hi there!'
```

Note   In web3.js, the arguments that are part of the contract function are set on the corresponding contract method, while the transaction options are passed in the send or call methods.

As mentioned, we can also manually craft the data to be sent in the transaction to invoke a function in our contract and then use a low-level sendTransaction (Listing 5-10). It is unlikely that you will actually use this pattern, but it is useful to know what happens behind the scenes when you send a transaction from a web3 contract object.

Listing 5-10. Using a low-level sendTransaction to call setGreeting. Note that we need to specify the target address as another option

```
> let to = ADDRESS
> let data = greeter.methods.setGreeting('Hi!').encodeABI()
> web3.eth.sendTransaction({ from, value, data, to })
```

Note   If you are curious about the contents of `data`, you can check out that it contains the following hexadecimal sequence:

0xa4136862000000000000000000000000000000000000000000000000 000000000000020000000000000000000000000000000000000000000000000000 000000000000000034869210000000000000000000000000000000000000 00000000000000000000000

While intimidating, this sequence corresponds to the ABI call with the RLP-encoded data we provided. RLP, or Recursive Length Prefix, is a method to encode arbitrarily nested data of arbitrary length.[7] In this scenario, the first 8 bytes (a4136862) are the function selector, which tell the contract that `setGreeting` must be called. The rest of the payload corresponds to the RLP encoding of "Hi!".

Estimating Gas

Let's try the `setGreeting` method again, but this time using a longer string as an argument to the function.

```
> const longGreeting = 'Hi there! This is a very long and costly greeting
to set which will require more gas.'
> await greeter.methods.setGreeting(longGreeting)
    .send({ from, value})
Error: Returned error: VM Exception while processing transaction: out of
gas
```

Remember from Chapter 3 that executing a transaction in Ethereum costs gas. The total gas cost of a transaction is proportional to the accumulated cost of all operations executed, where different operations have different gas costs. Writing to storage is a particularly expensive operation, since it implies persisting new state in the blockchain. And the larger the data, the more `store` operations involved.

---

[7]https://github.com/ethereum/wiki/wiki/RLP

In the preceding example, by attempting to save a very large string to this contract's state, we exceeded the gas allowance for our transaction (which in web3@1.2.0 defaults to 90,000), and thus the transaction failed.

We can make this transaction work by allocating a larger supply of gas for its execution (Listing 5-11). For instance, let's try with 1 million gas units. Keep in mind that this does not mean that the transaction will actually use 1 million gas – only that we are willing to spend up to that much in its execution.

Listing 5-11. Running the previous transaction with a higher gas allocation. Note that the returned transaction receipt includes the actual gas used by the transaction, which is well under 1 million

```
> let gas = 1e6
> await greeter.methods.setGreeting(longGreeting)
    .send({ from, value, gas })
{ transactionHash: '0x6eb0fa...',
  transactionIndex: 0,
  gasUsed: 98097,
  ... }
> await greeter.methods.greet().call()
'Hi there! This is a very long and costly greeting to set which will
require more gas.'
```

This begs the question of how we can know how much to allocate to a transaction. An option could be to simply specify a very high gas allowance: the block gas limit in most networks is between 4 and 8 million gas, so we could simply use a value in that order.

However, if we do so, our users will be asked to accept a transaction that may potentially drain more funds than they are willing to part with (Figure 5-3). Any user who takes a look at the gas fee numbers will most likely refuse to run a transaction under these conditions.

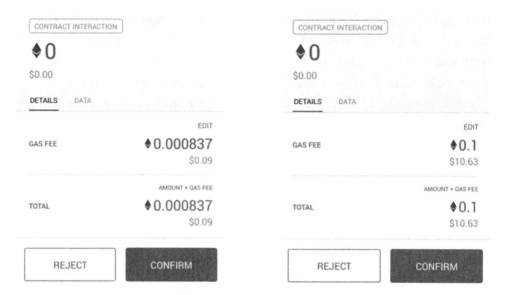

Figure 5-3. *Metamask confirmation dialog for the same transaction using different gas allowances: on the left, using the default amount of gas; on the right, using 5 million. Note the differences in the fee costs in USD: the user is asked to invest up to 9 cents vs. 10 dollars*

To solve this situation, we can *estimate* the gas a transaction will cost before actually needing to send it (Listing 5-12). Ethereum nodes implement an `estimateGas` method that accepts a transaction and runs it locally to determine how much gas it is needed to run it.

Listing 5-12. Using `estimateGas` to calculate how much gas is required for a transaction. In this case, the returned value for `estimateGas` was around 98K

```
> gas = await greeter.methods.setGreeting(longGreeting)
    .estimateGas({ from, value })
> await greeter.methods.setGreeting(longGreeting)
    .send({ from, value, gas })
```

In some cases, the returned value from `estimateGas` may not be exactly equal to the gas actually used. This is because the estimation relies on the state of the network at the time it is called, whereas the actual amount of gas is only determined when the transaction is actually mined. Between these two events, the state of the contract may have changed, which could alter the amount of gas required.[8]

Because of this, it is a good practice to allocate a slightly higher amount of gas than the one returned from the estimate gas call (Listing 5-13). A 20% more is usually good enough, though your mileage may vary depending on the contracts you are working with. Also, make sure not to set a gas allowance above the block gas limit, or the transaction will be simply rejected.

Listing 5-13. Calculating the actual amount of gas to use in a transaction

```
> let lastBlock = await web3.eth.getBlock('latest')
> let limit = lastBlock.gasLimit
> gas = Math.min(limit - 1, Math.ceil(gas * 1.2))
```

It is worth noting that if the transaction fails during its gas estimation, the estimate call will fail with an "always failing transaction" error. This prevents you from sending a transaction to the network that would ultimately fail.

Choosing a Gas Price

Transactions require not just a gas limit but also a gas price. Remember from Chapter 3 that the gas price indicates how much (in Wei) is paid per unit of gas used during the execution of a transaction. While this value is unimportant in development or testing networks, they are critical to get right on the main network – or any network where its native currency holds actual monetary value.

Needless to say, using higher gas prices will result in more costly operations. On the other hand, a higher-than-average gas price means that the transaction will be picked up by miners earlier; this reduces the amount of time a user must wait until their transaction is included in the blockchain.

Gas prices fluctuate depending on the total network load. At times of intensive usage of the Ethereum network, there is much more competition to get a transaction included in the next block, which drives gas prices higher.

---

[8]Unfortunately, sometimes the amount of gas estimated will not match due to a bug. In complex transactions, certain versions of ganache estimate a lower gas amount than what is actually required. If you run into an "out of gas" error when running a transaction using the estimated gas, try updating your ganache version or switching to geth or parity in development mode.

Estimating gas prices is much more difficult than estimating gas allowance, since an estimation cannot be obtained by just making a dry run of the transaction and checking the total usage. Instead, estimating prices requires an analysis of past and pending transactions.

The most direct way to obtain a gas price estimate is by relying on the gasPrice API method of an Ethereum node (Listing 5-14). Nodes keep a gas price value, which is updated with a preconfigured frequency and is calculated based on a percentile of the gas price of the transactions from recent blocks.

Listing 5-14. Querying the Ethereum node for gas price. Note that ganache returns a constant value for gas price, which can be configured at startup

```
> await web3.eth.getGasPrice()
'20000000000'
```

Note   When running getGasPrice via Metamask, a subprovider intercepts the call and manually calculates the gas price as the median of the last N blocks.

However, this method only considers data from transactions already mined, disregarding any information from pending transactions on the mempool awaiting to be included in the blockchain.

As an alternative, there are centralized services that provide real-time gas estimates for the Ethereum main network (Listing 5-15), based on more complex calculations. These services often return better results, but at the cost of introducing a centralized dependency on your application. Such services are offered by Etherchain or EthGasStation, among others, and provide gas prices for low, standard, fast, or fastest transaction processing.

Listing 5-15. Retrieving gas price from the Etherchain API and using it in a transaction. This snippet uses the axios package for performing a standard HTTP GET request to the API

```
$ npm install axios@0.18.0
$ node --experimental-repl-await

// Setup web3 provider and contract
> Web3 = require('web3')
> GreeterJSON = require('./artifacts/Greeter.json')
```

```
> let web3 = new Web3('http://localhost:8545')
> let abi = GreeterJSON.compilerOutput.abi
> let greeter = new web3.eth.Contract(abi, ADDRESS)

// Retrieve gas price and send transaction
> axios = require('axios')
> let URL = 'https://www.etherchain.org/api/gasPriceOracle'
> let { data: gasData } = await axios.get(URL)
> let gasPrice = gasData.fast * 1e9
> await greeter.methods.setGreeting('Hello!')
    .send({ from, value, gas, gasPrice })
```

Lifecycle of a Transaction

Now that we know how to configure the main components of a transaction, it is time to review what happens once a transaction is sent and how do we interact with it.

A Transaction is Sent

When a transaction is sent to a node, the node performs some basic checks to make sure the transaction is valid and can be broadcasted. For instance, the node checks that the sender account has enough funds, and that the gas allowance and price values are reasonable.

If the transaction is accepted by the node, it returns a hash of the transaction. This transaction hash acts as a globally unique identifier of the transaction on the blockchain, and can be used to retrieve information on the transaction later.

```
> let txHash = null
> greeter.methods.setGreeting('Hello!')
    .send({ from, value })
    .on('transactionHash', (hash) => txHash = hash)
```

Note   If needed, the transaction hash can be calculated offline by a client, as long as the client has the sender's private key, since it depends exclusively on its parameters and signature.

By the time the transaction hash is returned, the transaction info can be retrieved from any node that has *seen* this transaction (Listing 5-16), regardless of the transaction having been mined or not. This info includes the sender, recipient, gas allowance, price, nonce, input data, and everything that you may have specified when sending the transaction.

Listing 5-16. Transaction information returned right after the transaction is sent. Note that all block-related information is empty, since the transaction has not been mined yet

```
> await web3.eth.getTransaction(txHash)
{ blockHash: '0x0000...0',
  blockNumber: null,
  from: '0x...',
  gas: 90000,
  gasPrice: '1000000000',
  hash: '...',
  input: '0xa41368620...',
  nonce: 470,
  to: '0x...',
  transactionIndex: 0,
  value: '1000'
}
```

At this point, the transaction has not yet been mined and is said to be in *pending* state. Any attempts to retrieve the transaction receipt will simply return null.

A Transaction is Mined

After a while, depending on the gas price used and the network load, the transaction should be mined. Note that a transaction gets mined regardless of it being successful or not: reverted transactions are also included in the blockchain and consume a gas fee from their sender.

Once the transaction is mined, its getTransaction information will include the block number and hash in which it was included, plus its index in the block. Also, at this point, the transaction receipt becomes available.

```
> await web3.eth.getTransactionReceipt(txHash)
{ transactionHash: '0x...',
  transactionIndex: 0,
  blockHash: '0x...',
  blockNumber: 29,
  gasUsed: 23235,
  cumulativeGasUsed: 23235,
  logs: [ ... ],
  status: true}
```

The receipt includes information generated when the transaction was executed during mining, such as the gas actually used, whether it succeeded (the status flag is true if the transaction did not revert), and the logs it emitted.

Note   If you inspect the logs in a transaction receipt obtained via a getTransactionReceipt call, you will only be able to fetch the raw data of an event. This is because the client library does not have enough context to understand how to *decode* the logs. It requires an ABI to indicate what are the event names and argument types.

We can await for a transaction to be mined by checking for new blocks (either via polling or subscribing to newBlockHeaders) and attempting to retrieve the transaction receipt whenever a new mined block is seen (Listing 5-17). If the transaction was successfully mined in the new block, then its receipt will be available.

Listing 5-17. Subscribing to new block headers to check when a transaction is successfully mined. Note that if you have multiple transactions in-flight, it may be worthwhile to share a single newBlockHeaders subscription among all of them

```
// Sends a transaction to the network and returns its hash
function sendTransactionReturnHash(opts) {
  return new Promise((resolve, reject) => {
    web3.eth.sendTransaction(opts)
      .on('transactionHash', hash => resolve(hash))
      .on('error', err => reject(err));
```

```
    })
}

// Sends a transaction and awaits for it to be mined
function sendTransactionAwaitReceipt(opts) {
  const BLOCKS = 'newBlockHeaders';
  return new Promise((resolve, reject) => {
    sendTransactionReturnHash(opts).then(hash => {
      const sub = web3.eth.subscribe(BLOCKS, (err) => {
        if (err) reject(err);
        // Check for the receipt on every new block
        // If available, it means the tx was mined
        web3.eth.getTransactionReceipt(hash).then(receipt => {
          if (receipt) {
            sub.unsubscribe();
            resolve(receipt);
          }
        });
      });
    }).catch(reject);
  });
}
```

If using web3, the transaction receipt can also be obtained by simply awaiting on the sendTransaction method (both for sending plain transactions and for triggering transactions on a contract function). This also provides easy access to the events, which are decoded based on the ABI of the contract object in which the transaction was issued.

```
> let receipt = await greeter.methods.setGreeting('Hey!')
    .send({ from, value: 10000 })
> let { events } = receipt
> let { greeting, balance } = events.GreetingSet.returnValues
> greeting
'Hey!'
> balance
'30000'
```

Being able to process transaction events is particularly important because *there is no way to retrieve the return value of a function called in a transaction.* If you go back to the code of our contract, you will see that our function actually returned the greeting string and the contract balance. However, by design, those values are not part of the transaction receipt and cannot be obtained from the client.

Note   The only way to get the return values from a function in a transaction is to call them from another contract: a contract that invokes `setGreeting` will have access to them, but an `off-chain` client that sends a transaction to the `Greeter` will not.

Because of this reason, it is a common pattern in smart contract design that public state-changing functions emit an event with their return values (Listing 5-18). This allows an externally owned account to call into such functions and retrieve the return values from the event arguments.

Listing 5-18. Emitting an event with data that mimics the return values, to make them accessible from a client

```
function setGreeting(string memory _greeting)
  public payable returns (string memory, uint256)
{
  greeting = _greeting;

  // This can only be accessed by a client off-chain
  emit GreetingSet(_greeting, address(this).balance);

  // This can only be accessed by another contract calling
  return (_greeting, address(this).balance);
}
```

A Transaction is Confirmed

While it may be tempting to act upon a mined transaction immediately, transactions may be moved out of the blockchain due to reorganizations. This means that a mined transaction can go back to pending state and then either mined again or dropped – and can even produce different state changes when it is mined in a different context.

Because of this, it may be prudent to wait for a certain number of confirmations before actually acting upon a transaction. What *acting upon* means depends on your use case, as well as the number of confirmations to wait. Remember that a confirmation is the number of blocks mined after the one that included a transaction: every new mined block is a new confirmation for your transaction. A reorganization becomes less and less probable as more blocks are added to the chain.

Transaction confirmations can be measured by subscribing to new blocks on the network (see Chapter 4), and counting the blocks since the transaction receipt. We can modify the code from the previous section to return only once a certain number of confirmations have occurred (Listing 5-19) instead of when the receipt is immediately available.

Listing 5-19. Modifying the sendTransactionAwaitReceipt function to wait for a specific number of confirmations before returning the receipt. Note that it is important to fetch the transaction receipt again on every block, since it may have changed due to a chain reorganization

```
function sendTransactionAwaitConfirmations(opts, confs) {
  const BLOCKS = 'newBlockHeaders';
  return new Promise((resolve, reject) => {
    sendTransactionReturnHash(opts).then(hash => {
      const sub = web3.eth.subscribe(BLOCKS, (err, block) => {
        if (err) reject(err);
        // Instead of just checking that the receipt exists,
        // now we also check its age in blocks
        web3.eth.getTransactionReceipt(hash).then(receipt => {
          if (receipt &&
              block.number > receipt.blockNumber + confs) {
            sub.unsubscribe();
            resolve(receipt);
          }
        });
      });
    }).catch(reject);
  });
}
```

Alternatively, web3 also provides an event to track confirmations once the transaction was sent (Listing 5-20), which performs a similar logic under the hood.

Listing 5-20. Awaiting 12 confirmations before acting upon a transaction using the confirmation event handler from web3

```
> greeter.methods.setGreeting('Hello!')
    .send({ from, value })
    .on('confirmation', (number, receipt) => {
      if (number === 12) {
        console.log(receipt.events.GreetingSet.returnValues)
      }
    })
```

Replacing a Transaction

Transactions pending to be mined can be *replaced* by their sender, by hacking the nonce and gas price parameters. Remember that for a transaction to be valid, its nonce cannot have been previously used by its sender. Therefore, if the sender broadcasts a second transaction with the same nonce while the first one is still pending, both transactions will be eligible to be mined, though only one will. To enforce the second one to be picked, the sender only needs to issue it with a higher gas price than the first one.

An easy way to test this is to issue a first transaction with a very low gas price to ensure it takes several blocks to be mined, so we have enough time to send the second one to replace it. Make sure to test this in a network without instant seal; otherwise, the first transaction will be mined immediately.

```
// Send first transaction for a value of 0.02 ETH
> let to = accounts[1]
> let value = 2e16
> let gasPrice = 100
> let txOpts = { from, to, value, gasPrice };
> let txHash = await sendTransactionReturnHash(txOpts)

// Retrieve nonce
> let { nonce } = await web3.eth.getTransaction(txHash)
```

```
// Send replacement with different value and higher gas price
> value = 1e16
> gasPrice = 20e9
> txOpts = { from, to, value, gasPrice, nonce}
> let txHashReplace = await sendTransactionReturnHash(txOpts)

// Verify that only the replacement tx got mined
> await web3.eth.getTransactionReceipt(txHash)
null
> await web3.eth.getTransactionReceipt(txHashReplace)
{ status: true, ... }
```

Replacement transactions have multiple uses, since the second transaction does not need to have anything in common with the original one, except for the nonce and the sender account:

- The most common usage for replacement transactions is to speed up the original one. If you detect that a transaction is taking too long to be mined, you may simply resubmit it with the exact same parameters but a higher gas price to make it more attractive to miners. This is also a simple pattern to implement in terms of UX: if you are showing a loading indicator to your user while the tx is processing, you could display an option to resubmit it, after a long period of time without news. Metamask already includes this feature in its UI out of the box.

- Another usage is to simply cancel a transaction. If the user wants to undo a transaction already sent, a viable option is to send a no-op replacement transaction that removes the previous one. A no-op transaction can be as simple as a transaction of 0 ETH with no data where the recipient address is the same as the sender.

- Alternatively, a replacement transaction can be sent to change a parameter of a previous transaction, as a means to amend the previous one. This will depend heavily on your use case, and needs to be executable by the user quickly, since the window for getting a transaction replaced may be short if the original gas price was already high.

Error Handling

When sending a transaction to the network, there are many things that can potentially go wrong. Your application should be prepared to handle them, and inform your user accordingly:

- At any point in time, you may lose the connection to the node. Needless to say, this will impact not just sending transactions but also any kind of operation, read or write, with the network. You will typically get an *Invalid JSON-RPC response* error in these scenarios, since your library will get an empty response from the unreachable node.

- The transaction being sent may not be valid. This could be due to one of its parameters not being well-formed, such as a non-hexadecimal string for an address, or an outright invalid value. As an example of the latter, if you try to send a transaction with a gas allowance of 1, you will get an *intrinsic gas too low* error. These errors are usually caught by your library, while trying to build the transaction to send.

- The sender account may not have enough funds for the specified value, gas allowance, and gas price of the transaction. These errors are generally reported by the node before the transaction is even broadcasted.

- When replacing transactions, attempting to replace a mined transaction will yield a *nonce too low* error even before the transaction is sent to the network. Similarly, most clients will prevent you from trying to replace a transaction without increasing the gas price.

- Transactions that execute contract code may fail due to a REVERT or an ABORT raised by the contract. Contracts written in Solidity 0.4.22 and up can include a revert reason, which can be used to determine the cause of the error. This is only detected once the transaction has been actually mined, and the sender funds have been spent to pay for the gas of the execution.

- When estimating the required gas for a transaction, an *always failing transaction* error means that the estimation fails since the transaction raises an error. This can be used to detect a failing transaction before actually sending it to the network and spending gas.

- Even if you estimate the gas required for a transaction, the conditions under which the transaction is mined may differ to the ones when the gas was estimated. An out-of-gas error will be raised in these scenarios, and only once the transaction was already mined.

- After the transaction is sent, if the gas price was too low or the network too busy, it may fail to be mined. Most libraries will eventually time out, and inform you that the transaction was not found after a certain number of blocks. Be aware that if the node your user is connecting to is out of sync, then the transaction may actually get mined, but the node will never see it, raising this error.

Note   Keep in mind that the actual error messages may depend on the library you are using, and in some cases, the client you are connecting to (Geth, Parity, or Ganache).

Most of the preceding errors can be caught in web3 using an `error` event handler, similar to the transaction sent, receipt, or confirmation events. Input formatting errors, on the other hand, will raise an exception immediately.

```
> let [from, to] = await web3.eth.getAccounts()
> web3.eth.sendTransaction({ from, to, gas: 1 })
  .on('error', err => console.error(err.message))
Returned error: intrinsic gas too low
```

Example Application

As in the previous chapter, we will now set up a sample application that covers many of the concepts we have reviewed in this chapter. In this case, we will set up a simple interface for allowing a user to create (*mint*) new digital collectibles using a modified ERC721 contract.

Setup

Our setup will be similar to that of previous chapters, relying on `create-react-app` for the client boilerplate,[9] as we will be building a client-side-only application.

```
npm init react-app erc721-app
```

Dependencies

Along with the same set of dependencies as in our ERC20 app, we will also install the solidity compiler, and the `axios` library for performing HTTP requests.

```
$ npm install web3@1.2.0 openzeppelin-solidity@2.1 bignumber.js@8.0
axios@0.18.0
$ npm install --save-dev @0x/sol-compiler@2.0.2
```

Make sure you have also installed either ganache-cli, Geth, or Parity, as described earlier in this chapter, in order to spin up a local development network.

Contract Deployment

For this application, we will code, compile, and deploy our own contract `contracts/ERC721PayPerMint.sol` (Listing 5-21). This will be a contract based on the default ERC721 implementation, which we will pull from the OpenZeppelin contracts library, with an additional method to create new instances in exchange for a fee in ETH. The ETH will remain in the contract until its owner decides to withdraw it.

Listing 5-21. Modified ERC721 token that will back our application. It provides a public minting function so users can create new tokens for a fee, as well as a view function to check for the existence of a token

```
// contracts/ERC721PayPerMint.sol
pragma solidity ^0.5.2;

import
"openzeppelin-solidity/contracts/math/SafeMath.sol";
import
```

---

[9]https://facebook.github.io/create-react-app/

```
"openzeppelin-solidity/contracts/ownership/Ownable.sol";
import
"openzeppelin-solidity/contracts/token/ERC721/ERC721.sol";
import
"openzeppelin-solidity/contracts/token/ERC721/ERC721Enumerable.sol";

contract ERC721PayPerMint
  is ERC721, ERC721Enumerable, Ownable {
  using SafeMath for uint256;

  function exists(uint256 tokenId)
    public view returns (bool) {
    return _exists(tokenId);
  }

  function mint(address to, uint256 tokenId)
    public payable returns (bool) {
    require(msg.value >= tokenId.mul(1e12), "Insufficient payment");
    _mint(to, tokenId);
    return true;
  }

  function withdraw()
    public onlyOwner {
    msg.sender.transfer(address(this).balance);
  }
}
```

We can now try compiling our contract using the sol-compiler.

```
$ npx sol-compiler
Artifact for ERC721PayPerMint does not exist
Compiling 1 contracts (ERC721PayPerMint.sol) with Solidity v0.5.2...
ERC721PayPerMint artifact saved!
```

There should now be an ERC721PayPerMint.json file in the artifacts folder. Let's add a short script scripts/deploy.js for retrieving the compiled bytecode and deploying the contract to the local network, using a modified version of the deployment code we wrote earlier in this chapter (Listing 5-22). We will also store the deployment address in a Deploys.json file, which we will then retrieve from the application.

Listing 5-22. Script for deploying the ERC721PayPerMint contract to a network specified by the PROVIDER_URL environment variable, and storing the deployment address indexed by network ID. Note that the main function can be modified to easily deploy other contracts

```
// scripts/deploy.js
const Web3 = require('web3');
const fs = require('fs');
const path = require('path');

// Deploys any artifact from the default account
async function deploy(artifact, arguments, opts) {
  const providerUrl = process.env.PROVIDER_URL
                      || 'http://localhost:8545';
  const web3 = new Web3(providerUrl);
  const from = (await web3.eth.getAccounts())[0];
  const data = artifact.compilerOutput.evm.bytecode.object;
  const abi = artifact.compilerOutput.abi;
  const Contract = new web3.eth.Contract(abi, null, { data });
  const gasPrice = 1e9;
  const instance = await Contract.deploy({ arguments })
                         .send({ from, gasPrice, ...opts });
  const address = instance.options.address;
  const network = await web3.eth.net.getId();
  save(network, address);
  console.log(address);
}

// Saves deployment address to a Deploys.json file
function save(network, address) {
  const file = path.join(
    __dirname, '..', 'artifacts', 'Deploys.json'
  );
```

```
  const deployments = fs.existsSync(file)
    ? JSON.parse(fs.readFileSync(file)) : {};
  deployments[network] = address;
  const content = JSON.stringify(deployments, null, 2);
  fs.writeFileSync(file, content);
}

// Deploys our ERC721PayPerMint contract
function main() {
  const artifactPath = '../artifacts/ERC721PayPerMint.json';
  const artifact = require(artifactPath);
  return deploy(artifact, [], { gas: 5e6, gasPrice: 1e9 });
}

main();
```

Now, with the ganache-cli process (or the Geth or Parity development node) listening on port 8545, try running the deployment script.

```
node scripts/deploy.js
```

You should then see a Deploys.json file in the artifacts folder with the network ID and the deployment address. Note that the ID and deployment address you get may differ.

```
$  cat artifacts/Deploys.json
{
  "155164184873": "0x0E696947A06550DEf604e82C26fd9E493e576337"
}
```

Now that we have our contract set up on our local network, we can start working on the web application itself.

The Application

Our application will follow a similar structure than the previous one. We will have separate folders for interacting with the Ethereum network, for managing contract artifacts, and for the React components.

Initializing the Web3 Instance

We will set up a src/eth/network.js file (Listing 5-23) with the code necessary to instantiate a new web3 object from the injected provider, along with a few methods that we will be using later throughout the app.

Listing 5-23. Network file to initialize a new web3 object given the injected provider

```
// src/eth/network.js
import Web3 from 'web3';

let web3;
export function getWeb3() {
  if (!web3) {
    web3 = new Web3(Web3.givenProvider);
  }
  return web3;
}

export function hasProvider() {
  return !!Web3.givenProvider;
}

export async function getAccount() {
  const accounts = await window.ethereum.enable();
  return accounts[0];
}

export async function getBlockNumber() {
  return web3.eth.getBlockNumber();
}

export async function getNetwork() {
  return web3.eth.net.getId();
}
```

Note that the getAccount method is especially important, since it includes the call to *enable* the provider. This is what allows us to access the list of accounts of the user.

Creating the Contract Object

We will now create a `src/contracts/ERC721.js` file that will initialize the web3 contract object, and load the deployment address from the `Deploys.json` file.

However, that file is in the `artifacts` folder in our project root, outside the `src` folder. Unfortunately, the `create-react-app` template prevents us from importing anything outside the `src` folder. If we tried to import it from our react application, we would get the following error.

```
You attempted to import ../../artifacts/Deploys.json which falls outside
of the project src/ directory. Relative imports outside of src/ are not
supported.
```

The easiest way around this is to create a symlink to the `artifacts` folder from within the `src` folder. We can do this with the following commands.

```
$ cd src
$ ln -ns ../artifacts
```

We can now load both the compiler output and the deployment files in our app. Note that the limitation of loading files from outside the source folder is exclusive to react-app. If you used any other app template, you will probably not face this issue.[10]

```
// src/contracts/ERC721.js
import Artifact from '../artifacts/ERC721PayPerMint.json';
import Deploys from '../artifacts/Deploys.json';
```

By retrieving the ABI from the first, we can write a function to create a web3 contract instance for our ERC721PayPerMint.

```
// src/contracts/ERC721.js
export default function ERC721(web3,address=null,options={}) {
  const abi = Artifact.compilerOutput.abi;
  return new web3.eth.Contract(abi, address, { ...options });
}
```

---

[10]You may also eject your react-app, which allows you to manually modify the webpack configuration, in order to remove this limitation. Alternatively, the `react-app-rewired` package lets you do the same without ejecting.

We can then retrieve the deployment address from the second and use it to instantiate an ERC721 contract at that address (Listing 5-24). Note that since the deployments file is indexed by network, we need to retrieve the network ID via the web3 object.

Listing 5-24. Returning a web3 contract that represents the deployed instance of the ERC721PayPerMint in the current network

```
// src/contracts/ERC721.js
import {
  getWeb3, getAccount, getNetwork
} from '../eth/network.js';

export async function getDeployed() {
  const web3 = getWeb3();
  const from = await getAccount();
  const network = await getNetwork();
  const address = Deploys[network];
  if (!address) throw new Error(`Could not find address for contract in
    network ${network}`);
  return ERC721(web3, address, { from });
}
```

Root App Component

Our root App component (Listing 5-25) will be similar to the one from our previous chapter. This component will have the responsibility of loading both the default account and the contract instance, and injecting it into a main ERC721 component to be defined in src/components/ERC721.js.

Listing 5-25. Main methods of the root App component

```
// src/App.js
import React, { Component } from 'react';
import { getDeployed } from './contracts/ERC721';
import { hasProvider, getAccount } from './eth/network';
import ERC721 from './components/ERC721';
```

```
class App extends Component {
  async componentDidMount() {
    if (hasProvider()) {
      const contract = await getDeployed();
      const sender = await getAccount();
      this.setState({ contract, sender });
    }
  }

  render() {
    const { contract, sender } = this.state;
    return (
      <div className="App">
        { (hasProvider() && contract && sender)
          ? <ERC721 contract={contract} owner={sender} />
          : <div>Please enable Metamask and reload</div>
        }
      </div>
    );
  }
}
```

Keep in mind though that if the user changes the current account in Metamask, we need to refresh the info displayed, since we will be listing the user's tokens. We can detect account changes by installing a listener on the ethereum object and force a reload of the ERC721 component by attaching the sender as a React key[11] (Listing 5-26).

Listing 5-26. Updated methods from Listing 5-25 to monitor for account changes. When the account is changed, the entire ERC721 component is automatically reloaded

```
// src/App.js
class App extends Component {
  async componentDidMount() {
```

---

[11]See https://reactjs.org/blog/2018/06/07/you-probably-dont-need-derived-state. html#recommendation-fully-uncontrolled-component-with-a-key

```
  // ...
  window.ethereum.on('accountsChanged', async (accounts)=>{
    this.setState({ sender: accounts[0] });
  });
}

render() {
  // ...
  <ERC721 contract={contract} owner={sender} key={sender} />
  // ...
  }
}
```

Main ERC721 Component

This component will contain most of the logic in our application: it will list the user's tokens and allow the user to mint new ones via a simple *Create* button. Let's start by listing existing tokens when the page loads.

Listing Existing Tokens

Enumerating the non-fungible tokens of a user can be tricky. The ERC721 standard exposes two functions to do this: `balanceOf` and `tokenOfOwnerByIndex`. The former returns the number of tokens of a user, and the latter returns the token ID given an index between zero and the user's balance. In order to avoid the two methods falling out of sync, it's important to run all queries specifying a single block number.

```
// src/components/ERC721.js
class ERC721 extends Component {
  async getTokensAtBlock(blockNumber) {
    const { contract, owner } = this.props;

    // Load number of tokens of the user
    const strBalance = await contract.methods.balanceOf(owner)
                          .call({}, blockNumber);
    const balance = parseInt(strBalance);
```

```
  // Retrieve the id of every token
  const queries = Array.from({length: balance}, (_,index)=>(
    contract.methods.tokenOfOwnerByIndex(owner,index)
      .call({}, blockNumber)
  ));
  return await Promise.all(queries);
 }
}
```

Given the preceding function, we can now load the tokens into the component's state on its *didMount* lifecycle event (Listing 5-27).

Listing 5-27. Loading the user tokens into state. Note that we are adding a `confirmed` flag to these tokens to distinguish them from the newly minted ones that we will be adding later

```
async componentDidMount() {
  const currentBlock = await getBlockNumber();
  const tokenIds = await this.getTokensAtBlock(currentBlock);
  const tokens = tokenIds.map(id => ({id, confirmed: true}));
  this.setState({ tokens, loading: false });
}
```

We will also initialize the component's state in its constructor to the following default, so the component starts in a loading state until the user's tokens are loaded.

```
constructor(props) {
  super(props);
  this.state = {
    tokens: [],
    loading: true
  };
}
```

Let's test this with a simple `render` method that will just render the list of tokens by presenting their IDs, reusing them as React keys as well.

```
render() {
  const { tokens, loading } = this.state;
  if (loading) return "Loading";
  return (
    <div>
      <h1>Collectible Numbers</h1>
      <div>
        { tokens.map(token => (
          <div key={token.id.toString()}>
            { token.id.toString() }
          </div>
        ))}
      </div>
    </div>
  );
}
```

If you check your react application in your browser, you should now see the list of tokens that belong to the current user, assuming there are any. We can now move onto the main feature of this app: sending a transaction to mint a new token.

Minting New Tokens

We will first create two methods in our ERC721 component: one for checking whether the user can mint a specific token and another for actually minting it. Whether a user can mint a token depends on whether a token with that ID already exists or not.

```
// src/components/ERC721.js
class ERC721 extends Component {
  // ...
  async canMint(id) {
    const { contract } = this.props;
    const exists = await contract.methods.exists(id).call();
    return !exists;
  }
}
```

Minting will require actually sending a transaction to the contract, including the ID to be minted. As we have seen throughout this chapter, this requires estimating the gas and choosing a gas price to use. For the latter, we will define a getGasPrice helper function that will retrieve the current price from the Etherchain oracle.

```
// src/eth/gasPrice.js
import axios from 'axios';
import BN from 'bignumber.js';
const URL = 'https://www.etherchain.org/api/gasPriceOracle';
async function getGasPrice() {
  const { data: gasData } = await axios.get(URL);
  const bn = new BN(gasData.fast);
  return bn.shiftedBy(9).toString(10);
}
```

Using this helper, we can now define our mint function in the ERC721 component. Remember that the value we need to send is directly proportional to the ID we are attempting to create, so higher numbers will actually cost more ETH to mint.

```
// src/components/ERC721.js
import { getGasPrice } from '../eth/gasPrice';
import BN from 'bignumber.js';

class ERC721 extends Component {
  // ...
  async mint(id) {
    const { contract, owner } = this.props;

    const from = owner;
    const value = new BN(id).shiftedBy(12).toString(10);
    const gasPrice = await getGasPrice();
    const gas = await contract.methods.mint(owner, id)
                  .estimateGas({ value, from });

    contract.methods.mint(owner, id)
      .send({ value, gas, gasPrice, from });
  }
}
```

We will now define a new small `Mint` component with a form with a controlled component, use `canMint` to check whether the create action is enabled, and trigger `mint` when the user chooses to create a token. We will pass the `mint` and `canMint` methods as props.

```
// src/components/Mint.js
import React, { Component } from 'react';
export default class Mint extends Component {
  constructor(props) {
    super(props);
    this.state = { value: "" };
    this.handleChange = this.handleChange.bind(this);
    this.handleMint = this.handleMint.bind(this);
  }

  async handleChange(event) {
    const value = event.target.value;
    this.setState({ value, mintable: false });

    if (value && value.length > 0) {
      const mintable = await this.props.canMint(value);
      if (value === this.state.value) {
        this.setState({ mintable });
      }
    }
  }

  async handleMint(event) {
    event.preventDefault();
    this.props.mint(this.state.value);
    this.setState({ value: "", mintable: false });
  }

  render() {
    const { value, mintable } = this.state;
    return (
      <form onSubmit={this.handleMint}>
        <input type="numeric" value={value}
```

```
                onChange={this.handleChange} />
        <button disabled={!mintable}>Create</button>
      </form>
    );
  }
}
```

We can wire this component into our main ERC721 by adding the following markup
in its render function. Note that this requires binding both functions to this in the
ERC721 constructor.

```
// src/components/ERC721.js
class ERC721 extends Component {
  constructor(props) {
    // ...
    this.mint = this.mint.bind(this);
    this.canMint = this.canMint.bind(this);
  }

  render() {
    // ...
    <Mint canMint={this.canMint} mint={this.mint} />
    // ...
  }
}
```

Give this new version a try, and you should see the Metamask dialog when you hit
the Create button in the Mint component. If you accept, a new token will be minted, but
it will not be added to your list until you reload the page. Let's fix that now.

Reacting to Transaction Events

The last piece of the puzzle is for our application to react to the lifecycle of the
transactions issued. Whenever a new transaction is sent to mint a new token, we will add
a new tentative token to our list and increase its confirmations as new blocks are mined.
To do this, we will attach handlers to the transaction events for each of these scenarios in
the mint method of the ERC721 component.

```
// src/components/ERC721.js
class ERC721 extends Component {
  async mint(id) {
  // ...
    contract.methods.mint(owner, id)
      .send({ value, gas, gasPrice, from })
      .on('transactionHash', () => this.addToken(id))
      .on('receipt', () => this.confirmToken(id, 0))
      .on('confirmation', (n) => this.confirmToken(id, n))
      .on('error', (error) => this.failToken(id, error));
  }
}
```

Each of the handlers will respectively add a token to the list, mark it as confirmed, or flag it as errored. We are assuming that six confirmations is good enough for our current use case.

```
// src/components/ERC721.js
class ERC721 extends Component {
  addToken(id) {
    this.setState(state => ({
      ...state,
      tokens: [ ...state.tokens, { id }]
    }));
  }

  confirmToken(id, confirmations) {
    const confirmed = confirmations >= 6;
    this.setState(state => ({
      ...state,
      tokens: state.tokens.map(token => (
        token.id === id ? { id, confirmed } : token
      ))
    }));
  }
```

```
  failToken(id, error) {
    this.setState(state => ({
      ...state,
      tokens: state.tokens.filter(token => (
        token.id !== id
      ))
    }));
  }
}
```

We now have a list of Token objects, where each token is defined by its ID and whether it is pending, mined, or confirmed. Let's use this information to display each token via a simple Token visual component in src/components/Token.js, which we can use instead of just displaying the token ID.

```
// src/components/Token.js
export default function({ token }) {
  const { id, confirmed } = token;
  const pending = typeof(confirmed) === "undefined";

  let status;
  if (pending) {
    status = "Pending";
  } else if (!confirmed) {
    status = "Awaiting confirmation";
  } else {
    status = "Confirmed";
  }

  return (
    <div>
      <h3>{id.toString()}</h3>
      <div>{status}</div>
    </div>
  );
}
```

In your own app, you may want to use other visual hints to report the status of each token, such as a color code – assisted by tooltips for explaining the concept of confirmation to the user.

Confirmations for Existing Tokens

When loading the initial list of tokens in this component, we assumed that all of those tokens were already *confirmed*, that is, they were already mined several blocks ago. However, this may not be the case. You can easily test this yourself by simply reloading the page right after sending a transaction and seeing how a token awaiting confirmation incorrectly goes into confirmed state.

There are many techniques for dealing with these situation, some of which we will see in the next chapter. We will go with a simple approach in this case, and favor simplicity over efficiency.

First of all, instead of loading all tokens from the current block on page load, we will load two sets of tokens: one from the current block and one from six blocks ago. We will consider all tokens from six blocks ago as confirmed, while all new tokens from the current block will be flagged as unconfirmed. Let's update the didMount handler on the ERC721 main component (Listing 5-28) to implement this change.

Listing 5-28. Get confirmed and unconfirmed token lists, and set the confirmed flag accordingly on the token collection. Note the catch block when querying the confirmedTokenIds, as the call will throw if the contract had not been created at confirmedBlock, in which case all tokens should be unconfirmed

```
// src/components/ERC721.js
const CONFIRMATIONS = 6;
class ERC721 extends Component {
  async componentDidMount() {
    const currentBlock = await getBlockNumber();
    const confirmedBlock = currentBlock - CONFIRMATIONS;

    const confirmedTokenIds = await this
      .getTokensAtBlock(confirmedBlock)
      .catch(() => []);
    const latestTokenIds = await this
      .getTokensAtBlock(currentBlock);
```

```
    const unconfirmedTokenIds = latestTokenIds
      .filter(id => !confirmedTokenIds.includes(id));

    const tokens = confirmedTokenIds
      .map(id => ({ id, confirmed: true }))
      .concat(unconfirmedTokenIds
        .map(id => ({ id, confirmed: false })
      ));

    this.setState({ tokens, loading: false });
  }
}
```

This will allow us to properly display the status of each token when the page loads. However, any tokens listed as unconfirmed will remain on that state until a full page reload. We need to update their status once they reach the required number of confirmations.

We will do that by subscribing to new blocks and re-checking the ownership of each of the unconfirmed tokens *six blocks ago*. Once enough new blocks are mined, we will be able to move these new tokens to a confirmed state. Let's add a new method (Listing 5-29) to be called from the didMount handler.

Listing 5-29. Subscribe to new blocks, and re-check the ownership of each token six blocks before the current one. If a token belongs to the current user six blocks ago, we consider it to be confirmed. Once all pending tokens have been processed, we close the subscription

```
// src/components/ERC721.js
class ERC721 extends Component {
  subscribeUnconfirmedTokens(unconfirmedIds) {
    if (unconfirmedIds.length === 0) return;
    const { contract, owner } = this.props;

    this.newBlocksSub = getWeb3().eth
      .subscribe('newBlockHeaders', (err, { number }) => {
      unconfirmedIds.forEach(async (id) => {
```

```
      const confirmedOwner = await contract.methods
        .ownerOf(id).call({}, (number - CONFIRMATIONS))
        .catch(() => null);
      if (areAddressesEqual(confirmedOwner, owner)) {
        this.confirmToken(id, CONFIRMATIONS);
        unconfirmedIds = unconfirmedIds.filter(i => id!==i);
        if (unconfirmedIds.length === 0) {
          this.newBlocksSub.unsubscribe();
        }
      }
    });
  });
  }
}
```

Keep in mind that in this example, we are only tracking new tokens created by minting, and any new tokens *transferred* to the user will not be shown until the page is reloaded. We are also assuming that the user does not transfer out their own tokens. If your application needs to handle these scenarios, then monitoring Transfer events is a much safer approach than only watching transactions sent by the user from the application. We will build around that concept in the next chapter.

Next Steps   The next steps for your app would be to move to a more interesting network, starting with a testnet such as Rinkeby, and eventually move onto Mainnet. You can spin up a local Geth or Parity node connected to such network (using the light syncmode to speed up the sync process) and rely on the deploy. js script or use an online tool like MyCrypto[12] or Remix for deploying the contract. Once deployed, all interactions will be managed by Metamask – just remember to switch to the correct network.

---

[12]https://mycrypto.com/contracts/deploy

Summary

In this chapter, we reviewed how to set up a local development environment by relying on either ganache or a full Ethereum client. We then went through the process of compiling and deploying contracts to the network, either via using the vanilla solc compiler or the sol-compiler wrapper. We also reviewed how Metamask works when using it for sending transactions and unlocking the user accounts.

Once we had ironed out the details of setting up the environment, we went in-depth on the process of sending a transaction, focusing especially in gas estimation and defining a gas price. We then reviewed the lifecycle of a transaction and how we can access specific events such as when it is mined or confirmed. We also went through a few of the most common errors when sending a transaction and how the process of replacement works.

To illustrate all these concepts, we built a small application, similar to the one from the previous chapter but this time around non-fungible tokens. Starting from a list of the user's existing tokens, we allowed the user to mint new ones and monitored the lifecycle of such transactions. In the next chapter, where we will cover concepts such as indexing and storage, we will also learn some additional techniques regarding handling reorganizations and testing, which can also be applied to this kind of applications.

CHAPTER 6

Indexing and Storage

In the last two chapters, we learned how to read from and write to the Ethereum network. Reads can be made as regular calls to contracts, or by querying logged events, while writes are always performed in the context of a transaction. However, these operations only accommodate for basic use cases. If we want to display aggregate data from the blockchain, querying events client-side quickly falls short. Similarly, if we want to store large amounts of information in a contract, gas costs make it economically infeasible. In this chapter, we will work with off-chain components to solve both problems. We will first go through the process of indexing blockchain data in a server to query it from a client application and then go into off-chain storage solutions. We will also review techniques for handling reorganizations and testing along the way, as well as discussing the value of centralized vs. decentralized solutions.

Indexing Data

We will begin with the problem of indexing blockchain data. In this context, by *indexing* we refer to the action of collecting certain pieces of information from the network (such as token balances, sent transactions, or contracts created) and storing them in a queryable data store, such as a relational database or an analytics engine like ElasticSearch, in order to perform complex queries. Throughout this chapter, instead of attempting to index the entire chain, we will choose a specific dataset and build a solution tailored for it.

Indexing is necessary whenever you need to perform any kind of *aggregation* over logged data, such as a sum or an average, since the Ethereum events API is not fit for doing so. For instance, it is not possible to easily obtain the number of unique addresses that hold more than a certain balance of an ERC20 asset – a query that is trivial to run on a relational database.

© Santiago Palladino 2019
S. Palladino, *Ethereum for Web Developers*, https://doi.org/10.1007/978-1-4842-5278-9_6

Indexing can also be used to improve performance when querying large numbers of events, by acting just as a query cache. A dedicated database can answer event queries much faster than a regular Ethereum node.

Note   Certain public node providers, such as Infura, actually include an events query layer,[1] separate from their nodes, in order to greatly reduce their infrastructure footprint for serving logs.

We will now focus on a specific indexing use case and design a solution for collecting the information to index.

Tracking ERC20 Token Holders

We will track the token holders of a specific ERC20 coin. Remember that ERC20 non-fungible tokens can act as a coin, where each address has a certain balance. However, the contract offers no methods to actually list them. Even if it did, some tokens have a user base that would vastly exceed the capabilities of a client-side-only application querying an Ethereum node. For example, at the time of this writing, the OmiseGO (OMG) token has over 650,000 unique holders.[2]

Revisiting the ERC20 Interface

We will review the ERC20 contract interface to identify the building blocks we will be using. Leaving aside functionality related to allowances, the ERC20 standard includes these methods and events.

```
function transfer(address to, uint256 value) returns (bool);
function totalSupply() view returns (uint256);
function balanceOf(address who) view returns (uint256);

event Transfer(
  address indexed from, address indexed to, uint256 value
);
```

---

[1]See https://blog.infura.io/faster-logs-and-events-e43e2fa13773
[2]See https://etherscan.io/token/0xd26114cd6EE289AccF82350c8d8487fedB8A0C07

As mentioned, unlike the extended ERC721 standard, ERC20 does not provide a method to list all token holders. The only way to build such a list is by going through every *Transfer* event and collect all recipient addresses.

Caution   Certain ERC20 contracts do not emit a Transfer event when minting new tokens, but rather emit a non-standard Mint event. In such cases, we would need to track both events in order to build the complete set of holders.

Querying Transfer Events

We will begin by querying all transfer events from a given contract. We will build an ERC20Indexer class, relying on a web3 connection provider, an ERC20 token address, and a block number to start querying from (Listing 6-1). This last parameter is added only for performance reasons: it does not make sense to query any blocks before the token contract was deployed.

Listing 6-1.   Constructor for the ERC20Indexer class we will be working on. We are once again depending on openzeppelin-solidity@2.2.0 to get the ERC20 contract ABI. We will store the list of all token holder addresses on the holders set, and the lastBlock field will keep track of the last block we have processed

```
// 01-indexing/simple-indexer.js
const ERC20 = require('openzeppelin-solidity/build/contracts/ERC20.json');
const BigNumber = require('bignumber.js');
const Web3 = require('web3');

class ERC20Indexer {
  constructor({ address, startBlock, provider } = {}) {
    this.holders = new Set();
    this.startBlock = startBlock;
    this.lastBlock = this.startBlock;
    this.web3 = new Web3(provider);
```

```
    this.contract = new this.web3.eth.Contract(
      ERC20.abi, address
    );
  }
}
```

We can now add a first method to this class to get the list of transfer events from a given contract (Listing 6-2). Since that list is potentially larger than what we can fit in a single request (OMG has over 2 million transfers up to date), we will need to break it into multiple requests, so we will start with a method that processes all events in a range of blocks.

Listing 6-2. Querying all transfer events from a range of blocks in batches. Here BATCH_SIZE should depend on the volume of transactions per block of the contract

```
async processBlocks(startBlock, endBlock) {
  for (let fromBlock = startBlock;
       fromBlock <= endBlock;
       fromBlock += BATCH_SIZE) {

    const toBlock = Math.min(
      fromBlock + BATCH_SIZE - 1, endBlock
    );

    const events = await this.contract
      .getPastEvents('Transfer', { fromBlock, toBlock });

    events.forEach((e) => this.reduceEvent(e));
  }
}
```

This method will get all transfer events in a block range from a contract and send them to a reduceEvent function (Listing 6-3). This reducing function should receive an event and use it to update the current list of token holders.

Listing 6-3. Retrieving the recipient of a token transfer to add it to the list of token holders. Transfers to the zero address are usually tokens being burnt, so we will keep it out of our list

```
const ZERO_ADDRESS = '0x0000000000000000000000000000000000000000';

async reduceEvent(event) {
  const { to } = event.returnValues;
  if (to !== ZERO_ADDRESS) {
    this.holders.add(to);
  }
}
```

> **Note** In a production implementation, you will not want to store the list of holders in a javascript data structure in memory that is wiped out whenever the process is stopped. You should rather use a database for storing all data and serving your clients' queries. The choice of the database engine is out of the scope of this book, and depends heavily on your use case.

However, this method may yield some false positives. If an address ever held some balance but then transferred it all, it will be added to our list of holders but never removed. This means that we need to check that an address balance is non-zero for listing it. Since we are at it, we will go an extra mile and track the current balance for each holder. We have two options to do this, each with their own pros and cons:

- We can rely on the ERC20 `balanceOf` method to check the balance of each address we add to our list. We can do this as soon as we find a new address to add to our set, and have a holder with its balance ready. However, this means that we are making an additional request for each token holder and that we also need to re-run this query whenever we see a new block with new transfers.

- We can use the fact that the balance of any address in an ERC20 contract can be determined by just looking at the transfer events. Since we are already querying them, we can track all movements to and from each address and update them accordingly. This will

require a bit more logic on our end, but does not need any extra
requests to the Ethereum network. Its downside is that we cannot rely
on the balance of an address until we have finished scanning until
the latest block in the chain.

To prioritize reducing the number of requests, we will go with the second strategy
(Listing 6-4). This means that our function to reduce an event will also need to account
for the *value* of each transfer.

Listing 6-4. Reducing an event to update the balances of each holder. Here
balances is an object that replaces the former set of holders. Note that we are
excluding the zero address both as sender and recipient, since transfers from it
represent minting events and transfers to it represent burns

```
async reduceEvent(event) {
  const { from, to, value } = event.returnValues;

  if (from !== ZERO_ADDRESS) {
    this.balances[from] = this.balances[from]
      ? this.balances[from].minus(value)
      : BigNumber(value).negated();
  }

  if (to !== ZERO_ADDRESS) {
    this.balances[to] = this.balances[to]
      ? this.balances[to].plus(value)
      : BigNumber(value);
  }
}
```

Armed with a class that can generate the list of holders and their balances for a
given range of blocks, we now need to keep this list up to date as new blocks are mined
(Listing 6-5). We will use polling for getting new blocks, though subscription is also a
viable alternative.

Listing 6-5. Polling for new blocks and retrieving any new transfer events. The processNewBlocks function will query the latest block and call into processBlocks with the new blocks range, while the start function kicks off an infinite loop that constantly polls and then sleeps for 1 second

```
const CONFIRMATIONS = 12;
const INTERVAL = 1000;

async processNewBlocks() {
  const lastBlock = this.lastBlock;
  const currentBlock = await this.web3.eth.getBlockNumber();
  const confirmedBlock = currentBlock - CONFIRMATIONS;
  if (!lastBlock || confirmedBlock >= lastBlock) {
    await this.processBlocks(lastBlock, confirmedBlock);
    this.lastBlock= confirmedBlock + 1;
  }
}

start() {
  this.timeout = setTimeout(async () => {
    await this.processNewBlocks()
    this.start();
  }, INTERVAL);
}
```

An important detail of our implementation is that we will not process up to the latest block, but only until a certain number of blocks ago. This ensures that any transfer events we have processed are confirmed and will not be rolled back as part of a reorganization. We will later look into strategies for querying up to the most recent block and handling reorgs as we detect them.

Sharing Our Data

The last step is to actually provide access to the data we have gathered (Listing 6-6). We will set up a simple express server that exposes the set of balances in JSON format upon an HTTP GET request.

Listing 6-6. Simple express server that exposes the balances from the indexer in an HTTP endpoint. The `mapValues` lodash helper is used to format the BigNumber values before serializing them in JSON. Make sure to get an Infura token to set the `API_TOKEN` variable

```
const express = require('express')
const mapValues = require('lodash.mapvalues');

// Sample values for testing a mainnet token
const API_TOKEN = 'YOUR_INFURA_API_TOKEN';
const PROVIDER = 'https://mainnet.infura.io/v3/' + API_TOKEN;
const ADDRESS = '0x00fdae9174357424a78afaad98da36fd66dd9e03';
const START_BLOCK = 6563800;

// Initialize express application and indexer
const app = express()
const indexer = new Indexer({
  address: ADDRESS,
  startBlock: START_BLOCK,
  provider: PROVIDER
});

// Register route for querying balances
app.get('/balances.json', (_req, res) => {
  res.send(
    mapValues(indexer.balances, b => b.toString(10))
  );
});

// Start!
app.listen(3000);
indexer.start();
```

We can test this script by running it using node and in a different console use `curl` to query the balances (Listing 6-7). Make sure to wait a few seconds so the script can process some blocks to gather transfer data.

Listing 6-7. Querying the express endpoint to retrieve the token balances. We are using the jq[3] utility just to pretty-print the JSON output

```
$ curl -s "localhost:3000/balances.json" | jq .
{
  "0xB048...": "26000000000000000000000000",
  "0x58b2...": "779977075353909983471493397",
  "0x352B...": "46666670000000000000000000",
  "0xBC96...": "30000000000000000000000000",
  ...
}
```

This naive implementation makes use of the fact that all indexed data is stored in the indexer instance. Keep in mind that for actual deployments you will want to store all data in a separate datastore, such as a relational database. This will allow you to run queries directly to the database and decouple the web server and indexer processes so they run separately. It will also allow you to add aggregations, filters, sorting, and paging from the client as needed: returning a list of half a million token holders in a single request may not fare well in some scenarios.

Handling Chain Reorganizations

Up to this point, we have avoided the issue of chain reorganizations by only processing transfers that can be considered to be finalized, in other words, transfers that occurred enough blocks ago that the chance of those blocks being removed from the chain is negligible. We will now remove this restriction and see how we can safely process the latest events by reacting properly to a reorg.

Using Subscriptions

The easiest way to detect and react to a reorg is through subscriptions. A subscription on an event, such as on the ERC20 `Transfer`, will not only push new events to our process in real time but will also notify on any events *removed* due to a reorganization. This means that we can write the counterpart of our `reduceEvent` function to also undo an event and run it whenever the Ethereum node pushes an event removal (Listing 6-8).

---

[3]https://stedolan.github.io/jq/

Listing 6-8. Reverting a transfer event in our list of balances. The logic here is the reverse of that in the reduceEvent method

```
// 01-indexing/subs-indexer.js
undoTransfer(event) {
  const { from, to, value } = event.returnValues;
  if (from !== ZERO_ADDRESS) {
    this.balances[from] = this.balances[from].plus(value);
  }
  if (to !== ZERO_ADDRESS) {
    this.balances[to] = this.balances[to].minus(value);
  }
}
```

This way, instead of polling for new blocks relying on the getPastEvents method, we can simply open a subscription and listen for events additions and removals (Listing 6-9).

Listing 6-9. Using subscriptions for monitoring new events and tracking removed ones due to reorganizations. The data handler fires whenever there is a new event and the changed one when the event is removed from the chain due to a reorganization

```
async function start() {
  // Process all past blocks
  const currentBlock = await this.web3.eth.getBlockNumber();
  await this.processBlocks(this.startBlock, currentBlock);

  // Subscribe to new ones
  this.subscription = this.contract.events
    .Transfer({ fromBlock: currentBlock + 1 })
      .on('data', e => this.reduceEvent(e))
      .on('changed', e => this.undoTransfer(e.returnValues))
      .on('error', err => console.error("Error", err));
}
```

However, this approach has a major downside. If the websocket connection to the node is lost when a reorg occurs, our script will never be notified of the removed events. This means that we will not roll back the reverted transfers and end up with an invalid state. Another issue is that subscriptions only return new events, so if any blocks are minted between the `processBlocks` call and the time the subscription is installed, we may miss some events. Let's try a different, simpler approach then. We will first need to manually detect when a reorg has happened.

Detecting a Reorganization

A reorganization occurs when a chain fork gathers more accumulated hash power than the current head, and that fork becomes the official chain. This can happen if different sets of miners work on different forks.

This means that in a reorganization, one or more blocks (starting backward from the current head) will be replaced by others. These new blocks may or may not contain the same transactions as the previous ones and may also be ordered differently,[4] yielding different results.

We can detect a reorganization by checking the block identifiers. Recall from Chapter 3 that each block is identified by its hash. This hash is calculated from the block's data and the hash of the previous block. This is what constitutes a blockchain in its essence: the fact that each block is tied to the previous one. And this means that an old block cannot be changed without forcing a change in the identifiers of all subsequent blocks.

This is exactly what allows us to easily detect a reorganization. When the hash of a block at a given height changes, it means that that block and potentially other blocks before it have changed as well. We can then just monitor the latest block we have processed, and if its hash changes at any point, we then scan backward for other changed hashes, until we detect a common ancestor (Listing 6-10).

Let's modify our script to add a check for reorgs using this strategy, which will require us to keep track of the block hashes we have processed.

---

[4]Note that the order of the transactions sent within each account will be preserved, thanks to the nonce mechanic.

Listing 6-10. Updated processNewBlocks function that checks for reorgs on every iteration. The function undoBlocks (Listing 6-12) should undo all transfers related to removed blocks, returning the most recent block not affected by the reorganization

```
// 01-indexing/reorgs-indexer.js
async processNewBlocks() {
  // Track current block number and its hash
  const currentBlockNumber =
    await this.web3.eth.getBlockNumber() - CONFIRMATIONS;
  const currentBlockHash =
    await this.getBlockHash(currentBlockNumber);

  // Check for possible reorgs
  if (this.lastBlockNumber && this.lastBlockHash) {
    const newLastBlockHash
      = await this.getBlockHash(this.lastBlockNumber);

    if (this.lastBlockHash !== newLastBlockHash) {
      // There was a reorg! Undo all blocks affected,
      // and reprocess blocks starting by the most recent
      // one that was not removed from the main chain
      const lastBlock = await this.undoBlocks();
      this.lastBlockHash = lastBlock.hash;
      this.lastBlockNumber = lastBlock.number;
    }
  }

  // Process blocks from lastBlockNumber until currentBlock
  // Update this.lastBlockNumber and this.lastBlockHash
  // ...
}

async getBlockHash(number) {
  const { hash } = await this.web3.eth.getBlock(number);
  return hash;
}
```

Note that we are now keeping track of not just the latest block number but also its hash. Whenever we start a new iteration, we check if the hash for the block at that same height changed. If it did, then we have stumbled upon a reorganization and must revert all changes from the removed blocks.

Reverting Changes

When the reorganization is detected, we need to revert any transfers we have processed from the blocks removed. To do that, we first need to keep track of which transfers we processed on each block (Listing 6-11).

We will add a new field to our Indexer class: a stack containing one item per each block we have seen when processing a transfer event. Each item will hold the block number, hash, and the list of transfers it included. We will add new items to it whenever we reduce a new event

Listing 6-11. Keeping track of transfer events per block. This function is called from `reduceEvent`. Note that this function must be invoked in order as new events are being processed to ensure the list of blocks remains sorted with the most recent block at its end

```
const last = require('lodash.last');

async saveEvent(event) {
  // Add a new block if this event happened on a new one
  if (!last(this.eventsBlocks)
      || last(this.eventsBlocks).hash !== event.blockHash) {
    this.eventsBlocks.push({
      number: event.blockNumber,
      hash: event.blockHash,
      transfers: []
    });
  }

  // Include the transfer event on the latest block
  last(this.eventsBlocks)
    .transfers.push(event.returnValues);
}
```

Now that we have a list of the blocks we have processed, we can iterate it starting from the end and undo all the transfer events we have aggregated on our list of balances (Listing 6-12).

Listing 6-12. Walk backward the list of processed events and undo all transfers. This function must return the most recent block that was not removed in the reorganization, so the script can reprocess the chain from it. The function undoTransfer is analogous to the one presented in the subscriptions subsection earlier in this chapter

```
async undoBlocks() {
  while (this.eventsBlocks.length > 0) {
    // Check if the hash of the last block changed
    const lastBlock = last(this.eventsBlocks);
    const hash = await this.getBlockHash(lastBlock.number);

    // If it did not, then we know that all previous ones
    // have not changed either
    if (lastBlock.hash === hash)
      return lastBlock;

    // If it did, we undo all transfers for that block,
    // and iterate
    this.eventsBlocks.pop();
    lastBlock.transfers.forEach((t) =>
      this.undoTransfer(t)
    );
  }

  // We return an empty block if there are no more
  return { hash: null, number: null };
}
```

To recap, the changes we have implemented to make our script robust against reorganizations are the following:

1. When processing a transfer event, save its block number and hash on a list, appending the most recent ones at the end.

2. When checking for new blocks, verify if the hash of the latest block we have processed has changed.

3. If it did change, undo each transfer event that happened on each changed block, starting from the most recent one. When we reach an unchanged block, stop.

4. Reset the latest block to the unchanged block, and resume processing from there.

While these changes have introduced much complexity to our solution, they ensure that its state does not fall out of sync because of reorganizations. It will depend on your use case how you choose to handle them: ignoring the most recent blocks until they become confirmed, using subscriptions to let the node track removed events assuming a stable connection, or implementing a client-based design similar to this one.

Unit Testing

Up until now, we have overlooked a critical aspect of software development: tests. While testing is not substantially different in Ethereum than in other applications, we will use our indexer example to introduce some useful techniques specific to blockchain testing.

Choosing a Node

The first decision lies in choosing which node to use for our tests. Recall from earlier chapters that we can work with ganache, a blockchain simulator, or on an actual node, such as Geth or Parity, running on development mode. The former is lighter and provides additional methods for manipulating the blockchain state which are useful in unit tests. On the other hand, using an actual node will be more representative of the actual production setup for your application.

A good compromise is to use ganache with instant seal for unit tests, while a Geth or Parity development node can be used for end-to-end integration tests, running with a fixed block time. This allows more fine-grained control in the unit tests and a more representative environment on integration.

> **Note**   Whether unit tests should be allowed to call external services is typically a contentious issue in software development. In traditional applications, some developers prefer to set up a testing database to back their unit tests, while others stub all calls to it in order to test their code in isolation, arguing that a unit test must only exercise a single piece of code. Here, we will side with the former group and will connect to a ganache instance in our unit tests. Either way, this is only a matter of semantics on what we understand for a unit test.

Testing Our Indexer

We will now write some unit tests for our indexer. We will use ganache as a back end, mocha[5] as a test runner, and chai[6] with the bignumber plugin[7] for writing assertions.

The first step is to deploy an ERC20 token for our indexer to monitor (Listing 6-13). We will extend the default ERC20 implementation from OpenZeppelin with a public minting method, so we can easily mint tokens for any addresses we want to test.

Listing 6-13. ERC20 token contract with a public minting method, which allows anyone to create new tokens. Do not use in production!

```
// 01-indexing/contracts/MockERC20.sol
pragma solidity ^0.5.0;
import "openzeppelin-solidity/contracts/token/ERC20/ERC20.sol";

contract MockERC20 is ERC20 {
  constructor () public { }
  function mint(address account, uint256 amount) public {
    _mint(account, amount);
  }
}
```

---

[5]https://mochajs.org/
[6]www.chaijs.com/
[7]www.chaijs.com/plugins/chai-bignumber/

Let's create the boilerplate for our test file (Listing 6-14). We will need to import all the relevant components, create a new instance of web3 for interacting with our ganache instance, and deploy the new contract.

Listing 6-14. Boilerplate code for a test suite for the Indexer. It initializes a new web3 instance and deploys an instance of the ERC20 token contract. Note that some require statements were removed for brevity

```
// 01-indexing/test/indexer.test.js
const expect =
  require('chai').use(require('chai-bignumber')()).expect;
const ERC20Artifact =
  require('../artifacts/MockERC20.json').compilerOutput;

const Web3 = require('web3');
const web3 = new Web3('http://localhost:9545');
const ERC20 = new web3.eth.Contract(
  ERC20Artifact.abi, null,
  { data: ERC20Artifact.evm.bytecode.object }
);

describe('indexer', function () {
  before('setup', async function () {
    this.accounts = await web3.eth.getAccounts();
    this.erc20 = await ERC20.deploy().send({
      from: this.accounts[0], gas: 1e6
    });
  });
});
```

Using this template, we can now write our first test within our *describe* block, to check that any balances minted in our contract are correctly picked up by the indexer (Listing 6-15).

Listing 6-15. Test for checking that transfers from minting are correctly processed. We initialize a new Indexer instance for the newly deployed token contract, mint some tokens for an address, and execute the indexer to check the result

```
it('records balances from minting', async function () {
  const indexer = new Indexer({
    address: this.erc20.options.address
    provider: 'http://localhost:9545'
  });

  const [from, holder] = this.accounts;
  await this.erc20.methods.mint(holder, 1000).send({ from });

  await indexer.processNewBlocks();
  expect(indexer.getBalances()[holder])
    .to.be.bignumber.eq("1000");
});
```

We can run this test with mocha. Make sure to have a ganache instance running in another terminal and listening on port 9545 (Listing 6-16).

Listing 6-16. Starting a ganache instance and running the test suite respectively. Each command should be run on a different terminal

```
$ ganache-cli -p 9545
$ npx mocha
```

However, if we run our test, it will fail – the indexer will not pick up any balance for the holder address. This is because we built our indexer to ignore any information from the latest blocks and only consider transfers after a certain number of confirmations.

We will fix this using the *mine* method from ganache (Listing 6-17). This method, not available in Geth or Parity, tells ganache to simulate a new block being mined. It is sent as any other message via the low-level JSON-RPC interface.

Listing 6-17. Helper method to instruct ganache to mine a certain number of blocks. The code in `mineBlocks` fires a chosen number requests in parallel and returns when all of them have succeeded

```
function rpcSend(web3, method, ... params) {
  return require('util')
    .promisify(web3.currentProvider.send)
    .call(web3.currentProvider, {
      jsonrpc: "2.0", method, params
    });
}

function mineBlocks(web3, number) {
  return Promise.all(
    Array.from({ length: number }, () => (
      rpcSend(web3, "evm_mine")
    ))
  );
}
```

We can now add a call to `mineBlocks` right before instructing our indexer to process new blocks in our test, run it again, and see it pass.

Using Snapshots

We can now write more tests that exercise other scenarios of our indexer. However, in any good test suite, all tests should be independent from each other, which is not the case here since we are deploying a single instance of our ERC20 contract. This means that any minting or transfers that occur in a test will be carried on to the following ones.

While the obvious solution is to just replace our `before` step with a `beforeEach` step,[8] so a new ERC20 is deployed for each test, we will use this opportunity to introduce a new concept specific to ganache: snapshots (Listing 6-18). Snapshots allow us to save the current state of the simulated blockchain, run a set of operations, and then roll back to the saved state.

---

[8]While *before* hooks run once before all tests in the suite, *beforeEach* hooks run once per each test, setting up a new state every time a new test starts. Read more at `https://mochajs.org/#hooks`

Listing 6-18. Helper functions for taking a new snapshot, which returns the snapshot id, and for reverting to a specific snapshot given its id

```
function takeSnapshot(web3) {
  return rpcSend(web3, "evm_snapshot").then(r => r.result);
}

function revertToSnapshot(web3, id) {
  return rpcSend(web3, "evm_revert", id);
}
```

A good use case for snapshots is to save time by removing the need to re-create a new state for each test (Listing 6-19). Instead of deploying a new ERC20 contract on each test, we just deploy it once, save a snapshot, execute a test, and restore the snapshot to clear out any changes before running the next test. While this will not offer any performance improvements in our tests, suites with a more complex setup that require creating multiple contracts will benefit from it.

Listing 6-19. Taking a new snapshot before each test, and reverting back to it once the test has ended. Note that we cannot revert to the same snapshot more than once, so we need to create a new one for each test

```
beforeEach('take snapshot', async function () {
  this.snapshotId = await takeSnapshot(web3);
});

afterEach('revert to snapshot', async function () {
  await revertToSnapshot(web3, this.snapshotId);
});
```

Another interesting use case of snapshots is for testing *reorganizations.* Triggering a reorganization on a regular Geth or Parity node is complex, as it involves setting up our own private node network, and disconnecting and reconnecting nodes to simulate the chain split. On the other hand, testing a reorganization on ganache is much simpler: we can take a snapshot, mine a few blocks, and then roll back and mine another set of blocks with a different set of transactions.

> **Caution**   This will not be equivalent to an actual chain reorganization, since subscriptions will not report any *removed* events. Nevertheless, since our indexer relies on plain polling for detecting any changes, using snapshots will do in this case.

Let's write a test for checking that our indexer properly handles chain reorganizations by undoing any balance changes from removed blocks and processing new ones.

```
it('handles reorganizations', async function () {
  // Set up a new indexer
  const indexer = new Indexer({
    address: this.erc20.options.address
    provider: 'http://localhost:9545'
  });

  // Mint balance for sender account and take a snapshot
  const [from, sender, r1, r2] = this.accounts;
  await this.erc20.methods.mint(sender, 1000).send({ from });
  const snapshotId = await takeSnapshot(web3);

  // Transfer 200 tokens to r1 and r2, and mine confirmations
  const transfer = this.erc20.methods.transfer;
  await transfer(r1, 200).send({ from: sender });
  await transfer(r2, 200).send({ from: sender });
  await mineBlocks(web3, 12);

  // Run the indexer and assert that they were picked up
  await this.indexer.processNewBlocks();
  const balances = this.indexer.getBalances();
  expect(balances[sender]).to.be.bignumber.eq("600");
  expect(balances[r1]).to.be.bignumber.eq("200");
  expect(balances[r2]).to.be.bignumber.eq("200");

  // Rollback to simulate the reorg and send new transfers
  await revertToSnapshot(web3, snapshotId);
  await methods.transfer(r1, 300).send({ from: sender });
  await mineBlocks(web3, 15);
```

```
  // Check that the old state was discarded
  await this.indexer.processNewBlocks();
  const newBalances = this.indexer.getBalances();
  expect(newBalances[sender]).to.be.bignumber.eq("700");
  expect(newBalances[r1]).to.be.bignumber.eq("300");
  expect(newBalances[r2]).to.be.bignumber.eq("0");
});
```

Note   These testing techniques can be used to test not only components that interact with smart contracts but the smart contracts themselves. It is a good practice to have a good test coverage in any code you deploy to the network, especially considering you will not be able to modify it later (in most cases[9]) to fix any bugs.

A Note on Centralization

For the first time in this book, we have introduced a server-side component to our applications. Instead of just building a client-side-only app that connects directly to the blockchain, we now have a new centralized dependency that is required for our application to run. It can be argued that our application thus no longer qualifies as a decentralized app, as it blindly trusts data returned by a server run by a single team.

Depending on the kind of data being queried, this can be alleviated by having the client *verify* part of the data supplied by the server. Following with the ERC20 balance example, a client could request the top 10 holders of a token from the indexing server and then verify against the blockchain that their balances are correct. They may still not be the top 10 – but at least the client has a guarantee that the balances have not been tampered with.

However, this is not a solution to the problem, as not all data can be verified against the blockchain without having to re-query all events. Furthermore, our application now depends on a component that could go down at any time, rendering it unusable.

---

[9]We will briefly touch contracts upgradeability in the next chapter.

Let's discuss two different approaches to this problem. The upcoming discussion applies not just to indexing but also to any other off-chain service, such as storage or intensive computation.

Decentralized Services

One approach to this problem is to look for *decentralized* off-chain solutions. For instance, at the time of this writing, a GraphQL interface to blockchain data named *EthQL*[10] is under review. This could be added as part of the standard interface for all Ethereum nodes, allowing easier querying of events from any client. As another example, thegraph[11] is a project that offers customized GraphQL schemas for different protocols. They rely on a token-incentivized decentralized network of nodes that keep such schemas up to date and answer any queries from users.

While elegant, these decentralized solutions may not yet be ready for all use cases. Decentralized indexing or computing solutions are still being designed. And even when ready, a generic decentralized solution may not always cater for the specific needs of your application. With this in mind, we will discuss a second approach.

Centralized Applications

An apparent non-solution to the problem is to just accept that applications *can be centralized*. This may come as a controversial statement, having focused strongly on decentralized applications throughout the book, but it does not need to be.

It can be argued that the strength of a blockchain-based system lies not in the application but in the protocol layer. By relying on the chain as the ultimate source of truth and building open protocols that run on it, any developer can freely build an application to interact with such protocols. This gives a user the flexibility to move between different apps that act as *gateways* to their data in a common decentralized protocol layer. Decentralization is then understood as the freedom of being able to pack up and leave at any time while preserving all data and network effects that arise from the shared decentralized layers.

---

[10]See https://github.com/ConsenSys/ethql
[11]See https://thegraph.com/

This rationale gives us as developers the freedom to build solutions as powerful as we want in the application level by leveraging any number of centralized components for querying, storage, computing, or any other service we could need. These solutions have the potential to deliver a much richer user experience than fully decentralized ones.

As you can imagine, centralization is a contentious issue in the Ethereum development community. There is no right or wrong answer to this topic, and the discussion will probably keep evolving over time. Regardless of the approach you take, be sure to understand the pros and cons of it and weigh them against the requirements of the solution you are looking to build.

Storage

We will now focus on another problem in Ethereum: storage. Storing data on the Ethereum blockchain is very expensive, costing 625 gas per byte (rounded up to 32-byte slots), plus a base 68 per non-zero byte just for sending that data to the blockchain. At 1GWei gas price, this means that storing a 100kb PNG will cost about 0.07 ETH. On the other hand, saving data in logs for off-chain access is much cheaper, costing 8 gas units per byte, plus the base 68 for sending the data (this amounts to 1/10th of the cost for our sample image), but is still expensive as we start scaling up. This means we need to look into alternative solutions for storing large application data.

Off-chain Storage

Following a similar approach to the one we used for indexing, we can set up a separate centralized server that provides storage capabilities. Instead of storing the actual data on the blockchain, we can store the URL from which we can retrieve that data off-chain. Of course, this approach is only useful for data that is not needed for contract execution logic, but rather for off chain purposes - such as displaying an image associated to an asset.

Along with the URL, we should also store the hash of the data stored. This allows any client that retrieves that information to verify that the storage server has not tampered with it. Even though data may be rendered inaccessible due to the storage server going down, the hash guarantees that any client can check that provided the data is correct. In other words, **we may be sacrificing the availability of our data by moving it off-chain, but not its integrity**.

We will pick up our ERC721 minting application from the previous chapter as a sample use case to illustrate how this may be implemented and store metadata associated to each token (such as a name and description) in an off-chain site.

ERC721 Metadata Extension

Before we go into the implementation, we will briefly review one of the extensions of the ERC721 standard: the metadata extension (Listing 6-20). This extension specifies that every token has an associated *token URI* that holds its metadata. This URI, which could be an HTTP URL, holds a JSON document with information on each token. This metadata can range from a canonical name, some description text, tags, authoring information, images, or any other fields specific to the domain of the collectible.

Listing 6-20. Specification of the tokenURI method required by the ERC721 metadata extension

```
function tokenURI(uint256 tokenId)
  external view returns (string memory);
```

We will extend our ERC721 contract (Listing 6-21) to include the ERC721Metadata base contract provided by the openzeppelin-solidity@2.2.0 package, which tracks a URI per token.

Listing 6-21. Updated ERC721 contract that accepts an associated tokenURI when minting a token. Recall that this contract required an amount of ETH proportional to the ID of the token for fun and profit

```
// 02-storage/contracts/ERC721PayPerMint.sol
pragma solidity ^0.5.0;
// import SafeMath, ERC721, ERC721Enumerable, ERC721Metadata

contract ERC721PayPerMint
  is ERC721, ERC721Enumerable, ERC721Metadata {

  using SafeMath for uint256;
  constructor() public ERC721Metadata("PayPerMint", "PPM") { }

  function exists(uint256 id) public view returns (bool) {
    return _exists(id);
  }
```

```
function mint(
  address to, uint256 tokenId, string memory tokenURI
) public payable returns (bool) {
  require(msg.value >= tokenId.mul(1e12));
  _mint(to, tokenId);
  _setTokenURI(tokenId, tokenURI);
  return true;
}
}
```

Let's modify our application to save metadata in a storage server and add the URL with the data to the token contract, along with the content hash.

Saving Token Metadata

We will modify our main mint method in the ERC721 component so that it accepts not just an ID but also a title and description string fields (Listing 6-22). We will save this data off-chain, obtain an URL, and pass it along to the following contract *mint* call.

Listing 6-22. Updated mint method to handle token metadata. Note that this also requires modifying the Mint component by adding the title and description inputs, so the user can provide these values

```
// 02-storage/src/components/ERC721.js
async mint({ id, title, description }) {
  const { contract, owner } = this.props;
  const data = JSON.stringify({ id, title, description });
  const url = await save(data);
  const value = new BigNumber(id).shiftedBy(12).toString(10);
  const gasPrice = await getGasPrice();
  const gas = await contract.methods
    .mint(owner, id, url).estimateGas({ value, from: owner });
```

```
contract.methods.mint(owner, id, url)
  .send({ value, gas, gasPrice, from: owner })
  .on('transactionHash', () => {
    this.addToken(id, { title, description });
  })
}
```

The save function will calculate the hash of the data, use it as an identifier, and store it in a storage server (Listing 6-23). Note that by using the hash as an identifier,[12] any client can validate that the data retrieved has not been tampered with.

Listing 6-23. Saving data to a local storage server, using the data hash as an identifier

```
// 02-storage/src/storage/local.js
import { createHash } from 'crypto';
const server = 'http://localhost:3010';

export async function save(data) {
  let hash = createHash('sha256').update(data).digest('hex');
  let url = `${server}/${hash}`;
  await fetch(url, {
    method: 'POST', mode: 'cors', body: data,
    headers: { "Content-Type": "application/json" }
  });

  return url;
}
```

In this example, the server that receives the POST request is a NodeJS process that will accept arbitrary JSON data at an URL path, save it locally in a file, and then serve it upon a GET request. In an actual application, you may want to rely on real storage services.

---

[12]If the storage service you are using assigns random identifiers to content, a good practice is to add the content hash as the URL hash.

We can now load the tokens' metadata on the initial load (Listing 6-24). We will add a call to a new `loadTokensData` function when the main component loads and after the list of existing tokens has been retrieved.

Listing 6-24. Loop through all current tokens and load their metadata by querying the contract to retrieve the URL where it is stored and then the URL to retrieve the actual metadata.

```
// 02-storage/src/components/ERC721.js
loadTokensData(tokens) {
  const { contract } = this.props;
  tokens.forEach(async ({ id }) => {
    // Retrieve metadata url from the contract
    const url = await contract.methods.tokenURI(id).call();

    // Retrieve data from the url
    const data = await fetch(url)
      .then(res => res.json()).catch(() => "");

    // Validate data integrity and update state
    const hash = createHash('sha256')
      .update(JSON.stringify(data)).digest('hex');
    const path = new URL(url).pathname.slice(1);
    if (path === hash) this.setTokenData(id, data);
  });
}
```

Note that the metadata integrity is verified by calculating its hash before accepting it. You can test it by modifying the saved metadata in your local filesystem (look in the server/data folder of the project) and checking that no metadata is displayed for the modified token.

This allows us to associate additional data to each non-fungible token when we mint it, which can be actually leveraged by any application that displays token information. In that regard, you can think of token metadata as the equivalent of opengraph metadata[13] for a regular HTML page.

---

[13]Opengraph (http://ogp.me/) is a standard for HTML meta tags that provide information such as an image, description, or author name for a page.

Interplanetary Storage

As an alternative to centralized storage solutions, we can store our data in the *InterPlanetary File System* (IPFS). IPFS is "a distributed system for storing and accessing files, web sites, applications, and data."[14] In other words, it acts as a decentralized storage system.

What is IPFS?

IPFS acts as a peer-to-peer content distribution system. Any node can join the network, from a dedicated IPFS server to a regular user in their home computer. Whenever a user requests a file from the network, that file is downloaded from the nearest node that has the file and is made available for other users to download from this new location. Availability of a piece of content depends on having enough users willing to store the relevant files.

Any data unit in IPFS is not identified by its location, as it is in most traditional file systems, but by its content. When requesting a file from the IPFS network, you address it by its identifier, which is nothing else than a hash of the content. This guarantees integrity of all content, since a client will validate all content received against its identifier. It also allows a client to request a file without needing to know *where* it is stored in the network.

This implies that content in IPFS is immutable. Any changes to it require storing a new copy entirely under a new identifier. The previous file will be retained by the network as long as someone keeps a copy of it.

All these properties make IPFS a good match for blockchain applications. The content hash verification we manually built in the previous section is already provided by the protocol itself. And by indexing the content identifier in the smart contract instead of its location, we can decouple the blockchain data from any centralized content provider.

---

[14]https://docs.ipfs.io/

Note   IPFS relies on users willing to save and share content for availability, which may make it look like a poor choice for building critical applications. Nevertheless, data availability for your application can be provided by relying on an IPFS pinning service. These are services that act as traditional storage servers, but they take part on the IPFS network by making *your* content available to all users – for a fee, that is.

Using IPFS in Our Application

To enable IPFS support in our application, we first need to connect to an IPFS node. This is similar to connecting to an Ethereum node in order to access the Ethereum network, with the difference that we do not need a private key or a currency to write any data to IPFS.

We can either host our own IPFS public node as part of our application or rely on a third-party provider. As an example, Infura provides not only Ethereum public nodes but also IPFS nodes, meaning we can use their IPFS gateway directly.

However, it is also possible that a user is running their own IPFS node in their computer. IPFS provides a browser extension, the IPFS companion,[15] that connects to a local node and makes the browser IPFS-enabled. This includes adding support for ipfs links and injecting an `ipfs` object to the global window object in all sites – much like Metamask adds an `ethereum` provider object to all sites.

Note   There is also the option of running an IPFS node *within your own web site*. The `js-ipfs` library provides a browser-compatible implementation of the entire IPFS protocol, so you can start an IPFS daemon as a user accesses your app. However, this can make your application much heavier, and the in-app IPFS process is not as stable as a dedicated one. Because of this, the suggested method for interacting with the network is to use the IPFS HTTP API to connect to a separate node.

---

[15]https://github.com/ipfs-shipyard/ipfs-companion

Opening an IPFS connection in our app is very similar to opening an Ethereum connection: we first check if there is a global connection object available and, if not, fall back to a well-known public node (Listing 6-25). We will use the `ipfs-http-client@30.1` javascript library for accessing the network, which is an IPFS equivalent of `web3.js`.

Listing 6-25. Creating a new ipfs client instance. We first check whether the global object, injected by the companion extension, is available. If not, we fall back to a connection to the Infura IPFS gateway

```
// 02-storage/src/storage/ipfs.js
import ipfsClient from 'ipfs-http-client';

async function getClient() {
  if (window.ipfs && window.ipfs.enable) {
    return await window.ipfs.enable({
      commands: ['id', 'version', 'add', 'get']
    });
  } else {
    return ipfsClient({
      host: 'ipfs.infura.io', port: '5001',
      protocol: 'https', 'api-path': '/api/v0/'
    });
  }
}
```

Using this new IPFS client, we can now easily save our token metadata to the IPFS network instead to a centralized server.

```
export async function save(data) {
  const ipfs = await getClient();
  const [result] = await ipfs.add(Buffer.from(data));
  return `/ipfs/${result.path}`;
}
```

Fetching the result back from the IPFS network given the URL is straightforward as well. Note that we no longer need to verify its integrity, since the protocol takes care of that automatically.

```
export async function load(url) {
  const ipfs = await getClient();
  const [result] = await ipfs.get(url);
  return JSON.parse(result.content.toString());
}
```

Hosting Our Application on IPFS

IPFS can be used not only to store our application data but also the application itself, for maximum decentralization. All our application's client-side code can be uploaded to IPFS and served from there. But how can our users access it from a regular browser? Or address it without having to specify a hash?

The first problem can be solved via IPFS gateways (see Listing 6-26 for examples). An IPFS gateway is a regular web site that serves content from the IPFS network. It allows you to access any IPFS item at the path /ipfs/CID, where CID is the content hash that identifies each object on the network.

Listing 6-26. You can access an older version of the ipfs.io web site at the following addresses directly on your browser via any of the public gateways listed. Since the ID of the content is its hash, you can be certain that all gateways will serve exactly the same object

```
https://gateway.ipfs.io/ipfs/
QmeYYwD4y4DgVVdAzhT7wW5vrvmbKPQj8wcV2pAzjbj886/
https://ipfs.infura.io/ipfs/QmeYYwD4y4DgVVdAzhT7wW5vrvmbKPQj8wcV2pAzjbj886/
https://cloudflare-ipfs.com/ipfs/
QmeYYwD4y4DgVVdAzhT7wW5vrvmbKPQj8wcV2pAzjbj886/
```

The second problem, having user-friendly names for IPFS sites, can be solved using *DNSLink*. DNSLink is a process for mapping DNS names to IPFS content using DNS TXT records.

Let's say we want to map our site in IPFS to the domain `example.com`. By adding a TXT record to `_dnslink.example.com` with the value `dnslink=/ipfs/CID`, any IPFS gateway will automatically map any requests to `/ipfs/example.com` to the specified content.

Not only that, but we can also specify a CNAME DNS record for our domain, pointing to a gateway. This allows us to automatically serve our page at `example.com` directly from the IPFS-specified gateway.[16] To sum up, the full process for accessing our site would be

- A user makes a request to `example.com`.

- The DNS query answers with a CNAME to `gateway.ipfs.io`.

- The user sends a request to the IP of `gateway.ipfs.io` using `example.com` as a Host header.

- The gateway makes a DNS TXT query for both `example.com` and `_dnslink.example.com` and obtains an IPFS CID as response.

- The gateway transparently serves the content from IPFS to the end user.

Another level of indirection can be introduced by relying on *IPNS*, the InterPlanetary Name System. This system allows you to have mutable links that refer to IPFS content, though IPNS links are also hashes. You can then have your DNSLink point to your IPNS name, instead of the IPFS ID, and update your site by just updating the IPNS link to a new version of your content. This saves you from having to modify your DNS TXT records whenever you deploy a new version of your site.

Summary

We have gone through two problems that arise when building non-trivial Ethereum applications: how to perform complex queries on chain data and how to store large amounts of data. Both of these problems require looking outside Ethereum itself and relying on other services – either centralized or decentralized. We also looked into how to write unit tests that interact with the Ethereum network, and some strategies for handling chain reorganizations.

---

[16]Read more about this at `https://docs.ipfs.io/guides/examples/websites/`

Besides the specific problems or strategies detailed in this chapter, perhaps the most important takeaway is that of defining the *decentralization* demands of your application. While we are used to traditional non-functional requirements such as performance, security, or usability, blockchain apps need to take decentralization into account as well. Decentralization is the core reason of why a blockchain is used in the first place, so it makes sense to pay special attention to it.

Like other non-functional requirements, decentralization is not binary. Our application can have different degrees of decentralization, depending on which components of the stack are centralized, how much trust we place on commercial third parties as opposed to peer-to-peer networks, or how much control our users have over their own data.

For instance, a financial application can be purely centralized except for the underlying protocol that manages the users' assets, allowing high performance and good user experience, and at the same time ensuring its users' that they can part with their assets at any point in time. On the other hand, an application focused on bypassing censorship may need to be purely decentralized to not risk being shut down by its hosting provider.

Different applications will have different requirements. It is important that you define yours, so you know which solutions you have access to, and build the architecture of your application accordingly.

CHAPTER 7

User Onboarding

The complex user onboarding experience is one of the main issues for achieving mass adoption in Ethereum. Users new to the space need to install a dedicated browser or extension, create and back up an account, and then acquire ETH just to begin interacting with a DApp. While in previous chapters we have worked with web3-enabled users, in this chapter we will look into ways for simplifying the onboarding experience for new ones.

We will begin by exploring scenarios for interacting with the blockchain without having to create an account or creating one for our users behind the scenes. We will take this one step further by moving account management itself to the blockchain with smart accounts while exploring contract upgradeability along the way. Then, we will shift our focus to the problem of requiring ETH to interact with Ethereum, and introduce gasless transactions: a technique that removes the need for your users to pay for gas fees. We will wrap up with a review of the Ethereum Name System, which hides raw addresses behind user-friendly names, making them more accessible to your users.

The Problem

Try to remember what your first steps were when using an Ethereum-powered app. The first one was probably acquiring ETH to fuel your transactions. If you were not lucky enough to have someone gift you some crypto, this requires signing up in an exchange and potentially verifying your account. Depending on the exchange, this sometimes even requires uploading a selfie holding your passport or a utility bill to prove your address. Once whitelisted, you need to send funds to the exchange old style, such as via a wire, to get your ETH.

Next step was getting your funds out of the exchange into an account you control. After careful research on hardware, mobile, desktop, and online wallets, you can settle for one and actually create your account. Regardless of the wallet you have chosen, this involves writing down a set of 12 random words and keeping them somewhere safe – but not too safe, because losing them means losing your only backup and thus all your

© Santiago Palladino 2019
S. Palladino, *Ethereum for Web Developers*, https://doi.org/10.1007/978-1-4842-5278-9_7

crypto. After choosing a passphrase for your wallet (but hadn't you just written down 12 words for security?), you are finally presented with your public address and can move your funds out of the exchange and under your control.

Armed with your funded account, you now open your browser at a DApp to try it out. But alas, the site cannot find a web3 provider and is asking you to install a dedicated browser extension (such as Metamask) or use a web3-enabled browser (like Opera) to interact. After doing so, you decide whether to trust this new component with your 12 words – that were supposed to be kept super safe, is it a good idea to enter them on a browser extension you just downloaded? – or set up another new account. Should you pick the latter, you need to go once again through the same process of backing it up via the 12 words, choosing a passphrase, writing down the new account, and transferring your ETH to it.

After these steps, you can now finally send your first transaction and buy a digital-collectible crypto hat from your favorite decentralized store. Hooray.

Now, if you are reading this book, you are most likely a programmer and have a knack for technical challenges. Setting up your own accounts can be cumbersome, though it comes with the thrill of becoming part of the vanguard in a decentralized revolution.

But put yourself in the shoes of your average user, who will outright close a page if it takes more than a few seconds to load. Most users demand immediate satisfaction, and requesting them to go through such a complex process just to start using your application is a recipe for disaster.

While it is not always possible to remove all of the preceding required steps, it is certainly possible to hide some of them to the user or delay them until they are involved enough in your application that they are willing to invest a few minutes to go to *the next level*. We will review some techniques for achieving this throughout this chapter. Be warned though – there is no silver bullet for this problem.

Interacting Without Accounts

We will start by tackling the task of setting up of an account – which involves choosing a wallet, writing down the mnemonic, setting up a passphrase, and so on. The easiest way around these steps is for your app to *not require an account at all* for interacting with it. While this does not fit all use cases, it can be tweaked to cover many more than you would expect.

Sending Funds from an Exchange

The simplest scenario to get started with this method is just receiving plain ETH at an address. For example, a donations application only needs to list a payment address where users can send plain transactions directly from an exchange or from any wallet they control without forcing them to use a web3-enabled browser. Certain services even provide embeddable widgets that you can integrate in your application, so users can buy the ETH they need using fiat without even leaving your site.

Plain Transactions and Fallback Functions

Just sending ETH is the simplest operation for a user (Figure 7-1). The recipient address listed can be either an externally owned account or a smart contract that performs some simple processing upon every transfer.

FOR ETHER DONATIONS, THE SPECIAL ACCOUNT IS:

0xfB6916095ca1df60bB79Ce92cE3Ea74c37c5d359

For information about larger donations, contact us

Figure 7-1. *Donations account for ethereum.org. This address may have changed since this screenshot was taken, so do not send any funds to it before checking it against the original source at* `www.ethereum.org/donate`

Caution   Keep in mind that exchanges do not generate unique ETH addresses for each user or transaction. This means that you cannot rely on `msg.sender` in your contracts to try to identify the user to trigger the transaction, if you expect your users to send funds directly from an exchange.

Remember that every time a contract receives a vanilla transfer of funds, the fallback function is executed, meaning that you can actually react to a transfer via a certain action. In particular, you can rely on the precise amount of ETH sent. However, some exchanges will only send the transfer with a minimal amount of gas, so it may not be possible to perform complex actions as a response to an ETH transfer.

Note   An exchange that fails to set a reasonable gas limit to its transfers can actually be exploited. As described in the vulnerability "Failure to set gasLimit appropriately enables abuse"[1] by Chris Whinfrey and others: "Many exchanges allow the withdrawal of Ethereum to arbitrary addresses with no gas usage limit. Since sending Ethereum to a contract address executes its fallback function, attackers can make these exchanges pay for arbitrary computation. This allows attackers to force exchanges to burn their own Ethereum on high transaction costs." All exchanges should set a strict gas limit to their outbound transactions.

Forwarding Contracts

A neat trick to allow the user to send additional information along with their contribution is to set up several contracts that act as forwarding proxies and execute certain functions in a main contract as their fallback function. Though this does not allow for arbitrary data to be sent, it allows for a predefined set of functions to be run.

As an example, let's suppose we have a contract that accepts funds for two competing parties (A and B). A simple implementation for such contract may look like Listing 7-1.

Listing 7-1. Sample implementation for a contract that accepts donations for one of two parties. The user must call either donateA or donateB when sending funds

```
// 01-forwarding-contracts/contracts/Donations.sol
pragma solidity ^0.5.0;

contract Donations {
  uint256 fundsA;
  uint256 fundsB;

  uint256 timeEnd;
  address payable walletA;
  address payable walletB;
```

---

[1]https://drive.google.com/file/d/1mULop1LxHJJy_uzVBdc_xFItN9ckO4Jj/view

```
  constructor(...) public { ... }

  function donateA() external payable {
    require(now <= timeEnd && msg.value > 0);
    fundsA += msg.value;
  }

  function donateB() external payable {
    require(now <= timeEnd && msg.value > 0);
    fundsB += msg.value;
  }

  function withdraw() external { ... }
}
```

As is, this contract requires your users to specify whether they are donating for A or B on every transfer – at a low level, this implies requesting them to add the data for the call to donateA or donateB. Remember that this data can be easily generated given the contract's ABI using web3js (Listing 7-2).

Listing 7-2. Obtaining the data component for a transaction to the donateA method of the Donations contract, given its ABI

```
> let donations = new web3.eth.Contract(DonationsABI)
> donations.methods.donateA().encodeABI()
0x63420a5c
```

However, asking the user to include an arbitrary hexadecimal string along with their transfer can be an issue, since most exchanges do not support including data along with their withdrawals. And, for regular wallets, including data is often presented as an advanced feature (Figure 7-2).

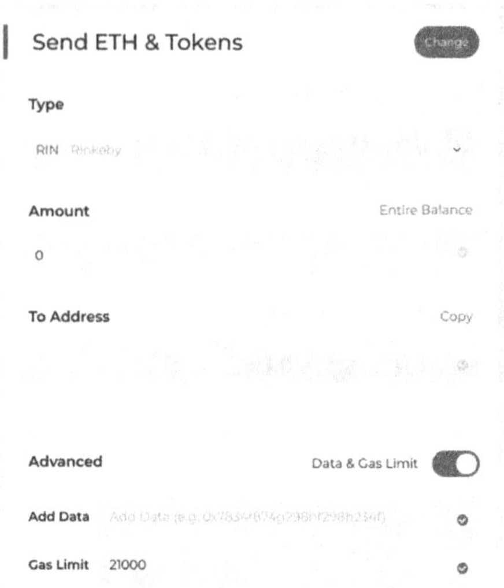

Figure 7-2. *Dialog for sending ETH from myetherwallet.com, an online wallet.*
Note that the option to include data in the transaction is placed under an
Advanced section, hidden by default

A much better alternative is to deploy two small contracts along with the main one,
whose only purpose is to forward every call to either the donateA or donateB functions
(Listing 7-3). This way, the user only needs to send their funds to one of two addresses –
those of DonateA or DonateB – to send their contribution to their party of choice, actually
executing one of two functions by just moving ETH to a certain address.

Listing 7-3. Sample DonateA contract that forwards all transfers to the main
Donations contract by calling donateA. The code for DonateB is equivalent

```
// 01-forwarding-contracts/contracts/DonateA.sol
contract DonateA {
  Donations donations;

  constructor(Donations _donations) public {
    donations = _donations;
  }

  function() external payable {
    donations.donateA.value(msg.value)();
  }
}
```

220

Single-use Addresses

As we have just seen, having a user move ETH directly from an exchange to a smart contract has several limitations:

- The msg.sender cannot be relied upon, since the exchange may use the same address for several withdrawals, or different ones for the same user.

- The gas included with the transaction may not be enough to perform a computationally intensive operation or even writing to storage.

- No data can be included in the transfer.

Users with their own wallets do not face these issues, since they hold an account of their own with its own funds, and from there they can send any arbitrary transaction. Though we could create an account for the user on the spot (as we will see later in this chapter), there is a simpler solution that works for short-lived interactions: *single-use addresses*.[2] These are externally owned addresses that can only issue a single predefined transaction on their lifetime. After that transaction is executed, the address cannot be used again.

How to Use a Single-use Address

Single-use addresses can be used as an intermediary account that receives the funds from an exchange and uses them to execute a predefined action. Such an action may set a gas allowance as high as needed and include arbitrary data as well. The user flow then looks like the following:

1. The user chooses which action they want to execute in the application, including any arbitrary data, funds to be transferred, or gas to be used.

2. A single-use address that can only execute that transaction is generated.

---

[2]The first reference to single-use addresses comes from the article "How to send Ether to 11,440 people" by Nick Johnson, and the trick itself is attributed to Vitalik Buterin (https://medium.com/@weka/how-to-send-ether-to-11-440-people-187e332566b7).

3. The user sends funds from an exchange to that single-use address.

4. Once the funds are received, the transaction is executed.

Note that if the transaction from the single-use address fails for any reason (whether it is a failed `require` in a contract or lack of gas), there is no way to issue a second transaction with the necessary fixes. This means that any funds that the user sent in step 3 will be effectively locked forever. As such, make sure to avoid using single-use addresses when a transaction could fail due to state changes.

As an example, the `Donations` contract from as in the previous section would be a poor choice, since the time while the donations are accepted is limited. A user may set up their single-use address while donations are open, but if they seed it after they close, then their funds will end up locked.

Another pitfall of single-use addresses is that they must be funded with the exact amount of ETH required for their execution. Any extra funds sent to the address are irretrievably lost. Make sure to clearly communicate this to your users!

Creating a Single-use Address

How are single-use addresses created? It is worth noting that they are not a special Ethereum construct, but the result of a clever hack. Also, creating them requires no initial gas at all.

Recall from previous chapters that all Ethereum transactions need to be signed with the sender's private key in order to be valid. The sender's address can then be derived from the transaction's signature, so the `from` is actually never included in the transaction's data – it's calculated from the signature when needed.

To recap, sending a transaction involves the following steps:

1. Pack the transaction parameters (recipient, gas, gas price, nonce, data, value, etc.) into a binary object.

2. Hash the transaction binary and sign it with the sender's private key.

3. Broadcast the transaction's binary and the signature.

On the other hand, processing a transaction involves the following:

4. Calculate the hash of the transaction binary.

5. Derive the sender's address (i.e., `from`) from the hash and the signature.

6. Unpack the transaction binary into its parameters (recipient, gas, gas price, nonce, data, value, etc.).

The trick for generating single-use addresses relies in sending a random signature with the transaction. Instead of actually signing the transaction in step 2, we just include a random set of bytes as a signature in step 3. This way, there is no private key associated with the process.

When processing the transaction, this results in a random sender address derived from the signature. And given that the private key associated with this address is unknown, it is not possible to generate any other transaction for the same address. This effectively yields a single-use address that can only broadcast one specific transaction. Then, as soon as the address is funded with ETH, the gas fees can be covered, and the transaction can be broadcasted to the network.

Sample Code

We will use a variant of the `Donations` example from the previous section, with a single beneficiary and a single donate method, which accepts a string to be emitted in an event along with each donation (Listing 7-4). We will then rely on a single-use address to interact with it.

Listing 7-4. Simplified Donations contract that accepts a custom string that is emitted in an event in every donation

```
// 02-single-use-addresses/contracts/Donations.sol
contract Donations {
  address payable wallet;

  event Donation(uint256 value, string text);

  constructor(address payable _wallet) public {
    wallet = _wallet;
  }
```

```
function donate(string calldata text) external payable {
  require(msg.value > 0);
  emit Donation(msg.value, text);
}

function withdraw() external { ... }
}
```

Let's assume that our user wants to send a 1 ETH donation with the traditional "Hello world". We need to first generate the encoded data that executes that function and estimate the gas cost for executing the call.

```
// 02-single-use-addresses/index.js
let donations = new web3.eth.Contract(abi, address);
let call = donations.methods.donate("Hello world");
let data = call.encodeABI();
let gas = await call.estimateGas({ value: 1e18 });
```

Caution   Keep in mind that actual gas usage may change depending on the state in which the transaction is executed. Due to the very nature of single-use addresses, if the transaction fails due to lack of gas, there is no way to execute it again with a higher allowance. This results in the user funds being locked in the address forever. If your function may end up consuming more gas in the future, make sure to account for it when building the transaction object in the upcoming steps.

We now have all the necessary parameters to craft our transaction with a random signature. To build this transaction object, we will use the ethereumjs-tx@1.3.7 library.

```
const Tx = require('ethereumjs-tx');
let tx = new Tx({
  value: 1e18,
  data,
  gas,
  gasPrice: 1e9,
  to: address,
```

```
  nonce: "0x0",
  v: networkId * 2 + 35,
  s: '0x' + '2'.repeat(61),
  r: '0x' + '3'.repeat(61)
});

let sender = tx.getSenderAddress().toString('hex');
```

Most parameters in the preceding snippet should be familiar by now: the recipient address, the amount of ETH being sent, the gas allowance and price, and the transaction data. Since this transaction will be sent from a new address that has sent no other transactions, the nonce must be zero.

The new parameters we see here are v, r, and s, which correspond to the transaction's signature. The first of them must be derived from the chain id,[3] while the two others are normally calculated from the user's private key – we will replace them by an arbitrary bytes sequence here.

Note   It is important to use a recognizable fabricated sequence as r and s, such as a clear repetition of the same set of bytes, or a large amount of leading zeroes. Otherwise, a third party cannot know whether the resulting transaction object belongs indeed to a single-use address, or the signature was obtained from an actual private key. If a private key was indeed used to generate the transaction, then its holder can generate a different transaction when the user sends their funds to the allegedly single-use address.

Now, if you try to run the preceding code to obtain the sender address, you will get an "Invalid Signature" error thrown by the getSenderAddress call. This is because not all signatures are valid in Ethereum – roughly half of them are. The easiest way around this is to just test with a few different values until we hit a valid arbitrary signature. For instance, we could increment r by one each time we get an invalid signature exception until we get to a valid value.

---

[3]See EIP 155 for more information (`https://github.com/ethereum/EIPs/blob/master/EIPS/eip-155.md`).

```
const BN = require('bignumber.js');
let sender = null;
while (!sender) {
  try {
    sender = '0x' + tx.getSenderAddress().toString('hex');
  } catch(ex) {
    const r = new BN('0x' + tx.r.toString('hex'));
    tx.r = '0x' + r.plus(1).toString(16);
  }
}
```

Armed with a valid pre-signed transaction, we can now try broadcasting it to the network.

```
const rawTx = '0x' + tx.serialize().toString('hex');
await web3.eth.sendSignedTransaction(rawTx);
```

However, since we have not yet funded the sender address, we will get a "sender doesn't have enough funds to send tx" error. Remember that the derived sender is a new account, so it will never have any previous funds.

At this point, we should ask our users to fund the derived single-use address and monitor for balance changes on the address to broadcast the transaction when it has enough funds. To do this, we first need to calculate the exact amount of ETH needed: this is the gas allowance multiplied by the gas price, plus any value sent in the transaction.

```
let required = (new BN(gas)).times(gasPrice).plus(value);
```

Caution   Remember that any extra ETH sent to a single-use address will be lost.

Let's now simulate that the user sends those funds to the single-use address.

```
const [funder] = await web3.eth.getAccounts();
await web3.eth.sendTransaction({
  from: funder, value: required, to: sender
});
```

We can now finally send our transaction to the network and verify that the event was correctly emitted.

```
let rawTx = '0x' + tx.serialize().toString('hex');
await web3.eth.sendSignedTransaction(rawTx);

let events = await donations.getPastEvents('Donation');
console.log(events[0].returnValues.text);
// prints "Hello world"
```

Application Local Accounts

While in the previous sections we saw a few tricks for interacting with a smart contract application without needing an Ethereum account, we will now look into another alternative: creating an account for the user *within* the application. Instead of asking the user to download a web3-enabled browser or install an extension, we can manage the entire flow of creating a wallet directly in our app. This allows any user who navigates to our application being instantly supplied with an Ethereum address to start interacting. On the other hand, we also need to provide means for our users to safely back up their new wallets – without becoming custodians of their funds.

Creating and Using a Local Wallet

Creating an Ethereum account requires a set of random bytes to derive a private key, from which the address is calculated. We can use the accounts set of methods from the web3@1.2.0 library to do so[4] (Listing 7-5), which will automatically pull the needed entropy from the browser's crypto API.

Listing 7-5. Creating an account using web3. Note that no connection to the network is needed to create a private key

```
let account = web3.eth.accounts.create();
```

---

[4]A lower-level alternative for creating and manipulating Ethereum accounts is the ethereumjs-wallet library (https://github.com/ethereumjs/ethereumjs-wallet).

We can now use the private key from this account object to sign a transaction and broadcast it to the network (Listing 7-6).

Listing 7-6. Signing a transaction for sending ETH with the account's private key and manually sending it to the network. Note that issuing this transaction requires seeding the sender address with some ETH

```
let tx = await web3.eth.accounts.signTransaction({
    to: account.address,
    value: 1e17,
    gas: 21000,
    gasPrice: 1e9 },
  account.privateKey);

await web3.eth.sendSignedTransaction(tx.rawTransaction);
```

To avoid having to generate, sign, and broadcast every transaction manually, the web3 library allows to register an account as a wallet (Listing 7-7), which will automatically use it for sending any transaction.

Listing 7-7. Registering an account as a wallet in web3. Any transaction sent from the wallet address will be automatically signed locally by the library and then sent to the network

```
web3.eth.accounts.wallet.add(account);
await web3.eth.sendTransaction({
  from: account.address,
  to: account.address,
  value: 1e17,
  gas: 21000
});
```

Note   Recall from previous chapters that Metamask achieves a similar behavior using a web3 subprovider. Instead of relying on the node to sign a transaction, the transaction is intercepted, signed client-side, and then broacbasted.

Encrypted Keystores

The following question is *how* to store the user's wallet after generating it. The most direct approach is to just keep the private key in the browser's local storage, so when the user visits our site again, we can easily reconstruct the account object.

```
// Store private key in local storage
localStorage.setItem("ethereum_pk", account.privateKey);

// Load private key from local storage and re-create account
let pk = localStorage.getItem("ethereum_pk");
let account = web3.eth.accounts.privateKeyToAccount(pk);
```

However, this option is extremely insecure, as the browser's local storage should never be used to keep sensitive information, since it is vulnerable to XSS attacks[5] – not to mention the fact that the keys are lost if the user clears the site data or loses the device. Storing plain private keys like this is only recommended when managing very low amounts of ETH and loss of funds is acceptable, in other words, when usability is prioritized over security.[6]

A safer approach is to encrypt the private key (Listing 7-8) before storing it – whether it is on the browser's local storage, on a remote server, downloaded to the user's computer, or synced across cloud storage. Ethereum's *wallet v3 format* is a standardized JSON that holds a private key encrypted with a password and is not easy to crack.[7] It is used under the hood by the nodes to store your keys and can also be used in the browser to encrypt your users' accounts before storing them.

---

[5]See the OWASP HTML5 security cheat sheet for more info (`https://github.com/OWASP/ CheatSheetSeries/blob/c8330995864c14ab2124e23f8fd48c201f522f05/cheatsheets/HTML5_ Security_Cheat_Sheet.md#local-storage`).

[6]A great example of such a project is Austin Griffith's Burner Wallet, which is designed to hold no more than 20 USD worth of ETH. It delivers an excellent experience by not getting in the way of the user asking for passwords or mnemonics (`https://github.com/austintgriffith/ burner-wallet`).

[7]See this answer by Taylor Monahan on the security of the Ethereum wallet v3: `https://ethereum.stackexchange.com/a/37177/8846`

Listing 7-8. Encrypting a user's private key with a password to generate a v3
keystore object. The converse method, decrypt, takes the keystore and password
and returns the decrypted account object

```
$ web3.eth.accounts.encrypt(account.privateKey, 'PASSWORD');
> { version: 3,
  id: 'b8c62b04-041c-49d6-966a-205bb5f70528',
  address: 'af0a9c8d7f74dff1ce64f9c322108c336502bbd4',
  crypto:
   { ciphertext: 'ba09a90b5...7b0e5e24da79d7f9efda613fd298',
     cipherparams: { iv: '2e72184026373b69d21ce157b1d93bba' },
     cipher: 'aes-128-ctr',
     kdf: 'scrypt',
     kdfparams:
      { dklen: 32,
        salt: 'eab3860a...d1d378abbc55a65cae3c83e0a39e',
        n: 8192,
        r: 8,
        p: 1 },
     mac: '60177f2af3...bd900315e46e2d' } }
```

While this is a much more secure option, it introduces additional complexity by
requesting a password from the user. Even though passwords are a common annoyance
to web users, they are also used to being able to *reset* them whenever they forget them –
an option that is not available in this case. If a user forgets the password to their keystore,
its contents are lost for good.

In addition to this problem, the keystore itself must not be misplaced. If you are
storing the encrypted private key just in the browser and the user happens to clear local
data or simply loses the device, then all funds are gone with it. You must ensure that
users perform proper backups (asking them to download the keystore from your page
and saving it elsewhere) or save them on a safe location in one of your application's
servers (assuming you have one!).

Note   There is a big difference between acting as a custodian of your users' funds and acting as a backup location for storing their encrypted private keys. While on the former any hack to your servers implies a loss of funds to your users, the latter is just a convenience for your users to keep their encrypted keys secure.

However, this difference may not be so big from a legal standpoint. Make sure to inform yourself on legal requirements in your jurisdiction if you do store users' encrypted keystores server-side.

Mnemonics

A decentralized alternative for backing up your user keys is to generate a *mnemonic*. Mnemonics are sequences of words (usually between 12 and 24) that can be easily written down by a human for safekeeping, and you have probably already stumbled upon them when creating an account in a wallet. Keep in mind that they are meant just as a means of backup if the keystore is lost, as it is not reasonable to ask your users for a 24-word sequence every time they want to use your application.

The main benefit of mnemonics is that they provide a way to store digital information (a private key) in a traditional physical medium (a piece of paper). This way, even if a user gets all their electronic devices stolen or hacked, they can still rely on an old-fashioned method for restoring their accounts.

Unfortunately, it is not possible to generate a mnemonic from a private key. As we have seen in Chapter 5, the derivation process is one way: the mnemonic is used to calculate an extended key, from which one or more private keys are derived in turn. This means that if you want to allow your users to back up their accounts via this method, you need to build it from scratch.

To create a mnemonic and derive a seed from it, we will use the `bip39` library. To create a hierarchical deterministic wallet from it and derive a private key, we will use the `ethereumjs-wallet` library (Listing 7-9).

Listing 7-9. Creating a mnemonic and deriving the corresponding private key. Note that more private keys can be generated from the same mnemonic by using different derivation paths

```
// 03-mnemonics/index.js
const hdkey = require("ethereumjs-wallet/hdkey");
const bip39 = require("bip39");

let mnemonic = bip39.generateMnemonic();
> sadness brief beauty strike donor capable recipe brand pretty hill orange
inflict

let hd = hdkey.fromMasterSeed(bip39.mnemonicToSeed(mnemonic));
let path = "m/44'/60'/0'/0/0";
let wallet = hdwallet.derivePath(path).getWallet();
let pk = wallet.getPrivateKeyString();
> 0xdc68f9ce62dd1f16eed...5f7feba7b3284d9
```

This snippet allows you to generate a mnemonic for your users' accounts. Just note that your users need to save the mnemonic somewhere safe before refreshing the page, since you should never store the plain sequence of words anywhere, as it is as insecure as storing the unencrypted private key.

Up to this point, we have added several mechanisms for ensuring the security of your users' funds, such as encrypting their private keys with a password, and providing an easy-to-write set of words for backing them up.

However, we have also reproduced the same complexity that we were trying to avoid in the first place – the complexity that prevents most users from actually getting onboard on Ethereum. Though we will see other approaches, the key takeaway from this section is for you to know the tools available, so you can settle for the proper balance between security, usability, and decentralization that best fits your application.

Smart Accounts

Local wallets have several shortcomings: not only they require additional steps for safekeeping, but they also offer very limited options for users accessing your application from multiple different devices. Even though you could rely on cloud services for synchronizing the encrypted private key across your user's devices, revoking access from a device is out of the question. To make matters worse, additional security measures such as two-factor authentication for critical transactions cannot be implemented without trusting funds to a custodian.

Fortunately, we already have a decentralized and secure computing platform we can rely upon for building any additional security or recovery features for our users' accounts. It is a matter of moving their very accounts to the blockchain as contracts.

Identities as Smart Contracts

The key concept behind *smart accounts*, also referred to as *identity contracts*, is that the user identity (along with its funds) is represented by a single smart contract instead of one or several externally owned accounts. The user controls a contract that forwards his or her calls to other applications and centrally holds the user's assets. Managing this identity from a new device is simply a matter of registering a new externally owned account as a manager of the contract.

Note   Research on these contracts has gone under the name of identity contracts, smart accounts, bouncer proxies, multisig wallets, or wallet contracts. These contracts have usually gone hand in hand with meta transactions or gas relays, which we will review later in this chapter. While it is difficult to identify the first person who came up with this idea, it is worth mentioning Alex Van de Sande, Philippe Castonguay, Panashe Mahachi, Austin Griffith, Christian Lundkvist, and Fabian Vogelsteller for their work on this topic. Work on this area has also been inspired by the Account Abstraction Proposal[8] by Vitalik Buterin, which aims at merging externally owned and contract accounts into a single type and moving the burden of signature verification onto the EVM.

---

[8] *Tradeoffs in Account Abstraction Proposals* by Vitalik Buterin (`https://ethresear.ch/t/tradeoffs-in-account-abstraction-proposals/263`).

Moving the user's identity to a smart contract allows us to implement any kind of account management features that our users are accustomed to, but in a trustless manner, directly on-chain:

- The user can register multiple devices, where each device has its own externally owned account, to manage the same identity contract.

- Different keys can have different access levels: from managing the identity contract itself to just being able to transfer a limited amount of funds.

- Major transactions can require more than one key to confirm the operation, effectively imposing a two-factor authentication (2FA) for critical operations.

- Social recovery of the account can be implemented by designating a group of trusted parties. This means you could pick a circle of close friends who could, all together, grant you access back to your identity contract in the event that you lose your keys. This could even be extended to testaments.

Keep in mind that using smart accounts does not remove the need for generating local externally owned accounts. Our application will still need to create a local key per device to manage the identity contract if the user does not already have a web3-enabled browser. The improvement on using smart contracts over regular accounts lies on the additional security and recovery features that can be implemented in a decentralized manner – for instance, social recovery can be used as a replacement for writing down a 24-word mnemonic.

Sample Implementation

The simplest version of an identity account (Listing 7-10) should handle two main concerns: managing the list of the user accounts authorized to operate on the contract and forwarding calls and transfers.

Listing 7-10. A very basic identity contract with support for managing user accounts and forwarding calls

```solidity
// 04-identity-contracts/contracts/Identity.sol
pragma solidity ^0.5.0;

contract Identity {
  mapping(address => bool) public accounts;
  event AccountAdded(address indexed account);
  event AccountRemoved(address indexed account);

  constructor(address owner) public payable {
    accounts[owner] = true;
    emit AccountAdded(owner);
  }

  modifier onlyUser {
    require(accounts[msg.sender], "Sender is not recognized");
    _;
  }

  function addAccount(address newAccount) onlyUser public {
    accounts[newAccount] = true;
    emit AccountAdded(newAccount);
  }

  function removeAccount(address toRemove) onlyUser public {
    accounts[toRemove] = false;
    emit AccountRemoved(toRemove);
  }

  // Forward arbitrary calls and funds to a third party
  function forward(
    address to, uint256 value, bytes memory data
  ) onlyUser public returns (bytes memory) {
    (bool success, bytes memory returnData) =
      to.call.value(value)(data);
    require(success, "Forwarded call failed");
    return returnData;
  }
```

```
  // Empty fallback function to accept deposits
  function() external payable { }
}
```

When this contract is first deployed, the user's first account is registered. Any new account from a new device can then be registered from a previous one (Listing 7-11).

Listing 7-11. Creating an identity contract funded with 10 ETH and adding a second device. In this example, `mainDevice` and `anotherDevice` are accounts created on the user's devices

```
// 04-identity-contracts/index.js
const identity = await new web3.eth.Contract(identityAbi)
  .deploy({ arguments: [mainDevice], data: identityBytecode })
  .send({ from: mainDevice, gasPrice: 1e9, value: 10e18 });

await identity.methods.addAccount(anotherDevice)
  .send({ from: mainDevice });
```

Any of the two registered accounts can then use the `forward` method to send funds from the identity to a third party (Listing 7-12).

Listing 7-12. Sending funds from the identity contract using `anotherDevice`

```
const emptyData = [];
await identity.methods
  .forward(thirdParty, 1e18.toString(), emptyData)
  .send({ from: anotherDevice });

await web3.eth.getBalance(identity.options.address);
// => 9 ETH

await web3.eth.getBalance(thirdParty);
// => +1 ETH
```

Calling into another contract is similar; it just requires encoding the call to the contract and providing it as data to the forwarding function (Listing 7-13). For example, we can call the setGreeter method from the Greeter contract we coded in previous chapters.

Listing 7-13. Calling the setGreeting method of a greeter contract instance from the identity, including 5000 Wei in the transaction

```
const data = greeter.methods.setGreeting("Hey").encodeABI();
await identity.methods
  .forward(greeter.options.address, "5000", data)
  .send({ from: anotherDevice });

await greeter.methods.greet().call();
// => "Hey"
```

Most of the features discussed previously can be implemented on top of this base contract: accounts can be assigned different clearance levels, while restrictions based on the value transferred can be imposed on the forwarding function.

A good example of this is a multi-signature wallet.[9] These contracts are designed to have a number N of accounts registered, and every transaction requires at least M (with M < N) confirmations. While they are often used for safekeeping of large amounts of funds by distributing the keys among different members of a team, they can also be used for managing personal funds by assigning different keys to different devices.

Deploying a Smart Account (Take One)

Given that the focus of this chapter is to make user onboarding easier, requiring the user to not only generate a local externally owned account but also to deploy a contract, fund it, and register their devices on it seems like a step (or many) on the opposite direction.

Nevertheless, many of these steps can be carried on by the application on behalf of the user – including deployments. After the user has performed a certain number of actions within our system, we can opt to deploy the identity contract on their behalf and transfer ownership of it to their account. Even though this implies costs in gas fees, in many cases this subsidy can be considered to be a necessary cost involved in user acquisition.

---

[9]See Gnosis' MultiSigWallet for an excellent implementation (https://github.com/gnosis/MultiSigWallet).

However, a more decentralized (and cheaper for us) option is to rely on single-use addresses for setting up the contract. Our application can generate a local wallet behind the scenes to act as the initial owner of the identity contract (if the user does not have a web3 browser already), as well as a single-use address that can trigger the deployment and configuration of the smart account once funded. When the single-use address is funded from an exchange, the identity is deployed and seeded with a predefined amount of ETH. From that point on, the user operates directly via their new identity contract.

Note   Remember from the single-use addresses section that any extra funds sent to the address are irretrievably lost. The user must choose how much ETH they want to initially send to their identity and then create the transaction and fund it with exactly the resulting amount.

Generating a single-use address for deploying a contract is similar to calling into a contract, with the difference that the transaction must be sent to the null address (Listing 7-14).

Listing 7-14. Transaction parameters for deploying a contract. Note that the recipient is set as null, as we are creating a new contract instead of interacting with an existing one. Signature parameters are set as shown in the single-use addresses section of this chapter

```
// 05-single-use-address-deploy-identity-contract/index.js
let call = new web3.eth.Contract(identityABI)
  .deploy({ arguments:[owner], data: identityBytecode });
let data = call.encodeABI(); // Encode data for deployment
let gas = await call.estimateGas();
let gasPrice = 1e9;
let value = 1e18; // Seed identity with 1ETH on deployment
let nonce = "0x00";
let to = null; // Set tx recipient to null
```

Another interesting property of this approach is that, since contract creation addresses are deterministic, it is possible to show the user their identity contract address *even before it is deployed* (Listing 7-15). The address where a contract is deployed is a function of the sender's address and nonce.

Listing 7-15. Precalculating the deployment address using the `ethereumjs-util` library

```
const Util = require('ethereumjs-util');
let deploymentAddress = '0x' + Util.generateAddress(
  Buffer.from(sender.substring(2), 'hex'),
  Buffer.from(nonce, 'hex')
).toString('hex')
```

However, an issue with this approach is that we are showing the user two different addresses: one address that he needs to fund one time for the deployment and another that will actually be their identity contract. This, compounded with the fact that any extra ETH sent to the address is lost, damages the user experience when setting up their smart account. We will analyze a more robust approach later in this chapter after we become familiarized with the concept of meta transactions.

Note   A much simpler option is to just have the user transfer their funds to their device account, whether it is local to our application or is managed by the web3 browser, and execute the deployment from it. However, this still has the issue of presenting two addresses to the user – one for initial funding and one for the identity.

Upgrading User Accounts

As we have seen, identity contracts can pack multiple features for your users, such as two-factor authentication, social recovery, daily transfer limits, and more. This begs the question of *what* to build into these contracts. As contracts are immutable, any change to add a new feature would require your users to ditch their current identity and deploy a new one. However, forcing a user to move all their assets to a new contract is the equivalent of forcing them to move to a new email account whenever they want access to a new feature – including changing their email in all online services they may be using.

Nevertheless, it is possible in Ethereum to actually upgrade a contract after it has been deployed, thus allowing iterative deployment and bugfixing as in traditional software development. To implement this, we first need to become familiarized with the concept of *delegate calls* in the Ethereum Virtual Machine, or EVM.

The DELEGATECALL Instruction

A regular CALL from one contract to another in the EVM works as a call from an actor or process to another: a new context is created, where the state (storage and balance) of the callee is loaded, the caller is set to `msg.sender`, and the code of the callee is executed. On the other hand, a DELEGATECALL works by executing the code of the callee but *maintaining the original context of the caller*. In other words, storage, balance, and even `msg.sender` are not changed by a DELEGATECALL – only the code being executed is.

This low-level instruction allows us to jump into an arbitrary contract and execute its code, where that code actually modifies the state of the current contract. The called contract then acts as a library,[10] being used only as a repository of shared code, but not using its state.

Delegating Proxies

The DELEGATECALL instruction allows us to build a contract that simply delegates all calls to another contract which holds the actual logic to be executed. These contracts are usually called *delegating proxies*, since they delegate all calls to another contract, or *transparent proxies*, as any client interacting with them is oblivious to their existence. The contract being called by the proxy that holds the code being actually executed is usually called *logic contract*, *implementation contract*, or *master copy*.

A delegating proxy (Listing 7-16) can be implemented in Solidity as a contract that keeps the address of its implementation contract as its only state variable and only has a fallback function in which it delegates all calls to it. The proxy will receive the implementation address in its constructor and optionally `calldata` to initialize it.

Listing 7-16. Implementation of a delegating proxy contract based on the code from `github.com/zeppelinos/zos`. Note the usage of assembly in the fallback function, since Solidity does not allow a fallback function to return arbitrary data. And if we did not return any data, then any calls to our contract would yield an empty response

```
// 06-upgrading-identity-contracts/contracts/DelegateProxy.sol
contract DelegateProxy {
  // Stores address in the first slot
```

---

[10]Calls to Solidity libraries are implemented using this instruction.

```
// Target contract must define address as the first variable
address private implementation;

constructor(
  address _implementation,
  bytes memory _data
) public payable {
  implementation = _implementation;
  if (_data.length > 0) {
    (bool success,) = _implementation.delegatecall(_data);
    require(success);
  }
}

// Fallback function delegates all calls to implementation
function () payable external {
  address impl = implementation;
  assembly {
    calldatacopy(0, 0, calldatasize)
    let result := delegatecall(
      gas, impl, 0, calldatasize, 0, 0
    )
    returndatacopy(0, 0, returndatasize)
    switch result
    case 0 { revert(0, returndatasize) }
    default { return(0, returndatasize) }
  }
}
}
```

Caution   Upgradeability in the EVM can be very tricky to implement correctly, and it imposes some restrictions. For instance, a proxy contract cannot execute a constructor of a logic contract when it is created, so any contract to be upgradeable needs to rely on regular functions that act as *initializers.* Another issue is that updating a proxy to a logic contract with a different set of state variables may also inadvertently corrupt the contract's state. If you are planning on relying on upgradeable contracts in your application, whether they are smart accounts or any other contract, it is strongly recommended that you use an existing upgradeability solution instead of rolling out your own.

The key concept here is that the address of the logic contract does not need to be hard-coded into the proxy – it can actually be kept in storage. When this address is changed, this effectively updates the code being executed by the proxy while keeping its state and address. We can now add this feature to our identity contracts.

Upgradeable Identities

Armed with this new building block, we can deploy a single identity contract to act as a logic contract and deploy one proxy for each of our users. Remember that since all state is kept in the proxy, there is no need for more than one copy of the logic contract, and a single one can be shared (like a library) among multiple proxies.

This not only saves gas in deployments, since proxy contracts are much smaller (and thus cheaper) than identity contracts, but also allows our users to upgrade to a different identity contract whenever they want. Let's build the *upgrade* feature into our new upgradeable identities (Listing 7-17).

Listing 7-17. Variant of the identity contract with support for upgradeability. Note that the first contract variable is the implementation contract address, and the constructor has been replaced by a regular function that relies on a flag to keep track of whether the instance has been initialized or not. Upgrading to a different identity implementation just requires changing the implementation address in the first position of storage

```
// 06-upgrading-identity-contracts/.../UpgradeableIdentity.sol
contract UpgradeableIdentity {
  // First variable is used for the implementation contract
  // Remember that the proxy uses the same variable position!
  address private implementation;

  // Keep track whether this instance has been initialized
  bool private initialized;

  // Initializer function instead of a constructor
  function initialize(address owner) public payable {
    require(!initialized);
    initialized = true;
    accounts[owner] = true;
    emit AccountAdded(owner);
  }
  // Upgrades to a new implementation
  function upgradeTo(
    address newImplementation
  ) onlyUserAccount public {
    implementation = newImplementation;
  }

  // The rest of the Identity contract code goes here...
}
```

Keep in mind that any state variables defined on this contract will not be actually stored on this contract's storage, but in the proxy's – thanks to the magic of delegate calls. For instance, the `initialized` flag is not actually set on the single `UpgradeableIdentity` contract deployed as a shared implementation, but is set on each of the proxies that are backed by it.

Because of this, the first variable declared on this contract must be the implementation address, as in the proxy. Also, the contract cannot extend from any base contract that defines additional contract variables. This ensures that the implementation address is stored in the same position in storage as where the proxy will look for it.[11]

Note   Contract upgradeability is a contentious issue for many in Ethereum. Having immutable contracts allows users to trust an application by knowing that the rules defined by it will not be subject to change. Adding upgradeability breaks this guarantee. However, this is not an issue with upgradeability itself, but with *who* can decide when a contract is upgraded. Having a decentralized token being controlled by a single developer who can unilaterally modify the contract by, let's say, adding a transaction tax, is definitely not good. On the other hand, a contract that has a clear owner (or set of owners) is a good candidate to be upgradeable – and in this an identity contract is a perfect example.

Creating an identity contract for a user now implies deploying not a contract instance but a proxy – assuming we have already deployed the single shared implementation contract (Listing 7-18).

Listing 7-18. Creating a proxy to an identity contract. Note that we need to use the logic contract ABI to build the initialization data and then use it when deploying the proxy

```
// 06-upgrading-identity-contracts/index.js
// Logic contract is a pre-deployed instance of Identity
let logic = new web3.eth.Contract(identityABI, identityAddr);

// Build initialization data to call initialize(user)
// when the proxy is created
let initData = logic.methods.initialize(user).encodeABI();
```

---

[11]Several proxy implementations avoid this issue by relying on the unstructured storage pattern for storing the implementation address, that is, storing it in a random place in storage that will never be allocated by the compiler. Read more about it at https://blog.zeppelinos.org/upgradeability-using-unstructured-storage/

```
// Deploy the proxy using the identity contract as
// its implementation, and setting user as its initial owner
let proxy = await new web3.eth.Contract(proxyABI, null, { data: proxyBin })
  .deploy({ arguments: [logic.options.address, initData] })
  .send({ from: application, gasPrice: 1e9, value: 1e18 });
```

After the proxy is deployed, we can interact with it as if it were a regular identity contract. We need to create a new web3 contract object using the identity contract ABI, with the proxy's address (Listing 7-19).

Listing 7-19. Interacting with the newly deployed proxy as if it were a regular identity contract. The proxy will delegate all calls to the logic contract and behave exactly like one

```
let proxyAddr = proxy.options.address;
let identity = new web3.eth.Contract(identityABI, proxyAddr);
await identity.methods
  .addAccount(anotherDevice)
  .send({ from: user });
```

As with any other method from the identity contract, the user can call into the upgrade function and switch to a different implementation (Listing 7-20). It is important to note though that the new implementation must have the same contract state variables as the original one; otherwise, the proxy's state may be corrupted.

Listing 7-20. Upgrading to a V2 of the identity contract. The user's identity address is unmodified, as is its balance and state, but it has access to new code with potentially new features and bugfixes

```
await identity.methods
  .upgradeTo(identityV2addr)
  .send({ from: user });
```

Implementing this pattern in smart accounts allows us to iteratively develop our application by gradually adding support for new features or fixing bugs and allows our users to adopt them when they want.

A good example of a feature we may want to add to our identity contracts is meta transaction support, which we will see in the next section.

Gasless Transactions

One of the root problems on user onboarding is that interacting with the Ethereum network requires ETH to begin with in order to be able to pay for gas fees. This involves an annoying set of steps just to make an initial ETH purchase with other currency. Gas fees are also problematic in multi-device solutions: all of a user's devices must hold a bit of ETH just to run any transactions, even when relying on a smart account to centralize the user identity.

All of the above means that removing the requirement of gas for issuing Ethereum transactions yields major benefits in terms of usability. *Gasless transactions*, also referred to as *meta transactions*, tackle this problem by offering a mechanism to decouple the author of the transaction from the payer of the gas. In other words, an account can issue a transaction, while other pays for its execution. This allows users in your application to execute any transactions without needing to worry about having ETH to pay for their gas fees.

Note   Gasless transactions is one of the most actively developed techniques in the Ethereum ecosystem at the time of this writing, and already has many different flavors. This makes this section one of the most complex ones in the book. Feel free to gloss over the technical details, and consider looking into already established libraries, such as Universal Login, Marmo, or the Gas Station Network.

Signatures in Ethereum

To understand gasless transactions, we first need to review how signatures work in Ethereum. As we have seen before, an Ethereum transaction needs to be cryptographically *signed* with the sender's private key in order to be valid. However, the user's key can be used to sign not just a transaction, but any arbitrary message (Listing 7-21).

Listing 7-21. Using web3 to sign a message from a user with their private key[12]

```
// 07-signing-messages/index.js
// Import web3 and create an instance without a provider
// since we will not be connecting to a node for now
> const Web3 = require('web3');
> const web3 = new Web3();

// Sample address and corresponding private key
> let address = '0xaca94ef8bd5ffee41947b4585a84bda5a3d3da6e';
> let pk = '0x829e924fdf021ba3dbbc4225ed' +
           'fece9aca04b929d6e75613329ca6f1d31c0bb4';

// Sign the hash of an arbitrary message
> let message = 'Hello world'
> let hash = web3.utils.keccak256(message);
> let signed = web3.eth.accounts.sign(hash, pk)
> signed.signature
0x7fcfb176706502a00e58f74c15cd8151309d8b8a777eefd387eabc760a1aa7f6705699
d1431155dfc7b1b1d7d88b3b24d07180107572b127a558b7a8b118cb4d1b
```

Note   Behind the scenes, web3 `sign` method prefixes the message with the string `"\x19Ethereum Signed Message:\n"` and its length and then hashes it before signing. This is done to avoid tricking users into signing an actual transaction. Most APIs, even those part of the nodes or in hardware wallets, will handle this automatically.

Given the original message and its signature, it is possible to recover the address that corresponds to the private key used to sign it in the first place.

```
> hash = web3.utils.keccak256(message);
> web3.eth.accounts.recover(hash, signed.signature)
0xACa94ef8bD5ffEE41947b4585a84BdA5a3d3DA6E
```

---

[12]Ethereum nodes also expose a method eth_sign that signs a message with an unlocked account in case the user's private key is not available in memory but is handled by the node.

The recovery can be done not just from an off-chain script but also from within a smart contract (Listing 7-22), as Solidity provides an `ecrecover` function that performs this task.[13] We will use it via the ECDSA contract from the `openzeppelin-solidity@2.2.0` library, which offers a friendlier interface and performs additional checks.

Listing 7-22. Simple contract that relies on OpenZeppelin's ECDSA to recover the signer from a message and its signature

```
// 07-signing-messages/contracts/Signatures.sol
pragma solidity ^0.5.0;

import "openzeppelin-solidity/contracts/cryptography/ECDSA.sol";

contract Signatures {
  using ECDSA for bytes32;

  function recover(
    string memory message, bytes memory signature
  ) public pure returns (address) {
    bytes32 hash = keccak256(bytes(message));
    return hash.toEthSignedMessageHash().recover(signature);
  }
}
```

We can check that calling the recover function from the preceding contract using the same parameters as before yields the same signer (Listing 7-23).

Listing 7-23. Recovering the signer from the original message using the smart contract listed before. Here, `signatures` is a web3 contract instance that represents a deployed instance of the smart contract

```
> await signatures.methods
    .recover(message, signed.signature).call();
0xACa94ef8bD5ffEE41947b4585a84BdA5a3d3DA6E
```

---

[13]Given the complexity of this function, it is implemented as a *precompiled contract*; otherwise, the math required to execute it would be prohibitive in terms of gas. When ecrecover is used in Solidity, it actually executes a call to a contract in address 0x1 that performs the calculation and returns the result. Each client implements the logic for that contract natively instead of via EVM assembly.

Ethereum signatures are typically used off-chain to verify that a user controls a certain account, or that the owner of an account signals an intention (for instance, in off-chain voting) by signing a specific message. But signatures can also be used on-chain to verify that the owner of an account intends to *execute* a certain action. This is where meta transactions come in.

Introducing Meta Transactions

A *meta transaction* or *gasless transaction* is similar to a regular transaction in that it is a signed tuple of a recipient, an amount of ETH transferred, a set of data included in the call, a gas allowance and price, and a nonce. However, instead of being broadcasted to the network, the meta transaction is wrapped within another transaction and sent to a particular contract. This contract knows how to unwrap the nested transaction, verify its signature, and execute the requested action.

Note that the contract that first receives and processes the transaction is actually reproducing the same behavior as the Ethereum protocol: it verifies the nested transaction signature and nonce and performs a call to a recipient with the specified value and data.

What is the value of meta transactions then? The key is that the meta transaction can be *relayed* to the network by a different account than the one who signed the original intent. This decouples the user who intends to execute an action and the user who pays for its gas, effectively *allowing any user to execute a transaction without requiring any gas*, that is, as long as another user is willing to pay for it. Meta transactions involve two main actors then:

- The user, who signs a meta transaction that they want to be executed, but does not send it to the network

- The relayer, who picks up that transaction, wraps it in another transaction of their own, and sends it to a contract, paying for its execution

We will go into relayers later in this chapter. Let's dive into the implementation of meta transactions first, at the smart contract level.

Building on Our Smart Accounts

Meta transactions require a contract that can process them, validate them, check that the signer is authorized to perform the action requested, and carry it out on their behalf. Fortunately, we already have a contract that can hold funds and carry actions on behalf of different accounts held by a user: the identity contract.

We will modify the identity contract we have been building to handle meta transactions. Our forwarding function will now receive a meta transaction pre-signed by one of the user accounts instead of a direct call from one of them.

This way, instead of having to actually send a transaction to the identity contract, the user can just sign an action and have a relayer send it. This allows the user to **hold all of their funds in a single smart account, without requiring any ETH on their devices to pay for gas fees**. Let's see how this looks like in a modified identity contract (Listing 7-24).

Listing 7-24. Modified forward function from the Identity contract (presented earlier in this chapter) to handle meta transactions

```
// 08-meta-txs/contracts/IdentityWithMetaTxs.sol
// Prevent replay attacks
uint256 public nonce;

// Use ECDSA library for retrieving the signer
using ECDSA for bytes32;

// Forward an action to a recipient validating the signer
// Note that the onlyUser modifier is no longer needed
function forward(
  address to, uint256 value, bytes memory data,
  bytes memory signature
) public returns (bytes memory) {
  // Get hash of the transaction that was signed
  bytes32 hash = getHash(to, value, data)
    .toEthSignedMessageHash();

  // Retrieve signer address and validate
  address signer = hash.recover(signature);
  require(accounts[signer], "Signer is not registered");
```

```
  // Increase nonce and execute the call
  nonce++;
  (bool success, bytes memory returnData) =
    to.call.value(value)(data);
  require(success, "Forwarded call failed");
  return returnData;
}

// Returns the hash for a pre-signed transaction
function getHash(
  address to, uint256 value, bytes memory data
) public view returns (bytes32) {
  return keccak256(abi.encodePacked(
    to, value, data, nonce, address(this)
  ));
}
```

The first thing to notice is that the forward method requires a `signature` as well as its original parameters. This signature is computed over a hash that includes all transaction parameters (recipient, value, and data), plus two additional items:

- The address of the validator, which is the contract checking the signature

- A nonce, increased on every transaction executed

The address of the validator is included to prevent a meta transaction sent to another validator to be reused in this one, while the nonce prevents replay attacks (i.e., relaying the same transaction multiple times). The resulting hash gets the magic prefix `"\x19Ethereum Signed Message:\n"` prepended, so it is distinguishable from a regular Ethereum transaction, and is then hashed again.

Note   Certain implementations track a nonce per signer instead of one global to the contract. This depends strictly on your use case: if it is possible that multiple whitelisted accounts will be sending meta transactions at the same time, then you should have signer-specific nonces.

Next is the validation of the sender. Note that the contract no longer checks that msg.sender is a registered account – it now checks that the *signer* of the transaction is. The msg.sender becomes irrelevant, since who relayed the transaction does not matter at this stage.

Finally, and before executing the transaction, the nonce is increased. This prevents the same transaction to be sent to the contract multiple times by a malicious relayer.

Note   It is worth mentioning that almost all smart account, identity contract, or bouncer proxy implementations include some variant of meta transactions. Once the user identity is moved on-chain, it does not make sense to keep them bound to the restrictions of the protocol, such as having the sender account pay for the gas of its transactions.

Sending Meta Transactions

We will pick up the example from the smart accounts section, this time by sending a meta transaction to a Greeter contract from our Identity contract. The first step (Listing 7-25) is for the user to sign the transaction to be executed.

Listing 7-25. User crafts and signs transaction to be relayed. Here pk is the private key of the user, and greeter is an instance of a contract which has a setGreeting method

```
// 08-meta-txs/01-identity-with-meta-txs.js
let recipient = greeter.options.address;
let value = 5000;
let data = greeter.methods.setGreeting("Hey").encodeABI();
let hash = await identity.methods
  .getHash(recipient, value, data).call();
let signature = web3.eth.accounts.sign(hash, pk).signature;
```

The resulting transaction, along with its signature, is then sent to a relayer via HTTP or another off-chain transport. The relayer should validate the transaction, wrap it, and then send it to the user's identity contract (Listing 7-26).

Listing 7-26. Relayer calls into the forwarding function of the identity contract with the parameters and the signature provided by the user. The identity contract will in turn call into the greeter, which changes its state

```
await identity.methods
  .forward(recipient, value, data, signature)
  .send({ from: relayer });

await greeter.methods.greet().call();
// => Hey
```

We are deliberately omitting from this example how the user communicates with the relayer or how the relayer decides whether to pay for the user's transaction. This will vary from application to application. For instance, an application could provide a centralized relayer at a well-known URL, which pays for every transaction to a contract in their system. It may also force users to go through a CAPTCHA to prevent spamming.

There are also efforts toward building fully decentralized relayer networks, in which the logic on whether paying for a user transaction is actually part of the application's smart contracts. These efforts also include approaches where the relayers are paid back for their execution, as we will see in the next section.[14]

Relayers and Rewards

The relayer is ultimately a process with a public interface (usually HTTP) that accepts signed messages from users, validates them, wraps them in a transaction, and pushes them to the network. For this last step, the relayer uses an account of its own – the gas fees are deducted from that account's balance.

In all of our examples so far, we have assumed that the gas cost for executing the meta transactions was covered by the owner of the application. This owner would spin up a relayer and freely forward all transactions for users of their own application.

However, it is possible for the users to actually *pay back* to the relayer serving them. An addition to the forwarding function is to send some ETH back to the relayer (i.e., the `msg.sender`) to cover the costs of the execution. This way, the user does pay the gas fees

---

[14]See `https://gasstation.network`

associated with their transactions – only that they are paid from their smart account, entirely removing the need to keep ETH for gas in each of their devices.

This opens the door for new incentive systems: the relayer does not need to be centralized by the application owner and subsidize the execution costs, but it can be decentralized and just profit from relaying transactions. This leads to a new concept of *desktop mining*, where users can earn fees not from computational-intensive proof-of-work, but from relaying meta transactions for other users.

Relayer Reward

The easiest way to implement a payback to the relayer is to include a *reward* along with each request for execution. The relayer can then decide whether to relay the transaction or not, depending on the estimated execution cost for it.

The user can even request a specific gas price and gas allowance for its transaction and verify that these are satisfied within the identity contract. This prevents relayers from sending transactions with very low gas prices, paying lower fees at the expense of a user's time.

Let's modify the forwarding function once again to account for all of the above (Listing 7-27). We will need to add parameters for specifying both the reward and the gas requirements and have these signed by the user as well.

Listing 7-27. Forwarding function of the identity contract with support for relayer rewards. The modified sections are highlighted in bold

```
// 08-meta-txs/contracts/IdentityWithRewards.sol
event Forwarded(uint256 nonce, bool success, address relayer);

function forward(
  uint256 reward, uint256 gasPrice, uint256 gasLimit,
  address to, uint256 value, bytes memory data,
  bytes memory signature
) public returns (bytes memory) {

  // Validate gas price of the transaction
  require(tx.gasPrice >= gasPrice, "Gas price too low");
```

```solidity
// Get hash of the transaction that was signed
bytes32 hash = getHash(
  reward, gasPrice, gasLimit, to, value, data
).toEthSignedMessageHash();

// Retrieve signer address and validate
address signer = hash.recover(signature);
require(accounts[signer], "Signer not registered");

// Increase nonce, execute call, and inform success
nonce++;
require(gasleft() >= gasLimit);
(bool success, bytes memory returnData) =
  to.call.value(value).gas(gasLimit)(data);
emit Forwarded(nonce, success, msg.sender);

// Pay back to the relayer
msg.sender.transfer(reward);
return returnData;
}

function getHash(
  uint256 reward, uint256 gasPrice, uint256 gasLimit,
  address to, uint256 value, bytes memory data
) public view returns (bytes32) {
  return keccak256(abi.encodePacked(
    reward, gasPrice, gasLimit,
    to, value, data, nonce, address(this)
  ));
}
```

An important change in the preceding snippet is that the function no longer requires the forwarded call to be successful (`require(success)`). The rationale for this is that if the forwarded call failed and reverted the entire transaction, then the relayer would not receive any reward, but would still lose the gas fees from the execution of the reverted transaction. To avoid punishing a relayer for a failed transaction that was correctly relayed, we drop that requirement. And to allow for determining whether forwarded call reverted, we add an event that reports the success in each transaction.

Also, note that the gas price validation is performed at the beginning of the method, since gas price is relative to the entire transaction, and cannot be changed in-between contract calls. Gas limit, on the other hand, can be enforced on each call within the transaction, so we can revert if there is not enough gas left. In this case, it is the relayer's responsibility to include additional gas on the request to account for the meta transaction processing (which is about 60K in this implementation).

Estimating Profits

The code for generating the signed transaction in this scenario is analogous to the previous one, with the only difference that the user now needs to include values for the gas price, the gas limit, and the reward. The first two can be estimated as seen in Chapter 5 by using a price oracle like the ethgasstation API or the gasPrice JSON-RPC method for the gas price and running an estimateGas on the transaction to be sent for the gas limit. The value for the reward may depend on other factors, but must be greater than the total execution cost for the relayer, to have an incentive to relay the transaction.

In this scenario, the relayer needs not only to relay the requested transaction but also to evaluate whether it should – by calculating the profit. Transactions with an estimated profit below a certain threshold should be dropped, and if multiple transactions (from different identities) are enqueued, the profit can be used to prioritize which to execute first.

The profit can be easily calculated by actually estimating the entire call, multiplying the estimate by the gas price, and subtracting that from the reward.

```
// 08-meta-txs/02-identity-with-rewards.js
let estimatedGas = await identity.methods
  .forward(reward, gasPrice, gasLimit,
          recipient, value, data, signature)
  .estimateGas({ from: relayer, gasPrice });

let estimatedProfit =
  BN(reward).minus(BN(estimatedGas).times(gasPrice));
```

Keep in mind that the transaction may actually require a higher gas value than the estimated if the user requested a higher gasLimit. To actually execute the transaction, the relayer should send a gas allowance equal to gasLimit plus the additional gas required to process the meta transaction. This additional gas can be roughly calculated as the difference between sending a transaction directly to the recipient contract and sending it via the identity as a meta transaction. In our implementation, that difference amounts to 60K gas approximately, though this value is not constant: it fluctuates slightly depending on the size of the transaction's data.

```
await identity.methods
  .forward(reward, gasPrice, gasLimit,
           recipient, value, data, signature)
  .send({ from: relayer, gasPrice, gas: gasLimit + 60000 });
```

Note that this difference may actually cause the transaction to cost more than the relayer expected in case the estimation and the actual usage differ, as the relayer could be setting a higher gas allowance.

Payment in Kind

Gas fees from transaction execution are paid in ETH, since it is the native currency of the Ethereum network. However, nothing forces us to pay the rewards to relayers in the same currency, as there are plenty of other media of exchange on Ethereum: every fungible token (ERC20) is a potential currency.

This opens the door to allowing our users to transact exclusively using a token, since ETH is no longer needed to pay for gas fees. This is especially interesting if our application is built on top of a token-based protocol: it allows us to send tokens to our users as they engage in our network, which are in turn used to pay for relayer rewards. Our users never need to hold or purchase any ETH; they only work with our application's token.

The code for supporting payment in tokens is a direct modification from the previous one. We add a new `rewardToken` parameter to the forwarding function and send tokens on that address or ETH if this parameter is set to the zero address.

```
// 08-meta-txs/contracts/IdentityWithTokenRewards.sol
import "openzeppelin-solidity/contracts/token/ERC20/IERC20.sol";

function forward(
  uint256 reward, address rewardToken,
  uint256 gasPrice, uint256 gasLimit,
  address to, uint256 value, bytes memory data,
  bytes memory signature
```

```
) public returns (bytes memory) {

  // Validate gas price of the transaction
  require(tx.gasPrice >= gasPrice, "Gas price too low");

  // Get hash of the transaction that was signed
  bytes32 hash = getHash(
    reward, rewardToken, gasPrice, gasLimit, to, value, data
  ).toEthSignedMessageHash();

  // Retrieve signer address and validate
  address signer = hash.recover(signature);
  require(accounts[signer], "Signer not registered");

  // Increase nonce, execute call, and inform success
  nonce++;
  require(gasleft() >= gasLimit);
  (bool success, bytes memory returnData) =
    to.call.value(value).gas(gasLimit)(data);
  emit Forwarded(nonce, success, msg.sender);

  // Pay back to the relayer
  if (rewardToken == address(0)) {
    msg.sender.transfer(reward);
  } else {
    require(IERC20(rewardToken).transfer(msg.sender, reward));
  }

  return returnData;
}
```

Keep in mind that while this mechanism is particularly useful when your application spins up relayers that trade tokens for executions, it imposes additional difficulties for decentralized relayers. A random relayer performing desktop mining now needs to check for the market value of the reward token against the execution cost to determine the profit. Not only that, but it also needs to ensure there is enough liquidity in the market to trade such token for ETH when they want to cash out their profits – and that is without considering the fees for that exchange.

In other words, paying relayer rewards in a protocol-specific ERC20 is useful if the relayer infrastructure you are using is specific to your application, but ETH or a widespread ERC20[15] may be a better option for working with decentralized relayers.

Native Meta Transactions

Meta transactions, as we have just seen, require the use of an identity contract to act as a bouncer proxy to the actual contracts the user is interacting with. The identity contract holds the logic to process the signed transactions and then calls into a third-party contract, which does not require to be aware of meta transactions.

However, it is possible to remove the need for identity contracts if the application contracts already have support for processing meta transactions. This approach is named *native meta transactions,*[16] since it is built-in natively on the application contracts, instead of requiring a proxy identity contract.

As an example, let's add native meta transactions to an ERC721 contract,[17] allowing any user who holds a non-fungible token to sign a transaction to have it transferred without expending gas (Listing 7-28). The code is similar to the forwarding function we have been working with, except that it is specialized to just perform token transfers.

Listing 7-28. Adding native meta transactions to an ERC721 contract. Note that the nonces now need to be tracked per signer

```solidity
// 08-meta-txs/contracts/ERC721WithNativeMetaTxs.sol
pragma solidity ^0.5.0;

import "openzeppelin-solidity/contracts/token/ERC721/ERC721.sol";
import "openzeppelin-solidity/contracts/cryptography/ECDSA.sol";
```

---

[15]A stablecoin, such as DAI, is an excellent candidate here.

[16]This term was coined by Austin Griffith (see https://medium.com/gitcoin/native-meta-transactions-e509d91a8482), though the approach can be traced back to being used in fungible tokens by Ludovic Galabru in EIP865 (see https://github.com/ethereum/EIPs/issues/865).

[17]This example is inspired by the MetaCoin code (see https://github.com/austintgriffith/native-meta-transactions/blob/6e1efc041ecf7e1665b5b0e986505c2598a86add/contracts/MetaCoin/MetaCoin.sol).

```solidity
contract ERC721WithNativeMetaTxs is ERC721 {
  using ECDSA for bytes32;

  // Track nonces per signer
  mapping (address => uint256) nonces;

  function signedTransferFrom(
    address from, address to, uint256 tokenId,
    uint256 nonce, bytes memory signature
  ) public {

    // Retrieve signer
    bytes32 hash = getTransferHash(
      from, to, tokenId, nonce, signature
    ).toEthSignedMessageHash();
    address signer = hash.recover(signature);

    // Ensure signer can handle this token
    require(_isApprovedOrOwner(signer, tokenId));

    // Validate nonce and increase it
    require(nonce == nonces[signer]);
    nonces[signer]++;

    // Execute the transfer
    _transferFrom(from, to, tokenId);
  }

  // Calculates the hash to be signed for a transfer
  function getTransferHash(
    address from, address to, uint256 tokenId, uint256 nonce
  ) public view returns (bytes32) {
    return keccak256(abi.encodePacked(
      from, to, tokenId, nonce, address(this)
    ));
  }
}
```

By bundling this logic in the reward token contract itself directly, our users can directly sign token transfers that are then sent by a relayer and executed by the ERC721 contract. This allows a user with an existing account to benefit from meta transactions (which could be subsidized by our application) without having to deploy an identity contract.

Rewards in Native Meta Transactions

While moving the meta transaction logic to the application contract directly reduces complexity for the user, it introduces an additional difficulty: how to handle rewards to relayers. Identity contracts did not face this problem since they already held all of the user's assets, so they could directly transfer them to relayers as payment.

In the case of ERC20 tokens, the solution is simple: the token contract can manage the signer's tokens and directly transfer the reward to the relayer of the transaction using those very tokens (Listing 7-29).

Listing 7-29. Sample signedTransfer function in an ERC20 contract that supports meta transactions and relayer rewards using the same ERC20 token

```
// 08-meta-txs/contracts/ERC20WithNativeMetaTxs.sol
function signedTransfer(
  address to, uint256 value,
  uint256 nonce, uint256 reward, bytes memory signature
) public {
  bytes32 hash = getTransferHash(
    to, value, nonce, reward
  ).toEthSignedMessageHash();
  address signer = hash.recover(signature);
  require(nonce == nonces[signer]);
  nonces[signer]++;
  _transfer(signer, msg.sender, reward);
  _transfer(signer, to, value);
}
```

However, this solution does not allow any rewards in any currency that is not that same token – for instance, ETH rewards are not possible under this scheme. It also does not translate well to other assets. What would be the reward for transferring an ERC721 non-fungible token? A digital collectible cannot have a piece removed and given to a relayer as a reward.

A way around this problem is to rely on ERC20 *approvals*. Recall from Chapter 3 that ERC20 tokens allow holders to appoint other addresses to manage their funds. This way, a user could grant an approval on their tokens to the application contract processing the relayer rewards, which then sends the tokens to the relayer as payment. This approach, however, still requires the user to have ETH to pay gas fees in the initial approve transaction – unless the reward token contract itself has native meta transaction support for approvals.

Another option is to simply subsidize the user's transactions and have the application itself pay out to the relayers. This requires careful logic in the application contract to determine *when* to accept a meta transaction – otherwise, a malicious relayer could spam the application with fake transactions and drain the entire reward pool. Such logic will depend entirely on your use case, but keep in mind that you have much flexibility: your contracts may require the meta transaction to have an additional signature by an application key, so you can perform validations off-chain to approve a transaction for execution.

Revisiting Smart Accounts Deployment

We will go once more through the process of deploying a smart account contract. In the "Smart accounts" section, we discussed how to do this using single-use addresses, though it had certain limitations. We will now explore another approach, with support for relayer rewards, based on a different EVM operation: CREATE2.

The CREATE2 Instruction

Ethereum has, since its first versions, provided a CREATE instruction for creating a new contract from another. The address of the newly created contract, as we saw earlier, is a function of the sender address and its nonce. While this allows for deterministic deployments, it also means that reserving an address is tricky, since the sender must not send any other transactions besides the deployment one to prevent changing its nonce.

To solve this, a new CREATE2 instruction was introduced. This low-level operation works similar to CREATE, but also accepts a *salt* parameter: the deployment address is now calculated as a function of the sender, the salt, and the contract creation code. This allows for much more interesting flows by setting up a factory contract that spins up contracts using this instruction.

```
Factory IdentityFactoryWithRewards {
  function deploy(
    bytes code, uint256 salt
  ) public returns (address) {
    address deployed;
    assembly {
      deployed:= create2(0, add(code,0x20), mload(code), salt)
      if iszero(extcodesize(deployed)) { revert(0, 0) }
    }
    return deployed;
  }
}
```

A user can now choose a contract, along with its constructor arguments, generate a random salt, and know the address where the resulting contract will be deployed. Not only that, but *anyone* who knows these parameters can now perform the deployment.

This means that the user can simply share the creation parameters and salt, plus the address of the factory contract to be used, and have any relayer execute the transaction, without even needing to sign the transaction – and certainly not paying any gas. Should a relayer attempt to modify the code or creation parameters, the contract would end up deployed at a different address. Let's use this approach to deploy our identity contracts, providing rewards to the relayers.

Deployment Rewards

Before going into the code, we need to define how the payments to the relayer will be managed and which addresses will be initially funded by the user.

Recall from the previous approach that one of the downsides of single-use addresses is that the user needs to fund from an exchange one address, but then his or her identity is spawned at a different one. Even worse, any additional funds sent to the single-use address are lost. Then, it is desirable if we can have the user fund the address of the identity contract directly.

The easiest way to solve this is by having the Identity contract pay the relayer reward upon deployment, that is, in its constructor (Listing 7-30). In this scenario, the relayer is by definition the account who initiated the transaction – or tx.origin in Solidity.

Listing 7-30. Modified Identity contract that pays out a reward to the relayer of the transaction

```
// 08-meta-txs/contracts/IdentityFactoryWithRewards.sol
contract IdentityWithReward is Identity {
  constructor(
    address owner, uint256 reward
  ) Identity(owner) public {
    tx.origin.transfer(reward);
  }
}
```

This approach allows the user to simply specify the owner account and the reward to be paid and broadcast those parameters along with the salt chosen, since these values alone are enough to determine the deployment address. Any relayer can then pick up this transaction, validate that there are enough funds on the deployment address to pay for the reward, and send the transaction to the factory contract. As a bonus, any surplus funds sent to the deployment address will still be there after the contract is created, ready to be used by their owner.

Identity Contract Factory

The factory contract then must provide a deployment function, callable by anyone, that accepts the Identity contract deployment parameters and salt (Listing 7-31). This function assembles the creation code and performs the actual creation using the CREATE2 instruction.

Listing 7-31. Deploy function of an IdentityFactory contract. The creationCode property of the contract type returns the bytecode used in the creation, and any constructor arguments just need to be appended at the end

```
// 08-meta-txs/contracts/IdentityFactoryWithRewards.sol
contract IdentityFactoryWithRewards {
  function deploy(
    address owner, uint256 reward, uint256 salt
  ) public returns (address) {
    bytes memory code = getCode(owner, reward);
    address identity;
    assembly {
      identity:= create2(0, add(code,0x20), mload(code), salt)
      if iszero(extcodesize(identity)) { revert(0, 0) }
    }
    return identity;
  }

  function getCode(
    address owner, uint256 reward
  ) internal pure returns (bytes memory) {
    return abi.encodePacked(
      type(IdentityWithReward).creationCode,
      abi.encode(owner, reward)
    );
  }
}
```

Note that there is no need to validate the owner's signature, since any change on the creation parameters would yield a different deployment address – one with no funds to pay back the reward to the relayer. Relayers should validate that the deployment address indeed has enough funds to pay back.

An addition to this contract is a view function to obtain the deployment address given the constructor parameters and salt. This function can be used to tell the user on which address their identity contract will be deployed, that is, which address they need to fund.

```
function getDeploymentAddress(
  address owner, uint256 reward, uint256 salt
) public view returns (address) {
  bytes memory code = getCode(owner, reward);
  bytes32 codeHash = keccak256(code);

  bytes32 rawAddress = keccak256(
    abi.encodePacked(
      bytes1(0xff),
      address(this),
      salt,
      codeHash
    )
  );

  return address(bytes20(rawAddress << 96));
}
```

Using this strategy, you can precalculate the address where a user's identity will be created given a salt and share the address with him or her. The user acknowledges that address as their own and seeds it with funds from an exchange. This in turn triggers a relayer to create an identity contract at that address once it is funded.

Note   This strategy can actually be carried out with single-use addresses instead of CREATE2 using a slightly more complex flow. The application can select a relayer and create a single-use address that will spawn a new identity contract and send a reward to the pre-selected relayer. After the user funds the address where the identity is to be deployed, the relayer in turn funds the single-use addresses, executes the deployment, and receives the reward.

Ethereum Names

The last onboarding challenge we will tackle in this chapter is that of Ethereum addresses themselves. While addresses are central to any Ethereum application, as they identify the actors of a decentralized system, they are far from user-friendly. Asking a user to understand their 40-character string of apparent gibberish as their global identifier is not good design. To solve this issue, we will look into ENS (Ethereum Name Service).

A DNS for Ethereum

Most web developers are familiar with the concept of DNS (Domain Name Service), a protocol for mapping easily recognizable domain names (like "google.com") to machine-friendly addresses (like 172.217.28.206) that identify a server in the Internet Protocol.[18]

The Ethereum Name Service[19] (or ENS) is an analogous protocol that resolves user-friendly names (like "ethereumfoundation.eth") to Ethereum addresses (0xfB6916095ca1df60bB79Ce92cE3Ea74c37c5d359 in this example, which is the Ethereum Foundation tip jar). Also like DNS, it supports registering non-address records (like content hashes or plain text), as well as reverse lookups.

The components involved in ENS loosely mimic those of DNS, with the difference that they are implemented as smart contracts within the Ethereum network. The ENS **registry** itself is a singleton contract that keeps track of all domain names and their owners and maps each domain to a **resolver**. A resolver contract provides methods for resolving a name to an address and optionally additional information such as text, content hashes, or public key records. Finally, the ENS registry is updated via **registrars**, contracts that manage the registration of subdomains at different levels of the tree, each with its own policy.

The most widely used top-level domain for ENS is `.eth`,[20] operated by the so-called *.eth permanent registrar*. This registrar uses a commit-reveal scheme for purchasing second-level domains and allows anyone to chip in for extending a name registration. While it is possible to interact with this contract directly, it is suggested to use a tool (such as mycrypto[21] or myetherwallet[22]) to purchase and manage your second-level domains.

---

[18]This is a gross oversimplification of the capabilities of DNS, but is good enough for establishing the analogy with ENS.

[19]See `https://ens.domains/` for more information.

[20]There are also other TLDs (such as .xyz or .luxe) that are implemented via a DNS integration, but we will focus on .eth in this book.

[21]`https://mycrypto.com/`

[22]`https://www.myetherwallet.com/`

Names Resolution

A key part of making your application ENS-aware is to allow your users to enter ENS names wherever an address is required. Allowing users to input ENS names in your application instead of addresses helps abstracting the complexity of Ethereum addresses, which means one less concept your users need to grasp to start using your app. This is the equivalent of allowing your users to navigate to "google.com" by entering the domain name in their browser instead of forcing them to type in its IP address.

As in DNS, translating from ENS names to addresses is a process called *resolution* (Listing 7-32). Given the architecture of ENS, resolving a name is a two-step process: we first need to query the central ENS registry to obtain the address of the *resolver contract* for the name and then query the resolver to obtain the actual *address* for that name. Domain names also need to be normalized and hashed via a process called *namehash*.[23]

Listing 7-32. Resolving a domain name to an address using the central ENS registry on mainnet

```
// 09-ens/01-resolve.js
const ensAddr = '0x314159265dd8dbb310642f98f50c066173c1259b';
async function resolve (domain) {
  let domainHash = namehash(domain);
  let ens = new web3.eth.Contract(ensABI, ensAddr);
  let resAddr = await ens.methods.resolver(domainHash).call();
  let resolver = new web3.eth.Contract(resolverABI, resAddr);
  return await resolver.methods.addr(domainHash).call();
}
```

Since name resolution is a common operation, several libraries implement this operation out of the box. In particular, the official `ethereum-ens@0.7.6` javascript package provides bindings for most operations, making name resolution much simpler.

```
$ let ens = new ENS(web3.eth.currentProvider);
$ let domain = "ethereumfoundation.eth";
$ await ens.resolver(domain).addr();
> 0xfB6916095ca1df60bB79Ce92cE3Ea74c37c5d359
```

---

[23]See `https://docs.ens.domains/contract-api-reference/name-processing` for a detailed explanation of the namehash algorithm.

Abstracting your users of Ethereum addresses also means that your application must use Ethereum names instead of raw addresses when displaying information. It is no good if your users enter a user-friendly Ethereum name, and your application answers with a plethora of 40-character hexadecimal strings.

Reverse resolution is supported in ENS by querying a special "addr.reverse" domain, which maps from addresses to full Ethereum names. This domain is managed separately from "eth," and users may choose not to register their addresses on it – so not every address with an Ethereum name will have a record for reverse resolution.

```
$ address = '0xfB6916095ca1df60bB79Ce92cE3Ea74c37c5d359';
$ await ens.reverse(address).name();
> "ethereumfoundation.eth"
```

Caution   ENS does not enforce the correctness of reverse records; this means that anyone could register that their address maps to "ethereumfoundation.eth". To protect against this, you should always run a forward name resolution on the result of a reverse resolution and verify that it matches the original address.

Giving Names to Our Users

ENS is a perfect match for smart accounts. Instead of requiring our users to remember the address of the smart contract that is their on-chain identity, we can allow them to assign it an Ethereum name.

As in DNS, instead of having them purchase a second-level domain directly from a network information center (NIC), we can allocate names within our own domain. Email is a good analogy of this and something users are accustomed to – most people have an email account with a provider, like john@gmail.com, instead of one managed by them, like hello@john.com. Similarly, in ENS, we can allocate a subdomain for each user of our application, like *john.myapp.eth*.

To implement this, we need to set up our own registrar contract to manage our Ethereum domain and manage all subdomain registrations. We will use a simple FIFS (first-in first-served) registrar contract that will freely accept all subdomain registrations.

Canonical implementations for this and other contracts we will be using can be found in the @ensdomains/ens@0.3.5 and @ensdomains/resolver@0.1.3 packages.

The first step is to actually acquire a domain. While this is a non-trivial process on mainnet, ENS offers FIFS registrars for .test domains in the test networks, with the restriction that these registrations expire after 4 weeks. Let's start by registering a test domain on the Rinkeby testnet (Listing 7-33).

Listing 7-33. Registering the Ethereum domain "myapp.test" on Rinkeby. The hash function in this code snippet is keccak256

```
// 09-ens/02-register.js
let [owner, user] = await web3.eth.getAccounts();
let ensAddress = '0xe7410170f87102df0055eb195163a03b7f2bff4a';
let ens = new web3.eth.Contract(ensABI, ensAddress);

// Get top-level registrar for test domains
let testRegistrarAddress = await ens.methods
  .owner(namehash('test')).call();
let testRegistrar = new web3.eth.Contract(
  fifsRegistrarABI, testRegistrarAddress);

// Register our domain name under our account
let name = 'myapp'; // try other names if already registered
let domain = `${name}.test`;
await testRegistrar.methods
  .register(hash(name), owner).send({ from: owner });
```

We can now deploy our FIFS registrar contract, which will freely allocate subdomains of "myapp.test," and transfer ownership of the domain to it.

```
// Deploy new registrar contract
let arguments = [ensAddress, namehash(domain)];
let myRegistrar = await
  new web3.eth.Contract(fifsRegistrarABI)
    .deploy({ data: fifsRegistrarBytecode, arguments })
    .send({ from: owner });
```

```
// Transfer ownership of our domain to our registrar
await ens.methods
let myRegistrarAddress = myRegistrar.options.address;
  .setOwner(namehash(domain), myRegistrarAddress)
  .send({ from: owner });
```

We can now augment our identity contracts with a method to register themselves on ENS using this registrar (Listing 7-34). This method takes three steps:

1. Registering a custom name (i.e., "john") in our registrar and appointing the Identity contract as the owner

2. Setting a resolver in the ENS registry for the new identity name ("john.myapp.test")

3. Setting the identity contract address in the resolver from the previous step

We will be using a *public resolver* for step 2 of the process. A public resolver is a public contract that accepts requests for managing the records of any address, but only from the owner of that address. This saves us the trouble of having to deploy a custom resolver for our app.

Note   An alternative is to add resolver methods to our identity contract and just let the identity return its own address upon a resolution request. However, this adds more complexity to our contract.

Listing 7-34. Identity contract function for registering a name and mapping it to the identity itself using our custom registrar and a public resolver. Code adapted from the UniversalLoginSDK repository[24]

```
// 09-ens/contracts/IdentityWithENS.sol
contract IdentityWithENS is Identity {
  function registerENS(
```

---

[24]See https://github.com/UniversalLogin/UniversalLoginSDK/blob/02025571ff8c1f256d47e 2e96bbcfda6f4a412c2/universal-login-contracts/contracts/ENSRegistered.sol

```
      bytes32 _hashLabel, bytes32 _node,
      ENS ens, FIFSRegistrar registrar, PublicResolver resolver
   ) onlyUserAccount public {
      registrar.register(_hashLabel, address(this));
      ens.setResolver(_node, address(resolver));
      resolver.setAddr(_node, address(this));
   }
}
```

Registering an identity contract on ENS is then just a matter of having our user call into this function from one of their external accounts (Listing 7-35). Note that the owner of the registered name is set to be the identity itself, so the user ultimately retains control of what to do with their subdomain.

Listing 7-35. Registering an identity contract as `john.myapp.test` using our custom registrar and a Rinkeby public resolver

```
const publicResolverAddress =
   '0xb14fdee4391732ea9d2267054ead2084684c0ad8';

let userName = `john`;
let userDomain = `${userName}.${domain}`;

await identity.methods.registerENS(
   hash(userName),
   namehash(userDomain),
   ensAddress,
   myRegistrar.options.address,
   publicResolverAddress
).send({ from: user });
```

Running this process for every new user allows them to refer to their identity using a friendly name provided by our application – a name that can be carried on to other applications and be used as a global Ethereum identity, handled by ENS.

Summary

We have gone through several tools and techniques for handling user onboarding and account management in general, making this one of the most content-heavy chapters in this book: fallback functions, forwarding contracts, single-use addresses, local accounts, mnemonics, smart accounts, upgradeability, meta transactions, native meta transactions, reserved deployment addresses, and Ethereum names, among others. All of these techniques help in different aspects of user onboarding, and their trade-offs make it difficult to settle for one solution that fits all use cases.

Work on user onboarding is still a very active field of research in Ethereum, and new mechanics to add to your toolbelt are bound to be developed in the near future. At the time of this writing, it is worth highlighting the work being done under Universal Logins.[25] Universal Logins is a framework that creates smart accounts for users, managed by local accounts automatically generated on each device, with support for meta transactions, as well as ENS for allowing users to easily connect to their accounts. It also promotes subsidizing early user actions to ease onboarding and reward users in-app who go the extra mile to strengthen the security of their accounts.

Whatever solution you implement, remember that the more steps a user must go through to start using your application, the most likely it is for them to drop. On the other hand, sacrificing security for usability is a huge risk, given that "the worst user experience is when people lose their crypto."[26] Striking the perfect compromise between the two for the use case you are building is no easy feat.

---

[25]See `https://universallogin.io`, developed by the EthWorks team, based on the work by Alex Van De Sande.

[26]Taylor Monahan, "The Impossible Balance Between Usability & Security," `https://medium.com/mycrypto/the-impossible-balance-between-usability-security`

CHAPTER 8

Scalability

In the previous chapter, we addressed user onboarding challenges, one of the two main issues for Ethereum mass adoption. The second of them, which we will tackle in this chapter, is scalability. The Ethereum network, as it is today, can handle about 15 transactions per second – and this throughput must be shared among all Ethereum applications globally. This has led to single applications cluttering the entire network due to a spike in their usage to the point of rendering all dapps unusable for brief periods. In this chapter, we will introduce state channels and sidechains, two of the most widely used scalability solutions.

What is Layer 2?

The Ethereum blockchain can be seen as a single global database, replicated across every node in the network, that needs to process every single transaction sent. This alone, without even considering block propagation times or proofs-of-work, already imposes a cap on the volume of transactions that can be processed.

> *The core limitation is that public blockchains like ethereum require every transaction to be processed by every single node in the network. (...) This is by design—it's part of what makes public blockchains authoritative. Nodes don't have to rely on someone else to tell them what the current state of the blockchain is. (...) This puts a fundamental limit on ethereum's transaction throughput: it cannot be higher than what we are willing to require from an individual node.*
>
> —Josh Stark, "Making Sense of Ethereum's Layer 2 Scaling Solutions: State Channels, Plasma, and Truebit"[1]

---

[1] https://medium.com/l4-media/making-sense-of-ethereums-layer-2-scaling-solutions-state-channels-plasma-and-truebit-22cb40dcc2f4

S. Palladino, *Ethereum for Web Developers*, https://doi.org/10.1007/978-1-4842-5278-9_8

But what if we do *not* require every transaction to be run through the whole network? For instance, a set of transactions, run between a small group of participants, could be processed on a separate network. And only after a certain period the resulting balances could be uploaded to the main Ethereum network.

These parallel (or *side*) networks require certain security guarantees – otherwise, we could just use a regular database. The key here is that these networks can rely on the main network to act as a secure decentralized base layer, on top of which new consensus mechanisms are built. Hence, these scalability solutions are said to belong to a *layer 2*, since they are not built as part of the Ethereum protocol itself, but rather on top of it. Today, there are three main types of layer 2 solutions:

- *Channels* are short-lived closed networks, typically between two participants, where they exchange multiple transactions between each other. Each party must acknowledge every transaction by signing it. To open the channel, they first must make a deposit on a smart contract on the Ethereum network. This contract can then validate their signatures to execute the payouts when needed.

- *Sidechains* are parallel networks that use a different consensus algorithm than the main network, such as proof of authority or stake. These are usually bridged to the main network, allowing users to move assets between the sidechain and the main chain. A variant of sidechains are *plasma chains*, in which the good behavior of the sidechain can be fully enforced by a smart contract on the main network.

- *External computation* solutions do not provide a higher transaction throughput, but they do allow for more interesting tasks to be performed in each transaction. They run computing-intensive tasks outside the main network, tasks that would be prohibitively expensive to run on the EVM, and then inject the result back.

In this chapter, we will explore the first two solutions. Today there are several teams working on implementations or new variations of each of them. We will mention some of them along the way, but not without making our own attempts at each solution first.[2]

---

[2]Note that these techniques are especially tricky to get right. While coding them ourselves are the best way to understand them, you may prefer using a vetted implementation by a third party instead of rolling your own for your app.

Channels

Channels are a family of layer 2 scalability solutions that span many different variants from unidirectional payment channels to counterfactual generalized state channels. They can also be extrapolated to full channel networks instead of isolated peer-to-peer solutions.

We will begin with *payment channels*.[3] In payment channels, two or more participants open a channel by making an initial deposit on the main network and then perform multiple payments off-chain over the channel. These payments are then settled trustlessly on a smart contract on the main network.

Unidirectional Payment Channels

The easiest variant of payment channels are *unidirectional payment channels*. Here, there are two distinct parties involved: a recipient and a sender. These are usually a provider that collects multiple payments in exchange for a service provided over time and a user performing these payments. A good example of this is a player performing microtransactions in a game.

How do Channels Work?

Let's suppose a scenario where a user needs to make several small purchases to a service provider. It does not matter what the service provider is offering, only that the user will need to perform *multiple payments to the same recipient over a period of time* and that the provider needs a proof of each small payment to continue providing the service.

If each and every one of these small payments is done as a transaction on the blockchain, the accumulated transaction gas fees would probably become considerable against the actual payments. Paying a 20-cent fee to the network for each 20-cent payment is not a good deal. Furthermore, since the service provider requires a proof after each payment, the confirmation times would constantly add significant delays to the service.

---

[3]As with many other techniques, payment channels were originally developed in Bitcoin and then migrated onto Ethereum and generalized.

A solution could be to have a trusted third party collect a large initial deposit from the user and monitor the service being provided. The user then signs each of these *microtransactions* with their private key, acknowledging each of the payments to be made. After all micropayments have been made, the third party issues a single on-chain transaction that includes the total payout to the service provider and returns the remainder of the initial deposit to the user. Assuming both the user and the service provider trust this party, this can reduce all micropayments to just two transactions on the network: one for the deposit and the other for the payout.

A *unidirectional payment channel* is an implementation of this solution using a smart contract as the trusted third party. The user is said to *open* a payment channel to the service provider as they deploy the payment channel contract with the initial deposit. The user sends each micropayment as a *signed message* directly to the service provider. These messages are not sent on the Ethereum network, but entirely off-chain via a separate protocol, such as HTTPS. When the service provider wants to cash out, they can submit the signed messages to the payment channel contract and collect their payments (Figure 8-1).

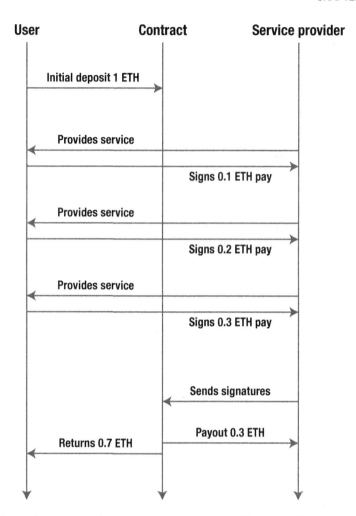

Figure 8-1. *Flow diagram of a payment channel. The user first opens the channel with an initial 1 ETH deposit. Every time the user needs to make a micropayment to the service provider, they instead sign a message with the accumulated amount to be paid and send it off-chain. When the provider wants to cash out, they submit the latest signed message to the contract and receive their payout*

Within a payment channel, most transactions happen completely off-chain, being sent directly from the user to the recipient. This is why channels are considered a *layer 2* solution, built on top of the main Ethereum network, the *layer 1*, while inheriting many of its security properties.

Channels have some very interesting advantages over layer 1. After a channel has been opened, any transaction sent through it has no gas fees, and once sent, they can also be considered to be instantly finalized, since there is no need to wait for any blocks to be mined to confirm it. Additionally, since transactions are exchanged within the two participants, they are entirely private until they are submitted to the blockchain.

Implementing a Unidirectional Channel

To illustrate how a unidirectional payment channel works, we will implement one from scratch (Listing 8-1). Our payment channel will have a sender and a recipient, will hold the initial deposit by the sender, and will have a predetermined end time. After this specified end time, if the recipient has not collected their payment, the sender is allowed to withdraw the deposit. This mechanism is required to prevent the user deposit to be locked into the contract forever, if the service provider never submits the payment messages.

Listing 8-1. Definition, state variables, and constructor for the unidirectional payment channel contract. We will be using the ECDSA library from openzeppelin-solidity@2.1 to verify the signatures on the contract. Note that the constructor is payable, so the sender can make the initial deposit upon deployment

```
// contracts/PaymentChannel.sol
pragma solidity ^0.5.0;

import "openzeppelin-solidity/contracts/cryptography/ECDSA.sol";

contract PaymentChannel {
  using ECDSA for bytes32;

  address payable sender;
  address payable recipient;
  uint256 endTime;
  bool closed;

  constructor(
    address payable _recipient, uint256 _endTime
  ) public payable {
    sender = msg.sender;
```

```
    recipient = _recipient;
    endTime = _endTime;
  }
}
```

Since most transactions in a payment channel occur off-chain, we will need to implement only two methods. The first method, `close`, will be called by the service provider to submit the sender's signature with the payout, collect their funds, and close the channel (Listing 8-2).

Note   We will require that the sender always signs messages for the total to be paid out to the recipient. This allows us to just submit a single signed message to the contract, instead of having to process multiple ones.

This method will only be callable by the recipient to prevent the sender from trying to prematurely close the channel with a message signed by them with zero value. Also, since the sender could sign a message for a total value greater than the deposit present in the channel, we need to limit the value transferred to the contract's balance. It is up to the recipient to decide whether they will accept a payment note for more value than can be actually paid by the channel.[4]

After the payout to the recipient is done, all the remainder of the deposit is returned to the sender. Since the channel contract is of no further use at this point, we also destroy the contract to get a small gas refund.

Listing 8-2. Closing the payment channel by the recipient. This requires submitting a signed message by the sender with the value to be transferred. Note that the signed message also includes the address of the contract to prevent replay attacks on other channels with the same sender

```
// contracts/PaymentChannel.sol
function close(
  uint256 value, bytes memory signature
) public {
  require(msg.sender == recipient);
```

---

[4]Note that we could also add a method for the sender to increase deposit if needed.

```
  bytes32 hash = keccak256(
    abi.encodePacked(value, address(this))
  ).toEthSignedMessage();
  address signer = hash.recover(signature);
  require(signer == sender);

  uint256 funds = address(this).balance;
  recipient.transfer(funds < value ? funds : value);
  selfdestruct(sender); // destroys contract, sending funds to sender
}
```

The second function to implement will correspond to the unhappy path, in which the recipient never calls the close function, and the sender terminates the contract after the predetermined end period (Listing 8-3).

Listing 8-3. Forcefully closing the channel by the sender to recover the deposit if the recipient never cashes out

```
// contracts/PaymentChannel.sol
function forceClose() public {
  require(now > endTime);
  require(msg.sender == sender);
  selfdestruct(sender);
}
```

This implementation can be modified to exchange ERC20 tokens instead of ETH, thus opening the door to *token payment channels*. Instead of making an initial deposit of ETH, the sender must transfer ERC20 tokens to the channel contract as a deposit. These tokens are then transferred again once the channel is closed. Refer to TokenPaymentChannel.sol in the code samples for an implementation.

Building a Payments App

We will now use our contract to build a simple application, where a sender can set up a payment channel contract with a recipient, send multiple micropayments via a direct off-chain connection, and eventually settle. As in previous chapters, we will use create-react-app for boilerplate.

To keep the application simple, we will establish a connection between two browser windows opened on the same app in the same computer, one of them acting as a sender and the other as receiver. We will use *broadcast channels*[5] to pass messages between the two browser windows. In a real app, you will want to use a different method, such as *WebRTC data channels,*[6] along with a server to manage discovery among your users.

We will make another simplification: instead of using Metamask, we will manage the accounts directly from the web application. This is to avoid difficulties with simulating two different accounts interacting with the same app on the same computer. We will call directly into ganache for sending transactions from both the sender and recipient accounts and for signing messages when needed.

Our application will be built out of two main views: one for the sender and one for the recipient, both set up by a root App component. It will be the App's responsibility to set up the web3 object and inject the sender and recipient addresses into the components. Refer to src/App.js in the code samples for its implementation.

Let's start with the Sender view. It will be the sender's responsibility to open the channel by deploying the smart contract and making the initial deposit (Listing 8-4). When this is done, we will notify the recipient via the broadcast channel. We will communicate using a custom protocol where we identify different message types by an action parameter, with a value of CHANNEL_DEPLOYED in this case.

Listing 8-4. Sender component function to deploy the payment channel contract, fund it, and notify the recipient of its deployment. The App component passes the web3 instance and the sender and recipient addresses as props. Here, PaymentChannel is a function that returns a new web3 contract instance, and BN is a BigNumber constructor

```
// src/components/Sender.js
async deployChannel(deposit) {
  const { web3, sender, recipient } = this.props;

  // Deploy the contract and transfer initial deposit
  const from = sender;
  const endTime = +(new Date()) +(300 * 1000); // 5 min from now
```

---

[5]https://developer.mozilla.org/docs/Web/API/Broadcast_Channel_API
[6]https://developer.mozilla.org/docs/Web/API/RTCDataChannel

```
const channel = await PaymentChannel(web3)
  .deploy({ arguments: [recipient, endTime] })
  .send({ value: deposit.toString(), from, gas: 1e6 });

// Notify the recipient via the broadcast channel
const address = channel.options.address;
this.broadcastChannel.postMessage({
  action: "CHANNEL_DEPLOYED", address
});

// Update sender state with deposit and channel object
this.setState({ channel, deposit, sent: BN(0) });
}
```

We will wire this function to a simple form (Figure 8-2), where we ask the user to choose the amount of ETH they want to deposit on the channel.

Sender

0xffcf8fdee72ac11b5c542428b35eef5769c409f0

Deploy payment channel

Deposit in ETH: 10   Deploy

Figure 8-2. *Simple payment channel deployment form. The code for this form can be found in* `src/components/CreateChannel.js`

Once the channel is deployed, our user should be able to send micropayments to the recipient[7] (Listing 8-5). This means signing messages (not sending transactions) that include the total amount of ETH to be paid out to the recipient once the channel is closed. These messages are sent to the recipient via the same broadcast channel using a different `action` identifier.

---

[7]The sender should also be able to force close the channel after the specified end period, but in this example, we will only focus on the main actions of sending payments via the channel and closing it on the recipient's side.

Listing 8-5. Sender function to send a micropayment to the recipient. Each message carries the total amount of ETH to be paid out. The component needs to keep track of the total sent so far, so the micropayment amount chosen by the user is added to that value before being signed and sent

```
// src/components/Sender.js
async sendEth(value) {
  const { web3, sender } = this.props;
  const { sent, channel } = this.state;

  // Calculate new accumulated ETH sent
  const newSent = sent.plus(value);

  // Sign it with the sender's key
  const signature = await signPayment(
    web3, newSent, channel.options.address, sender
  );

  // Send the message to the recipient
  this.broadcastChannel.postMessage({
    action: "PAYMENT", sent: newSent.toString(), signature
  });

  // Update state with new total accumulated ETH sent
  this.setState({ sent: newSent });
}
```

The signature is calculated on the hash of the total value to pay and the channel's address (Listing 8-6). Including the channel's address in the signature prevents *replay attacks*, that is, reusing the same message in another channel opened by the same user.

Listing 8-6. Signing each micropayment message using web3[8]

```
// src/contracts/PaymentChannel.js
async function signPayment(web3, value, address, sender) {
  const hash = web3.utils.soliditySha3(
    { type: 'uint256', value: value.toString() },
    { type: 'address', value: address }
  );
  const signature = await web3.eth.sign(hash, sender);
  return signature;
}
```

Similar to the channel deployment, this action is presented to the user in a simple form where they choose the amount to transfer (Figure 8-3). We can also show some basic stats on the channel, such as its address, the total deposit, and how much ETH has been committed so far.

Sender

0xffcf8fdee72ac11b5c542428b35eef5769c409f0

Channel

Deployed at 0x1967D06b1fabA91eAadb1be33b277447ea24fa0e

Deposit of 1 ETH

Sent 0 ETH

Send micropayment

Value in ETH: 0.1   Send

Figure 8-3. *Presenting the user the channel information and requesting the value to send via the channel. The code for these components can be found in* src/ components/ChannelStats.js *and* src/components/SendEther.js

---

[8]Certain geth, parity, or ganache versions may return a signature incompatible with the standard defined by EIP155, which is enforced on the contract when the signature is verified. If you find errors when validating the produced signatures, either update to a newer client version or include the following fix at end of the signPayment function.

```
const v = parseInt(signature.substr(signature.length-2), 16);
const fixedV = (v <= 1 ? v + 27 : v).toString(16);
return signature.slice(0, signature.length-2) + fixedV;
```

Note   For the sake of brevity, we will skip the implementation of the `forceClose` call by the sender in this example.

We can now turn our focus to the recipient view. Within our app, the recipient needs to do nothing but monitor the sender's actions until they decide to cash out. We will first install a listener for the sender's messages to react upon them (Listing 8-7), calling different functions depending on the message action (Listing 8-8).

Listing 8-7. Initializing a new broadcast channel for receiving messages from the sender and adding an event handler. This code is part of the `Recipient` component constructor

```
// src/components/Recipient.js
const bc = new BroadcastChannel('payments');
bc.onmessage = (evt) => this.handleMessage(evt.data);
this.broadcastChannel = bc;
```

Listing 8-8. Delegating to different handler functions, discriminating on the message action

```
// src/components/Recipient.js
handleMessage(data) {
  const action = data.action;
  switch (action) {
    case "CHANNEL_DEPLOYED":
      this.onChannelDeployed(data);
      break;
    case "PAYMENT":
      this.onPaymentReceived(data);
      break;
    default:
      console.error("Unexpected message", data);
  }
}
```

Let's see first how the recipient should react to a new channel deployed (Listing 8-9). Besides updating its own state by adding a reference to the channel, the recipient should inspect the channel's deposit to know up to how much the sender is able to pay. The recipient should also check that the contract deployed is indeed a payment channel. We can do that by checking that the bytecode deployed matches the code of the channel (Listing 8-10).

Listing 8-9. Recipient reacts to a new channel deployed by validating it, retrieving its deposit, and updating its own state. Here, `PaymentChannel` is a function that returns a web3 contract instance at the specified address

```
// src/components/Recipient.js
async onChannelDeployed(data) {
  const { web3 } = this.props;
  if (!await checkBytecode(web3, data.address)) {
    console.error("Contract bytecode does not match");
    return;
  }

  const deposit = await web3.eth.getBalance(data.address);
  this.setState({
    channel: PaymentChannel(web3, data.address),
    deposit: BN(deposit),
    received: BN(0)
  });
}
```

Listing 8-10. Checking the bytecode deployed at an address against the one in the contract compiled `Artifact`. Note that we check against the `deployedBytecode` of the contract, not the `bytecode`, since the latter includes the constructor code that is not saved in the blockchain

```
// src/components/Recipient.js
async function checkBytecode(web3, address) {
  const actual = await web3.eth.getCode(address);
  const { compilerOutput } = Artifact;
```

```
const expected = compilerOutput.evm.deployedBytecode.object;
return actual === expected;
}
```

The other message the recipient has to process is a payment message. Here, we need to validate the sender's signature and update the recipient state with the latest value transferred (Listing 8-11). We also need to save the associated signature, as we will need it to close the channel.

Listing 8-11. Recipient reacts to a payment message, updating the total ETH received and the corresponding signature. Validating each message implies recovering the signing address and checking it against the sender, since an invalid signature would yield a different signer address. We also discard any messages with a total payment less than the latest total

```
// src/components/Recipient.js
onPaymentReceived(data) {
  const sent = BN(data.sent);
  const received = this.state.received;

  if (this.verifyMessage(data) && sent.gt(received)) {
    this.setState({
      received: sent,
      signature: data.signature
    });
  }
}

verifyMessage(data) {
  const { web3, sender } = this.props;
  const { channel } = this.state;
  const signer = recoverPayment(
    web3, data.sent, channel.options.address, data.signature
  );
  return areAddressesEqual(signer, sender);
}
```

Recovering the sender's signature can then be implemented using the recover method from the web3 library (Listing 8-12).

Listing 8-12. Helper function to recover the signer of a payment message. Note that the hash over which the signature is recovered is calculated exactly like in the signPayment method

```
// src/contracts/PaymentChannel.js
function recoverPayment(web3, value, address, signature) {
  const hash = web3.utils.soliditySha3(
    { type: 'uint256', value: value.toString() },
    { type: 'address', value: address }
  );
  return web3.eth.accounts.recover(hash, signature);
}
```

The recipient is shown the current state of the channel, the total ETH received, as well as the option to close the channel at any time (Figure 8-4).

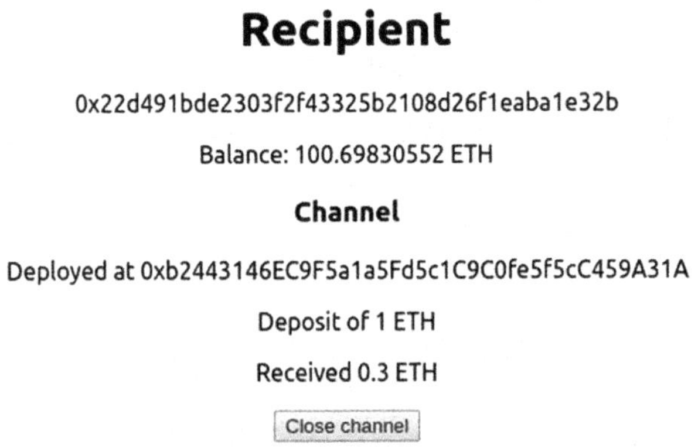

Recipient

0x22d491bde2303f2f43325b2108d26f1eaba1e32b

Balance: 100.69830552 ETH

Channel

Deployed at 0xb2443146EC9F5a1a5Fd5c1C9C0fe5f5cC459A31A

Deposit of 1 ETH

Received 0.3 ETH

Close channel

Figure 8-4. *Recipient interface with information on current balance and channel stats, including how much ETH has been sent via the channel*

The last step to implement on the recipient is closing the channel by sending a transaction to the channel contract with the latest value and signature (Listing 8-13). This settles all micropayments by sending the accumulated value to the recipient and the remainder of the deposit back to the sender.

Listing 8-13. Closing the channel by the recipient using the latest value and signature sent by the sender

```
// src/components/Recipient.js
async closeChannel() {
  const { web3, recipient } = this.props;
  const { channel, signature, received } = this.state;

  // Send closing transaction
  await channel.methods.close(
    received.toString(), signature
  ).send({ from: recipient });

  // Update the recipient's balance
  const balance = BN(await web3.eth.getBalance(recipient));
  this.setState({ channel: null, balance });
}
```

After this method is called, the channel contract should be destroyed, and the recipient should have received the sum of all micropayments made by the sender.

Now that we have a working application built on top of unidirectional payment channels, it's time to move into more interesting flavors of channels.

Bidirectional Payment Channels

Another scenario for payment channels is that of two equal parties exchanging funds between each other. Instead of having a distinguished sender and a recipient, both participants in the channel can send and receive funds.

This symmetry in the participants' roles makes the channel implementation more difficult. Which of the two participants should be allowed to close the channel in this model? Since they are equals, they both should be allowed to do so, but this introduces a problem.

Let's say Alice and Bob are exchanging microtransactions. At some point, Bob sends a very large payment through the channel to Alice, but before she can cash out, he submits an old message to the channel and closes it. The problem then is that a malicious participant can attempt to close the channel *at an older state* when it is convenient for them (Figure 8-5).

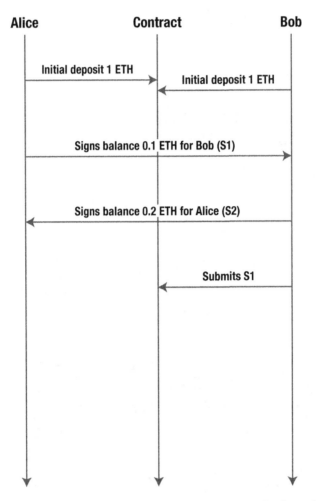

Figure 8-5. *Bidirectional payment channel scenario in which Bob attempts to close the channel with an older state, in detriment of Alice*

Challenge Periods

This situation is solved by adding a *challenge period* to the closure of the channel. When Bob requests the channel to be closed, it goes into a "closing" state for a fixed period of time. During this period, Alice can either confirm the closure of the channel, or she can submit a more recent state and start a new closing period (Figure 8-6).

If she fails to send any transaction to the channel during the challenge period, then the channel is closed and the payouts executed according to the state submitted by Bob. This last case is the equivalent of the recipient not submitting a message and having the sender run a forced close. So, adding a challenge period removes the need for having a predefined end time for the channel.

Note Challenge periods are a very common mechanism in layer 2 solutions, not just channels, as we will see later in this chapter. These allow an action to be carried away unilaterally without having to collect confirmations from every other party, but still let them watch for unlawful behavior and act upon it.

This mechanism requires the smart contract to recognize when a message is *more recent* than another. In other words, it requires adding a notion of *ordering* to the messages interchanged by Alice and Bob. In the previous example, this allows the channel to be able to verify that Alice's message is more recent than Bob's and hence discard Bob's in favor of Alice's.

This ordering is handled within the protocol by adding a counter or *nonce* to each message, which is increased with each message sent. Both parties should validate that the nonce is properly increased on each message: if one receives a signed message with a repeated nonce, they should immediately discard it.

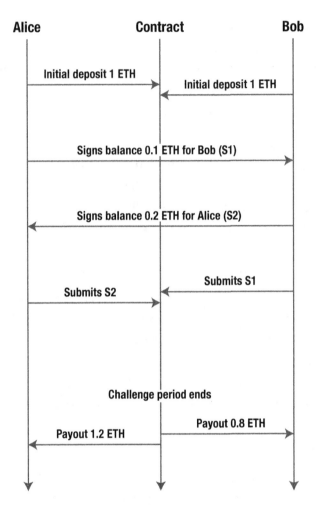

Figure 8-6. *Continuation of the previous scenario. Alice sees that Bob attempted to submit an older state and submits S2 in response. After the challenge period ends, the contract executes the payouts according to the most recent state submitted, S2*

These challenge mechanics have an important drawback: parties in the channel cannot be offline for any longer than the length of the challenge period. In our Alice and Bob example, if the channel has a challenge period of a few hours, Bob could just submit the state that is convenient for him while Alice is offline, so when she comes back online, the channel would already be closed. On the other hand, extremely long challenge periods can lead to locked deposits for long periods of time, if Bob attempts to rightfully close the channel and Alice never accepts the closure. Choosing the correct challenge period will depend heavily on the use case where the channel is deployed.

Note   As a complement to channels, there are *watchtower* services that can monitor a channel on behalf of the user in case they go offline and their counterpart attempts to unlawfully close the channel. These providers may demand a fee in exchange for their services proportional to the value locked in the channel.

A Sample Exchange

To ensure incentives are aligned, Alice signs messages where the balance changes in favor of Bob and the other way around. A sample scenario, where both start with a deposit of 1 ETH, could be the following:

- Alice signs 0.4 ETH by signing balances (0.6, 1.4)[9] with nonce 1.

- Bob signs 0.3 ETH by signing balances (0.9, 1.1) with nonce 2.

- Alice signs 0.1 ETH by signing balances (0.8, 1.2) with nonce 3.

- Alice signs 0.1 ETH by signing balances (0.7, 1.3) with nonce 4.

Let's go through some possible scenarios based on this set of messages:

- When the exchange ends, Bob rightfully picks the latest message signed by Alice and uses it to close the channel. Note that it never makes sense for him to pick nonce 3 over 4, since 4 has a balance more beneficial to him, as it corresponds to a payment made by Alice.

- Bob never signs another message and never closes the channel. In response, Alice uploads the last message that was beneficial to her: the last one signed by Bob (nonce 2). She has no reason to submit any of the more recent ones where she performs additional payments. Alternatively, she could also attempt to close the channel as if no messages were exchanged.

- Alice maliciously uploads the message with nonce 2 to try to close the channel. Bob should immediately submit a more recent message, preferably the one with nonce 4.

---

[9]Here, the notation (A, B) indicates the balances for Alice and Bob, respectively.

- Bob maliciously attempts to close the channel with the message
  with nonce 1, where the balance was most in his favor. Then, Alice
  should submit the message with nonce 2 in response, as it is a more
  beneficial situation to her. This takes us to the previous scenario,
  where Bob should submit nonce 4.

As we can see, by signing a message with increasing nonce with each micropayment, participants are then incentivized to always submit the latest message signed by their counterparty. This leads to the most recent message being used to close the channel.

Implementing a Bidirectional Channel

We will now implement a sample bidirectional state channel (Listing 8-14). In our implementation, any user can request the channel's closure by providing a signed message by the other user. The payouts can then be executed either when the other party confirms it or when the challenge period ends.

Our channel will keep track of the balance of each user, initialized to the deposit that each of them made. The channel is created by one of the users and then joined by the second as they make their own deposit.[10]

Listing 8-14. Contract variables and initialization functions of our bidirectional state channel implementation. We are using the same ECDSA library as in the unidirectional implementation

```
contract BidirectionalPaymentChannel {
  using ECDSA for bytes32;
  uint256 constant closePeriod = 1 days;

  address payable user1;
  address payable user2;
  uint256 balance1;
  uint256 balance2;

  uint256 lastNonce;
  uint256 closeTime;
  address closeRequestedBy;
```

---

[10]As in our unidirectional implementation, we could add support for any of the users to top up their initial deposit in the channel.

```
constructor(address payable _user2) public payable {
  balance1 = msg.value;
  user1 = msg.sender;
  user2 = _user2;
}

function join() public payable {
  require(msg.sender == user2 && balance2 == 0);
  balance2 = msg.value;
}
}
```

Having the setup ready, we can now look into the close function of our contract (Listing 8-15). This function is similar to the one from the unidirectional channel, in that it validates the user's signature over the state. However, instead of executing the payout on the spot, it starts the challenge (or closing) period.

Listing 8-15. Closing function for the bidirectional state channel. It can be called by any of the participants, as long as they submit a message signed by the other user, with a more recent nonce than the last one submitted (if there was one)

```
function closeWithState(
  uint256 newBalance1, uint256 newBalance2,
  uint256 nonce, bytes memory signature
) public {
  // Check that sender is a user, state is sound, and
  // the nonce is increased in case of a challenge
  require(msg.sender == user1 || msg.sender == user2);
  require(nonce > lastNonce);
  require(newBalance1 + newBalance2 == address(this).balance);

  // Validate that the signature belongs to the other user
  bytes32 hash = keccak256(abi.encodePacked(
    newBalance1, newBalance2, nonce, address(this)
  )).toEthSignedMessageHash();
  address signer = hash.recover(signature);
  require(signer == user1 || signer == user2);
  require(signer != msg.sender);
```

297

```
// Update balances, nonce, and start a challenge period
balance1 = newBalance1;
balance2 = newBalance2;
lastNonce = nonce;
closeRequestedBy = msg.sender;
closeTime = now;
}
```

Now we need to add a function to actually close the channel, callable either by the user who did not start the closure in the first place or after the challenge period ended (Listing 8-16).

Listing 8-16. Effectively closing a bidirectional payment channel and executing the payouts

```
function confirmClose() public {
  require(msg.sender == user1 || msg.sender == user2);
  bool challengeEnded = closeTime != 0
    && closeTime + closePeriod > now;
  require(closeRequestedBy != msg.sender || challengeEnded);

  user2.send(balance2);
  selfdestruct(user1);
}
```

Note   We are using `send` instead of `transfer` in `confirmClose` to protect against an attack. If user2 is a contract account instead of an EOA, it can be coded to revert on every incoming transaction. This would make it impossible for user1 to ever close the channel and recover the initial deposit, since the transfer call to user2 would fail, and revert the entire transaction. By using `send`, the sending of ETH may fail, but the close is allowed to succeed.

Our implementation needs one last function to be complete. In case one of the users never signed any messages, the other needs to be able to request a closure, transferring the initial deposits back to each user (Listing 8-17). Otherwise, the funds of the user who created the channel in the first place could end up locked for good.

Listing 8-17. Starting a channel closure from the initial state

```
function close() public {
  require(msg.sender == user1 || msg.sender == user2);
  require(closeTime == 0);
  closeRequestedBy = msg.sender;
  closeTime = now;
}
```

Note that any user could still call `closeWithState` after close, in case a party maliciously attempted to close the channel on the initial state.

Optimizations and Extensions

The implementations we have reviewed so far of payment channels are relatively simple, but there is much room for improvement:

- One possible optimization is having a *single contract* for managing all channels. Instead of deploying one contract per channel, each channel is actually a struct stored in a single payment channel contract. This greatly reduces the cost of creating a new channel, but at the expense of added complexity. Furthermore, it centralizes the funds of all participants in a single contract, opening the door for bugs that could let an attacker drain the funds from all channels simultaneously.

- Channels could also be modified to be reused. In our implementations, we required the channel to be closed to execute the payouts, but we could leave the channel open after a payout is executed. This allows for part of the funds to be withdrawn to be used in other applications, without having to destroy the channel contract.

- In the case of bidirectional channels, channel closure can be optimized by adding a special message, signed by both users, that signals the agreed finalization at a certain state. This message can be uploaded by any participant and does not require either a second transaction to confirm the closure or going through the challenge period.

- An interesting extension to channels is to increase the number of participants. While in all of our examples we explore peer-to-peer channels with two members, a larger number of users can be involved. Coordination may become more complex as the number of users increase, since messages may be required to be signed by several participants in the channel to be considered valid.

State Channels

Payment channels can be seen as a specific case of a more general class of channels called *state channels*. Instead of having two parties exchanging signed messages regarding the state of balance to be paid out, state channels allow users to exchange messages regarding *any state*.

As an example, a simple game could be carried over a state channel. The players can sign messages on the state of the game, such as the placement of the pieces in a board. Moving a piece is done by sending signed messages with the move or the new configuration of the board.

State channels typically involve an initial deposit and a payout, much like payment channels. The conditions that rule the payout are defined by a game and can be enforced on-chain by a smart contract.

Coding a Game into a State Channel

Turn-based games are an excellent use case for a state channel, since they have some useful properties. For one, all of the game state can be safely exchanged between messages and processed on-chain if needed. Also, at any point in time, it is well-defined which player should play next, and there can be no disputes regarding who made a move first. Furthermore, the game's state is all that is needed to resolve a challenge, as they do not depend on any external state.[11]

Let's use the tic-tac-toe game as an example. The state can be defined as a 3x3 matrix with three possible values per cell: circle, cross, or empty. The rules of the game are easy to encode, as well as the winning (or draw) conditions.

---

[11]These kinds of games are sometimes called force-move games, since at any point a player can *force* the other one to move by going on-chain. They have led to the development of a state channel framework named *ForceMove* by Tom Close and Andrew Stewart. `https://magmo.com/force-move-games.pdf`

Here, players will exchange messages with their moves, which can only be placing down one of their tokens. However, unlike in payment channels, each move (i.e., each message) is *beneficial to the player who plays (signs) it* and not to the recipient. This poses a major shift in mechanics: a player is no longer incentivized to post the latest state submitted by their opponent, but the last move made *by themselves*. Let's see an example:

- Alice plays X in the center, so she signs a message with only an X in the center and nonce 1, and sends it to Bob.

- Bob plays O in mid-right, signs with nonce 2, and sends it to Alice.

- Alice plays X in top-right, signs with nonce 3, and sends it to Bob.

- Bob plays O in mid-left, signs with nonce 4, and sends it to Alice.

- Alice wins playing X in bottom-left, signs it with nonce 5, and sends it to Bob.

The board would then look like the following, with subscripts noting the turn when each move was done:

$$
\begin{array}{ccc}
 & & X_3 \\
O_4 & X_1 & O_2 \\
X_5 & &
\end{array}
$$

After the last step, Bob should sign the message received by Alice and send it back to her, so she can upload it on-chain and claim her prize. However, if Bob was a sore loser, he could refuse to do so. In that case, Alice must be able to just upload the last state signed by Bob (4) on-chain, along with her winning move, and have the state channel verify that she has won. Note that this requires that **the state channel must be able to verify that her move is indeed a valid and winning move**.

Bob could also simply stall the game. For instance, when he receives message 3 from Alice, as he notices that he is going to lose the game, he could choose to stop playing. In this scenario, Alice must be able to go on-chain with the last state signed by Bob (2), along with her following move (3), and *challenge* Bob to move. If he does not respond on-chain within an allotted time, then the state channel should declare Alice winner. Here, we are using challenge periods not just for closures but also for enforcing moves.

As we said, the state channel must be able to *verify* that a move is valid on-chain. Let's see a scenario where this need becomes clear: instead of stalling as he receives winning message 5 from Alice, Bob decides to ignore that message. He then challenges her to move on-chain with a spurious state. He takes Alice's previous signed state (3) and submits a new state to the contract with the following invalid board:

$$X_3$$
$$X_1 \quad O_2$$
$$O_4$$

If the state channel contract were not able to verify that his move is invalid (he changed the location of X_3), then Alice would be forced to respond on-chain with a move on top of this invalid board.

Note   An alternative to having the state channel contract validate every transition is to have it accept all transitions by default, but accept proofs that a certain move was invalid. In some cases, verifying a proof that a transition is invalid can be much easier than verifying the transition itself. Chess is a good example: verifying checkmate can be prohibitively expensive in terms of gas usage. A way around this is allowing any player to claim checkmate and have the opponent prove that it is not the case by submitting any valid move.[12] This pattern is simply another form of challenge-response and follows the motto *"verify, don't compute"* of smart contracts.

State channels are then inherently more complex than regular payment channels, since they require the logic of the game being played to verify state transitions.

---

[12]See "Lessons learned from making a Chess game for Ethereum" by Paul Grau, https://medium. com/@graycoding/lessons-learned-from-making-a-chess-game-for-ethereum-6917c01178b6

Note   Most of the optimizations described for payment channels also apply to state channels. For instance, it could be possible to run multiple instances of a game between two participants over a state channel, without requiring to close and open a new channel every time a rematch is desired. Also, a state channel could be set up so its deposits are ERC20 or even non-fungible ERC721 tokens - imagine a representing a trophy as a digital collectible!

Generalized State Channels

As we have seen, a state channel for a given game has two main responsibilities: managing the channel itself and validating the game's transitions. This makes implementations more convoluted, as the logic for both responsibilities is intertwined. It also makes state channel contracts more expensive, as they need to include the logic on both the channel and the game.

This has led to the development of *generalized state channels* frameworks. Generalized state channels are channels that manage the users' deposits and allow new games or applications to be progressively *installed* on the channel. This effectively decouples the state channel logic from the application logic.

> *Generalized state channels move all of the on-chain stateful components for blockchain applications off-chain. Rather than require each application developer to build an entire state channel architecture from scratch, a generalized state channel generalized framework is one where state is deposited once and then be used by any application or set of applications afterwards.*
>
> —Jeff Coleman, Liam Horne, and Li Xuanji, "Counterfactual: Generalized State Channels"[13]

This opens the door to a new level of channel reuse. Users can now play multiple instances of a game and even play multiple different games over the same channel, thus creating several subchannels within a single channel. Furthermore, we can build dependencies between these subchannels, such as triggering a payment channel only upon the resolution of a set of game subchannels.

---

[13]www.counterfactual.com/statechannels/

Generalized state channel solutions are heavily under development by different teams, though there is work toward a common standard to provide some degree of interoperability among them. Several of these implementations, such as the one from the Counterfactual team, rely on the concept of *counterfactual* actions. Here, the term *counterfactual* is used to refer to an action that any participant in the channel could take on-chain but it is actually not and causes participants to act as if it had actually happened.[14] Let's see what this means.

In our tic-tac-toe state channel, we could say that Alice has *counterfactually* won if there is a state signed by both Alice and Bob with her winning the game. Both players know that any of them can submit the winning state to the smart contract on-chain to trigger the payouts at any time. However, they can also decide to keep playing a second match, knowing that Alice has already won the first and that it can be taken on-chain whenever needed. In other words, players are dealing with counterfactual state.

Applications in a generalized state channel can be *counterfactually installed*: if all participants play nicely and a dispute never arises, then the application contract never needs to be actually created, and the entire game can be resolved off-chain. This is also known as *counterfactual instantiation* of a contract: a contract that could be deployed, but it is not.

The fact that any player can go on-chain and enforce a certain action is enough to promote good off-chain behavior – as long as it is complemented with a set of penalizations for malicious players who force their opponents to waste gas going on-chain.

All in all, counterfactual generalized state channels provide an interesting framework that minimizes the number of on-chain actions and thus reduces the latency and gas fees that are incurred every time an action must be carried out on the Ethereum network. As an additional benefit, they also provide a layer of privacy over the participants' actions: if no transactions except for the deposit and payouts are taken on-chain, then only the participants know what messages were exchanged via the state channel.

Channel Networks

Channels are useful solutions when it comes to settling payments or state within a fixed small set of participants (typically two). However, the solution falls short when we want to connect a dynamic set of members: for each user we want to transact with, we would need to go on-chain and open a new channel.

---

[14]See Section 5 of the *Counterfactual Generalized State Channels* white paper for a more detailed definition. https://l4.ventures/papers/statechannels.pdf

To solve this problem, there are protocols for establishing *virtual channels* between two peers, which leverage a path of channels that goes through multiple intermediaries. This effectively creates a network built from point-to-point connections, where any participant can connect to another as long as there is a valid path between the two, much like the Internet itself.

Caution   This section covers topics currently under heavy research and in ongoing development. Use it as a starting point to run your own up-to-date research if you are considering building on top of a state channel network.

The easiest construction in networks comes once again from Bitcoin, which is *multi-hop payment channels*. This method allows to securely route payments through one or more intermediaries. For instance, Alice could send payments to an intermediary Ingrid with whom she has a payment channel set up and have Ingrid relay them to Bob (assuming that Ingrid had a channel with Bob as well). Due to how these channels are set up,[15] Ingrid has no way to take these funds for herself.

This type of channels leads directly to a simple and effective network layout, a *hub-and-spoke channel network*, where multiple clients connect to a single hub that acts as an intermediary for all of them. This way, setting up a single channel with the hub allows a user to transact with anyone else on the network. On the other hand, it has the downside of being centralized and requiring the hub to be available.

There are also several projects working on more interesting network layouts, such as the Raiden Network,[16] inspired by Bitcoin's Lightning Network. The ultimate goal for these networks is to allow for any two participants to establish a shared channel, usually called a *virtual channel* or *metachannel*, in a trustless manner. These need not to be just payment channels, but can be full generalized state channels, and can potentially run without active participation of the intermediaries on every exchange.

---

[15]The building block that makes this possible is called Hash Time Locked Contracts (https://en.bitcoin.it/wiki/Hash_Time_Locked_Contracts).

[16]See https://raiden.network/

Sidechains

At their most basic version, a *sidechain* is a parallel Ethereum network that potentially runs a different consensus algorithm, such as *proof-of-authority,* and is connected to the main network by a *bridge.* Working on smaller sizes allows sidechains to achieve much higher throughputs than the main Ethereum network.

Note   While it is technically possible for a sidechain to use proof-of-work, this is highly insecure. Remember that proof-of-work relies on an attacker being unable to produce more computing power than the rest of the network. Since sidechains tend to be small compared to the main network, their difficulty is also comparatively low, which makes it easier for an attacker to mount an attack on them. This is why most sidechains work with a closed set of miners or validators.

Proof of Authority

In proof-of-authority, or PoA for short, there is a predefined set of nodes that act as *validators* for the blocks being added to the network. Validators are the PoA equivalent of miners in PoW, in that they add new blocks. Every certain number of seconds, each of these validators, taking turns, proposes a new block. These blocks are broadcasted to the other validators and need to be approved by a majority of them to be added to the blockchain. The set of validators can be changed over time, with some validators being voted out and new ones allowed into the set.

How the blocks are broadcasted, approved, and agreed upon depends on the specific *consensus* algorithm being used. Though there are many different consensus algorithms, such as Clique,[17] Aura,[18] Raft,[19] or Istanbul BFT,[20] they all share the same basic scheme outlined previously. Different algorithms may offer different guarantees against malicious actors or nodes dropping from the network, as well as different performance.

---

[17]http://eips.ethereum.org/EIPS/eip-225
[18]https://wiki.parity.io/Aura
[19]https://raft.github.io/
[20]https://github.com/ethereum/EIPs/issues/650

Another component of a sidechain is the connection to a main network, often called *bridge*. A bridge is a mechanism for users to move their assets between the main chain and the sidechain. As an example, a simple bridge could allow users to move their assets in a specific ERC20 from the main network to a sidechain by having the users lock their funds in a specific mainnet contract. Sidechain validators watch this contract and create the corresponding funds in the sidechain whenever they register a user locking funds on the main chain. We will implement this mechanism later in this chapter.

Security and Trust

The security of a vanilla PoA sidechain depends entirely on its validators. If a majority of them collude, they can effectively steal all user funds locked in the sidechain. Because of this, it is critical that the set of validators is composed of multiple different parties and are not all controlled by a single organization. A user should trust a PoA network only if he or she trusts a majority of the validator nodes.

To disincentivize malicious behavior like this, some networks rely on proof-of-stake instead of proof-of-authority. In this scheme, the validator nodes are required to deposit (stake) a large amount of funds. If it is proven that they acted maliciously, then their stake is slashed as a penalty - though how this slashing is executed is another matter.

It is important that the value a validator could gain by attacking the network is less than what he would lose in stake in order to keep the incentives in line. There are currently different approaches to proof-of-stake. However, from a user's perspective, the experience is very similar to operating in a proof-of-authority network.

Note   Given that malicious validators may steal funds from users, the security guarantees from the sidechain are poorer than those of the main chain. This fact makes sidechains **not** to be considered layer 2 solutions under certain definitions. Nevertheless, there are constructs (such as Plasma, which we will see later) that allow the user to safeguard their assets by calling unlawful validator behavior on a main network contract.

Deploying Our Own Chain

To illustrate how a PoA network works,[21] we will manually set one up using the Geth
Ethereum node client.[22] While Geth can run in the proof-of-work main Ethereum
network, it can also be configured to run in PoA networks that use the Clique consensus
algorithm (such as the Rinkeby testnet) and act as a validator node.

Let's start by setting up three miner nodes, which will all run on the same computer.
We will first create new accounts for each miner. For convenience, we will use the same
password for all accounts, so create a file password.txt containing a random string to
be used as password. Then, create the addresses by running the following for each of the
three miners, replacing miner1 with miner2 and miner3. Make sure the password.txt file
is in the path where the command is run.

```
$ geth --datadir miner1 --password password.txt account new
> Address: {8305ccac...58269a7d}
```

You should get three different addresses, which we will set up as the validators of this
network (make sure to note them down). We will now create a *genesis* for our network.
The genesis is the configuration for the network and will include which is the set of
authorized validators, the consensus engine, the initial balances, the block gas limit, and
so on. In geth, this information is compiled into a JSON configuration file which is used
to bootstrap each node.

Geth includes a tool named puppeth that simplifies the creation of such a file. Simply
run puppeth in the console, and answer the questions prompted (Listing 8-18). Give
your network a name, create a new genesis, use clique proof-of-authority with 5-second
blocks, and choose your miners as "accounts allowed to seal." You should also pick a
fourth account to be pre-funded or choose one of the existing validators to hold the
initial ETH for your network.

---

[21]You may also be interested in checking out https://poa.network/, an excellent set of tools for
building and managing PoA-based sidechains.

[22]The Parity client also offers a similar capability, only that using a different consensus algorithm
(Aura). Check out https://wiki.parity.io/Proof-of-Authority-Chains to read more about
replicating this setup using Parity instead of Geth.

Listing 8-18. Fragment of the Geth puppeth configuration wizard to set up a PoA network with id 1212. You should have a new `mysidechain.json` genesis file after going through it

```
$ puppeth

Please specify a network name to administer (no spaces, hyphens or capital
letters please)
> mysidechain

What would you like to do? (default = stats)
 1. Show network stats
 2. Configure new genesis
 3. Track new remote server
 4. Deploy network components
> 2

What would you like to do? (default = create)
 1. Create new genesis from scratch
 2. Import already existing genesis
> 1

Specify your chain/network ID if you want an explicit one (default =
random)
> 1212
```

Before starting our Geth nodes, we will set up a *bootnode*. A bootnode is a node in the network whose sole purpose is to aid in the discovery of other nodes. We will use it to simplify the communication between our miner nodes.

To set up a bootnode, we first need to create a boot key and use it to derive the bootnode *enode address* (Listing 8-19). The enode address is a unique identifier of a node in the decentralized network, followed by the IP address and port where the node can be found. We will then start the bootnode using the generated boot key and have it listen on local port 30100.[23]

---

[23]You can pick pretty much any port number between 1024 and 65535 for this. Avoid port numbers that could be being used by other applications. In particular, Ethereum mainnet nodes listen on port 30303 by default, so you will want to pick a different one for your custom network.

Listing 8-19. Generating a boot key and running a bootnode

```
$ bootnode -genkey boot.key
$ bootnode -nodekey boot.key -writeaddress
> c190f2af...ee34b40a
$ bootnode -nodekey boot.key -addr :30100
```

Note   We did not need to use the genesis configuration file for the bootnode, since the bootnode does need any information on whether the network is running a proof of work or authority or who the validators are. It only needs to know where the nodes are to share this information with the network.

Now that we have a bootnode running and a genesis configuration file, it is time to actually start the network. In three different terminals, start the three different Geth validator nodes (Listing 8-20), configured to mine (i.e., seal) new blocks, and expose the JSON-RPC API locally over HTTP.

Listing 8-20. Starting the Geth validator nodes using the genesis configuration and bootnode ID generated earlier. Run this command three times in different terminals, one for each validator, changing the unlocked address, datadir, port, and rpcport

```
geth \
--datadir miner1 \
--port 30201 \
--rpc --rpcaddr localhost --rpcport 12001 \
--rpcapi 'eth,personal' \
--networkid 1212 \
--gasprice 10000 \
--unlock 8305ccac...58269a7d \
--password password.txt \
--mine \
--bootnodes 'enode://c190f2af...ee34b40a@127.0.0.1:30100'
```

Our network should be now running, sealing a new block every 5 seconds. Take a look at the logs from the three validators to see how they progress.

We can now spin up a new client node and connect to the existing network (Listing 8-21). Remember that even though the set of validators is limited, the network is still public and any node can connect to it. We can use its console to check how the latest block number increases every 5 seconds, running `web3.eth.blockNumber`.

Listing 8-21. Spinning a new node to join the network, with a console enabled. Note that we are not authenticating this new node in any way, since the network is public for anyone to join

```
$ geth \
--datadir node1 --port 30204 \
--rpc --rpcaddr localhost --rpcport 12004 \
--rpcapi 'eth,personal' \
--networkid 1212 \
--bootnodes 'enode://c190f2af...ee34b40a@127.0.0.1:30100' \
console
```

Let's now connect this network with an existing one, such as Rinkeby.

Building a Bridge

We will build a simple bridge, exclusively dependent on the validator accounts, using a contract deployed on both the main network and the sidechain, in addition to a script being run by each validator. In this model, the steps for a user moving into a sidechain and later exiting would be the following:

1. The user transfers funds to the bridge contract on mainnet.

2. The bridge contract retains the funds and emits an event.

3. The validators note the event, and each of them calls into the bridge contract on the sidechain side requesting to unlock the same amount of funds.

4. The user gets their funds in the sidechain and uses them to operate there.

5. Once the user wants to exit the sidechain, the same process is repeated by transferring the sidechain funds to the sidechain bridge contract and having the validators unlock them on the mainnet bridge contract.

We will begin by building the bridge contract. This contract will have two main responsibilities: (1) accepting and locking user funds and (2) unlocking them at the request of the validators. Note that we will deploy two instances of the contract, one in each chain. The locking function on one chain will have its counterpart on the unlocking function of the other chain and vice versa.

Note   In this example, we are building a bridge that accepts ETH and dispenses the native currency of the sidechain on the other end. However, we could also build bridges that accept a certain ERC20 token on the main chain or even non-fungible ERC721 assets.

To begin with, the bridge will need to know the validators' addresses (Listing 8-22). We will also specify how many validators need to agree to release a user's funds. In our scenario with three validators, we will release the funds with just two of them agreeing in case one of them drops.

Listing 8-22. Definition of the bridge contract, which is initialized with the validators' addresses

```solidity
pragma solidity ^0.5.0;

contract Bridge {
  uint256 threshold;
  mapping(address => bool) validators;

  constructor(
    uint256 _threshold,
    address[] memory _validators
  ) public payable {
    threshold = _threshold;
```

```
    for (uint256 i = 0; i < _validators.length; i++) {
      validators[_validators[i]] = true;
    }
  }
}
```

Note that we are making the constructor payable. When deploying the contract in the sidechain, we need to seed this contract with the maximum amount of ETH we want to allow our users to transfer from the main network (Rinkeby in this case) to our sidechain, so the contract can unlock those funds when prompted by the validators.

We will now go into the locking function (Listing 8-23), which is quite simple. We need to accept the sender's funds, allowing them to specify a recipient address on the other end of the bridge, and emit an event. We will assign an autoincremental ID to each locking operation, so the validators can refer to it when unlocking on the other end.

Listing 8-23. Lock function of the bridge contract

```
event Locked(uint256 id, uint256 amount, address recipient);

uint256 lastId;

function lock(address recipient) public payable {
  require(msg.value > 0);
  emit Locked(++lastId, msg.value, recipient);
}
```

Last but not least, we will work on the unlock function (Listing 8-24). This function will be called by the validators on the other end of the bridge. Each validator should authorize unlocking the funds that correspond to a locking operation that happened on the other end. Keep in mind that since there is no on-chain communication between both ends of the bridge, it is the validators responsibility to unlock the correct amount of funds to the address requested by the user.

Listing 8-24. Unlocking function of the token bridge. The first time a validator requests an unlock, we will create a new unlock request and then log an approval every time it is called again. When the required number of approvals is reached, the funds are unlocked

```
mapping(uint256 => Request) requests;

struct Request {
  uint256 amount;
  address payable recipient;
  bool paid;
  uint256 approveCount;
  mapping(address => bool) approvedBy;
}

event Unlocked(uint256 id, uint256 amount, address recipient);

function unlock(
  uint256 id, uint256 amount, address payable recipient
) public {
  Request storage request = requests[id];

  require(validators[msg.sender]);
  require(!request.approvedBy[msg.sender]);
  require(request.recipient == address(0)
    || request.recipient == recipient);
  require(request.amount == 0 || request.amount == amount);

  request.approveCount++;
  request.approvedBy[msg.sender] = true;
  request.recipient = recipient;
  request.amount = amount;

  if (request.approveCount >= threshold && !request.paid) {
    request.paid = true;
    recipient.transfer(amount);
    emit Unlocked(id, amount, recipient);
  }
}
```

Caution   This implementation allows a malicious validator to prevent a user's funds from being unlocked. The validator could spam the bridge contract with spurious unlock requests for upcoming request IDs. This way, when the honest validators actually try to honor the unlock request, the parameters (such as amount or recipient) will not match and the operation will fail. We will ignore this attack, since the purpose of this bridge is to just illustrate basic usage. Nevertheless, this serves as a reminder that even the most simple implementations may be hiding security issues, and you should always work with reviewed and audited contracts.

We can now deploy this contract on both networks (Listing 8-25), using the set of validators we defined earlier and choosing a required threshold of two approvals for unlocking. Remember to also transfer a large amount of funds to the contract when deploying it on the sidechain, so it has funds to unlock when requested.

Listing 8-25. Deployment script for the bridge contract. Run this twice with different PROVIDER_URLs: one for the Rinkeby Ethereum network and the other for the sidechain

```
const Web3 = require('web3');
const Artifact = require('../artifacts/Bridge.json');
const web3 = new Web3(PROVIDER_URL);
const abi = Artifact.compilerOutput.abi;
const data = Artifact.compilerOutput.evm.bytecode.object;
const Bridge = new web3.eth.Contract(abi, null, { data });

const bridge = await Bridge.deploy({
  arguments: [THRESHOLD, VALIDATORS]
}).send({
  from: FROM, gas: 1e6, gasPrice: GAS_PRICE, value: VALUE
});

console.log("Bridge deployed at", bridge.options.address);
```

Finally, we need to set up the watcher scripts that will be run by each validator (Listing 8-26). These scripts will watch the bridge contract in one network for Locked events and execute the corresponding unlock on the other side.

Listing 8-26. Watcher script to be run on each validator. Note that we create two web3 instances: one connecting to the main network, where we listen for events on the remote end of the bridge, and the other to the local network, where we execute the unlock operations. We then do the converse, allowing funds to go from the sidechain back to the main network

```
const Web3 = require('web3');
const Artifact = require('../artifacts/Bridge.json');
const abi = Artifact.compilerOutput.abi;

const remoteWeb3 = new Web3(REMOTE_PROVIDER_URL);
const localWeb3 = new Web3(LOCAL_PROVIDER_URL);
const remoteBridge = new remoteWeb3.eth.Contract(abi, REMOTE);
const localBridge = new localWeb3.eth.Contract(abi, LOCAL);

remoteBridge.events.Locked().on('data', function(e) {
  const { id, amount, recipient } = e.returnValues;
  localBridge.methods
    .unlock(id, amount, recipient)
    .send({ from: VALIDATOR, gas: 1e6, gasPrice: GAS_PRICE });
});

localBridge.events.Locked().on('data', function(e) {
  const { id, amount, recipient } = e.returnValues;
  remoteBridge.methods
    .unlock(id, amount, recipient)
    .send({ from: VALIDATOR, gas: 1e6, gasPrice: GAS_PRICE });
});
```

We can now run this script on each of the validator nodes (or at least on two of them). Once it is running, try calling the lock function in the Rinkeby end of the bridge. A few seconds later, you should have your funds ready to use on the chosen address in your sidechain.

In an actual application, you need to decide how much of this complexity you want to expose to your users. As we have seen in Chapter 7, onboarding is already troublesome enough, and adding another step requiring to send funds from one network to another is not a good idea.

However, you can actually leverage an application-specific sidechain for improving onboarding. You can directly fund your users' initial accounts on your sidechain or build a viral inviting scheme where existing users can invite new ones directly on the cheaper and faster sidechain. The bridge is then only used for advanced users who want to transfer value from or to the main network, but to an Ethereum neophyte the application simply runs smoothly and fast, without knowing how it is backed.

A good example of this, already mentioned in the previous chapter, is the Burner Wallet.[24] This wallet operates on a proof-of-authority sidechain[25] with four different teams acting as validators. Users are quickly onboarded by receiving a link with a pre-funded account on the sidechain and can easily transact with others thanks to low gas costs and 5-second blocks. For the most advanced users, there is an option to move the funds onto the main Ethereum network or even seed their burner wallets from their mainnet accounts.

Plasma Chains

The state of the art in terms of layer 2 solutions at the time of this writing are plasma chains,[26] originally designed by Vitalik Buterin and Joseph Poon in 2017.

Plasma chains are different from sidechains in that their security can be enforced by the main chain (or *parent chain*, in plasma terminology) and thus does not depend exclusively on the consensus mechanism of the sidechain. This means that if the set of validators on the child chain (called *plasma operators*) misbehaves, any user can build a cryptographic proof and take it to a smart contract on the main chain (called *root contract*). If there is no foul play, transactions on the child chain occur with the reduced gas cost and latency typical of a sidechain.

However, this additional security comes at a cost. Whenever a user wants to exit the child chain (i.e., transfer their assets back to the main chain), they must go through a *challenge period*, similar to the one we saw in state channels. If a malicious validator creates a fake block where he stole a user's assets and uses it to take over those assets

---

[24]https://burnerwallet.io/
[25]https://poa.network/xdai
[26]https://plasma.io/

in the main chain, the user can submit a fraud proof during this challenge period and regain their assets. As such, exiting a plasma chain is not instant and requires a user to wait a certain period of time.[27]

Also, since a smart contract needs to be able to process whether a set of transactions on the child chain was legitimate, the operations allowed on the child chain cannot be overly complex. In particular, no plasma implementations at the time of this writing support arbitrary smart contracts and only provide the means for exchanging assets between users. Research on this topic is done under *generalized plasma* implementations.

On the flip side, plasma chains are designed for having a tree-like structure. The parent chain of a plasma chain can be *another* plasma chain, allowing for massive scalability by simply composing plasma chains within others. This means that if an application-specific plasma chain becomes overcrowded, it can simply spawn new children and move clusters of users to them.

It is worth mentioning that plasma itself is not a specification but a framework for building scalable layer 2 infrastructure. This has led to the development of many different flavors of plasma by different teams, such as minimal viable plasma, plasma cash, plasma debit, or plasma prime.[28] It is most likely that by the time this book reaches your hands, there will be new major developments on this front.

Summary

Public blockchains like Bitcoin or Ethereum have traditionally sacrificed performance for trustlessness and security. While there are multiple efforts toward building Ethereum 2.0, which includes sharding mechanics that help the network scale, it is interesting to see many solutions sprouting that build on top of the existing infrastructure to solve the scalability problem.

Some of the solutions presented in this chapter, such as early versions of plasma or state channels, are ready to use and in production today, helping real-life applications scale beyond the limits of the main Ethereum network.

---

[27]There are new versions of plasma that remove this waiting period (see `https://ethresear.ch/t/plasma-snapp-fully-verified-plasma-chain/3391`).

[28]Head over to `https://www.learnplasma.org/` for an excellent overview of the available plasma implementations.

These solutions not only allow your application to achieve a higher transaction throughput, but they can also be used to provide a better user experience overall. Channels provide instant finality to peer-to-peer transactions if both parties behave appropriately instead of having to wait for a dozen confirmations. And sidechains can provide reliable block times much lower than the main network, with considerably lower gas fees.

These techniques can even be combined: you can set up state channels between parties in a sidechain or even use channels as the actual asset being traded in a plasma chain.[29] The sky is the limit here.

How you leverage these solutions and present them to (or hide them from) your users will depend on what you are building. Remember what your users need from your application, and use the building blocks available to you to create the best possible experience.

Happy coding!

---

[29]This is the model proposed by plasma debit: the child chain assets are not tokens but channels between the user and the chain operator, forming a hub-and-spoke channel network.

Index

A

Application Binary Interface (ABI), 23, 77
Application local accounts
    encrypted keystores
        password, 230
        private key, 229, 230
        XSS attacks, 229
    local wallet
        Ethereum account, 227
        private key, 228
        transaction object, 228
        web3 library, 228
    mnemonics, 231, 232
Archive nodes, 89
Auxiliary function, 116

B

Bidirectional payment channels
    challenge period, 292–294
    exchange, sample
        based on messages, 295, 296
        deposit of 1 ETH, 295
        implementation, 296–298
        optimizations/extensions, 299, 300
bip39 library, 231
Bitcoin, 7
Bitcoin blockchain, 7
Bitcoin to Ethereum
    gas fees, 8
    smart contract, 8

Blockchain
    advantages
        DAO, 13
        permanence, 13
        piece of data, 13
        smart contracts, 13
        trusted third party, 13
    blocks, 3
    chain of hashes, 4
    consensus algorithm, 5, 6
    DApps (*see* Decentralized
        applications)
    decentralized finance, 12
    defined, 2
    federated/consortium, 15, 16
    limitations
        transaction
            throughput, 14
        user onboarding, 14
    peer-to-peer network, 3
    reorganization, 6
    throughput, 6
    transaction, 3
Boolean literals, 61
Bridge mechanism, 307

C

Channels, 276
Contract upgradeability, 244
CREATE2 instruction, 263, 264

D

V

W, X, Y, Z

Printed in the United States
By Bookmasters